Somerville and Ross

by the same author

Autobiographies
TRIALS IN BURMA
THE JOURNEY OUTWARD
INTO HIDDEN BURMA

Histories
THE GREAT WITHIN
THE LAND OF THE GREAT IMAGE
FOREIGN MUD
THE FIRST HOLY ONE
LAST AND FIRST IN BURMA
THE HURLING TIME
BRITISH MERCHANT ADVENTURERS
(*Collins*)

Biographies
WAYFOONG
RAFFLES
SIAMESE WHITE
THE GRAND PEREGRINATION
MARCO POLO
CORTES AND MONTEZUMA
NANCY ASTOR
STANLEY SPENCER
(*Collins*)

Travel
LORDS OF THE SUNSET

Novels and Romances
SHE WAS A QUEEN
SANDA MALA
THE DARK DOOR
QUEST FOR SITA
THE DESCENT OF THE GOD
THE MYSTERY OF DEAD LOVERS

Drama
THE MOTHERLY AND AUSPICIOUS
WHITE OF MERGEN
LORD OF THE THREE WORLDS

Somerville and Ross

A BIOGRAPHY
BY
MAURICE COLLIS

FABER AND FABER
24 Russell Square
London

First published in mcmlxviii
by Faber and Faber Limited
24 Russell Square London WC1
Printed in Great Britain by
Ebenezer Baylis and Son, Limited
The Trinity Press, Worcester, and London
All rights reserved

Standard Book Number 57108430

In Memoriam
uxoris meae
Eleanor
Obiit. A.D. VIII Kal. Mar.
MCMLXVII

Contents

Preface   *page* 13
1 Violet Martin in youth   17
2 Edith Somerville's youth and meeting with
     Violet Martin   25
3 Edith and Martin become intimate friends   36
4 The Martins return to Ross   50
5 The Somerville-Martin Ross collaboration begins   64
6 Doings at Ross   73
7 Lady Zetland's visit to Ross   84
8 The Somerville family at Castle Townshend   89
9 The death of Edith's Mother   103
10 Edith becomes mistress of Drishane   112
11 Edith and Martin begin to write the R.M. Stories   123
12 The end of the Ross period   132
13 Edith and Martin's humour   141
14 From 1908 to the outbreak of War   157
15 The death of Martin   168
16 The Apotheosis of Martin   176
17 The meeting with Ethel Smyth   185
18 The Troubles   201
19 Attempt to materialize the spirit of Martin   219
20 Anecdotes   223
21 Edith in America   236
22 The calling up of Charles Bushe   246

Contents

23 D.Litt. Trinity College and Fellow, Academy of
      Letters   250
24 Edith fails as a playwright but succeeds as a
      horse dealer   254
25 The Murder of Admiral Boyle Somerville   257
26 The death of Cameron   263
27 Last Days   268
      Note on manuscript sources   279
      Chronological Tables   281
      Index   283

Illustrations

1 Grandpapa Somerville and Edith at twelve (1870) *page* 32
2 View of Drishane (1900)   33
3 Edith's portrait of Martin aged twenty-four
  (1886)   48
4 Aerial view of Castle Townshend   49
5 Edith and Martin composing in Drishane dining
  room (1888)   80
6 The Somerville brothers and sisters (1893)   81
7 Hildegarde Somerville and Egerton Coghill
  (1893)   96
8 Robert Martin (about 1900)   97
9 Hildegarde in the garden of Glen Barrahane
  after her marriage to Egerton Coghill   128
10 Edith on Bridget (1903)   129
11 Edith and Martin with Candy and Sheila (1907)   144
12 Uncle Kendal dancing with Hildegarde in the
   garden of Cosheen (1910)   145
13 The dying Martin, 18 December 1915. Drawing
   by Edith   160
14 Landscape in oils by Edith: Roger's Island in the
   Harbour   161
15 Tally Ho house, Castle Townshend   176
16 Edith autographing a copy of *Happy Days* at
   Tally Ho (1947–8)   177

[11]

Illustrations

Plan of Castle Townshend   26, 27

Plan of Ross and neighbourhood   47

Somerville family tree ⎫

Martin family tree   ⎬   281

Coghill family tree   ⎭

Preface

In December 1965 I received a letter from my old friend, Nevill
Coghill, then Merton Professor of English Literature at
Oxford, inviting me to write the biography of Edith Somerville
and Violet Martin who, as E. Œ. Somerville and Martin Ross,
are so widely known as the joint authors of *Some Experiences of
an Irish R.M.* and other stories. He told me, what I did not
know, that he and his brother, Sir Patrick Coghill, Bart, were
the nephews of Edith Somerville, whose sister Hildegarde, their
mother, married Sir Egerton Coghill, their father. Through her
they had inherited a very extensive collection of their aunt's
papers, which included those of Violet Martin. These they had
explored and arranged during the fifties, when they contemplated giving their contents to the world in some biographical
form, but abandoned the idea as they felt doubtful whether they
could write with sufficient objectivity on matters which touched
them so closely. Thus for years the papers had lain in their
custody at Sir Patrick Coghill's house in Gloucestershire. No
person outside the family had access to them nor was any part
of them made public. But now, wrote Professor Coghill, he
would like to hand them over to me to write from them the
biography which he and his brother desired.

I agreed to undertake the task and in April 1966 took over
from Sir Patrick the more important MSS., which included the
diaries of the two Irishwomen. Edith Somerville had kept a day

to day diary from 1873, when she was fifteen, till the year before her death in 1949, 76 volumes; Violet Martin did the same from 1875, when she was thirteen, till 1915 (the year she died), 40 volumes; a total of 116 volumes. A yet larger item of the MS. material was the letters. Edith Somerville was an indefatigable correspondent. Thousands of her letters are preserved, addressed to Violet Martin, to her sister Hildegarde, to two of her brothers, Cameron and Jack, and to friends, particularly to Dame Ethel Smyth, the celebrated musician. These letters are mostly long, running often to more than a thousand words. They amplify the diaries and exceed them in bulk. Violet Martin was also an active correspondent, but the greater part of her letters is lost. To this vast documentation are to be added letters received by Edith Somerville, particularly the hundreds from Dame Ethel Smyth, together with a quantity of miscellaneous papers. Few if any literary personages have left such a mass of autobiographical material. For a detailed list of these manuscripts, see the 'Note on MS. sources' on page 279.

My task has been to extract from this mine what is most characteristic of the two women. They were great humorists, and that mood pervades the documents at every turn. How they met and collaborated has been my first endeavour to explain, as the book turns on that collaboration. Their personalities emerge vividly as the story evolves. I have refrained from any general discussion of Irish politics except insofar as the troubled state of that country affected them personally. The facts of their lives are often surprising and always very Irish. Whatever I conceived to be tedious I have omitted, and given space to what is lively, curious, fantastic or tragic. My aim has been to make two remarkable Irishwomen speak for themselves and to avoid burying their story in piles of detail.

Sir Patrick Coghill and his brother Professor Coghill have been indefatigable in rendering help and advice, eliminating errors of fact and supplying information to clarify obscurities in the sources. I also received valuable hints from Miss Muriel Currey, a niece of Violet Martin's. She has both a practical and scholarly knowledge of the whole subject. Another niece, Miss Stella Martin, has been kind enough on several occasions to place her knowledge at my disposal. I have also to thank Mr Richard Martin, a nephew of Violet Martin's, and owner of the portrait of her reproduced in this book, for the loan of letters and some good advice, and Lady Violet Powell for writing to tell me that the house in Corfu where Edith was born (p. 28) is still standing and now used as the military telephone exchange.

Finally I have to thank my daughter, Louise Collis, for her assistance from first to last in reading sections of the MS. sources and annotating them and for her refreshing interest and readiness to discuss problems of interpretation as they arose.

1

Violet Martin in youth

Violet was born into the Martin family in 1862 at Ross House, near Oughterard, in the County of Galway, the youngest child of her father, James Martin. During the eighteenth century the Martins had been the greatest landed magnates in Connaught. They were of Norman origin. Oliver Martin, who was to found the Irish family, went as a youthful Norman squire to the Holy Land with Richard Coeur de Lion, who granted him a coat of arms with the motto: 'Sic itur ad astra'. Before he went on this crusade he joined the army of Strongbow for the invasion of Ireland in the reign of Henry II and went to Connaught with the de Burghs. The estate he acquired near Galway was the first land in Ireland to be owned by his family. It is impossible even to sketch the history of this powerful clan from the twelfth to the nineteenth century. Suffice it to say that when Violet was born their seat was Ross House on Ross Lake, twelve miles north of Galway town, a house built in 1777 on the site of an earlier Martin castle. During her father's time there occurred the disastrous famine of 1847/48, consequent upon the blighting of the potato crop, upon which the peasantry wholly depended for their food. Of this catastrophe Violet afterwards wrote: 'Despairing creatures flocked for aid into the yard and the long downstairs passages of Ross House. Corpses were buried where the starving fell dead at the avenue gate. A soup kitchen was established by my father.' But he could not feed the whole countryside. All he could hope to achieve was to keep his own tenants alive. In this effort he ruined himself, as, of course, no rents were coming in. Violet wrote: 'No adequate tribute has ever been paid to those Irish landlords—and they were men of every party and creed—who perished martyrs to duty in that awful time.' To make some money to pay his debts, James Martin was obliged to go over to London and write as a journalist for a while.

Up till the mid-nineteenth century the country people of Connaught lived as they had always lived. 'The old ways,' Violet records, 'were unchanged in Ross. My father came and went among his people as native as the soft air they breathed. All were known to the Master and he was understood by them.' He was a handsome man with a genial manner. Tenants whose rent was in arrears were given time or turf taken in place. Evictions were unknown. Indeed, the liberal way he managed his estate was hardly business, he was so soft hearted. Even before the famine he had incurred debts. But he had won all hearts. When Robert, his eldest son, was born in 1846 the tenantry celebrated the occasion in traditional style. To quote Violet again: 'The workmen in the yard kissed the baby's hands, the old women came from the mountains to prophesy and to bless and to perform the rite of spitting on the child for luck.'

In 1872 when James Martin died Violet was ten. 'With his death a curtain fell for ever on the old life at Ross, the stage darkened, and the keening of the tenants as they followed his coffin, a tremendous and sustained wail, like the voice of the grave itself, was the last music of the piece. My father was to all "The Masther, the Lord have mercy on him"; the Martins were "The Family" who could do no wrong. "The Martin family hadn't good sight," said a tenant, "but sure the people say that was a proof of their nobility".' The style 'Martin of Ross' was a princely title, like the style 'The Knight of Kerry' or 'The O'Donovan'.

When Violet speaks above of the curtain that fell, she is referring to the Home Rule movement under Parnell. A majority

of the Irish members elected to sit at Westminster became
Home Rulers. With Catholic emancipation and the extension of
the franchise, power passed gradually from the landed gentry to
the Catholic priesthood. Feudal power gave way to clerical. The
landed gentry no longer represented Ireland in the English
Parliament. The death of James Martin in 1872 coincided with
a general election when sixty Home Rulers were returned. The
people still were fond of the Martins, but there was a rift. As
Violet put it: 'The separation had begun and only those who
have experienced it will understand how strange, how wound-
ing it was.'

When Robert Martin succeeded to the Ross property he was
twenty-six, and was making his way successfully in London as a
journalist, where he was already very popular as a song writer
and a wit. He did not hear the call of Ross 'four hundred miles
away in the whispering stillness of its winter woods and the
monotony of its winter winds' as Violet has it in a lovely passage. Life in London was so attractive, things had changed so
much at Ross. So he resolved to shut the ancestral house, place
the collection of rents in the hands of an agent and himself continue his career in London. It was arranged that his mother
should take her five daughters to Dublin where they had many
relatives and the entry to the best society of the capital. She was
a remarkable woman. The grand-daughter of Charles Kendal
Bushe, Lord Chief Justice of Ireland (1822–1842), and one of
the most prominent men of his day, she was fifty at the time of
the move. Her name was Anna-Selina; in Violet's writings she
is always referred to as Mama. Her character was very marked,
an aristocrat, educated enough at seventeen, it was said, to have
translated into heroic couplets a Latin poem composed by the
Marquess Wellesley, the Duke of Wellington's elder brother,
which his lordship found very well done. Her daughters adored
her; Violet was closest to her.

Violet's diary opens in 1875, after they had been in Dublin
for a couple of years. The entry of the seventh of June in that
year shows her, at the age of thirteen, in command of a mature

style and with a penetrating eye for the amusing detail. It is an
astonishing bit of writing for a girl of her age and is here given
in part. The subject is a visit paid by her and her mother to
Bishop Darley of Cavan. At some railway station short of
Cavan, the bishop was on the platform. Violet's account begins
at this point. 'Old Darley got into our compartment. He is
rather deaf and after Mama had shouted at him for half an hour
they both gave up conversation and subsided into newspapers
and silence. A very small trap brought us from Cavan station to
the Palace, Mama admiring the drive to the old Bishop by saying every now and then whenever we passed a heap of stone,
"Oh a national school, oh lovely." At length we arrived utterly
done and were embraced by Nannie Darley (as Mrs Darley was
called) and two plump children who made a rush at me and
kissed me energetically. After unrobing we had high tea at
which neither I nor the other young ladies uttered a word. I
am much exercised as to what to call the bishop. I tried "Sir"
with splendid effect. I think I will adopt it for the future. It is
safe anyhow. This is a splendid house and a lovely wooded
country with no mountains but beautiful green slopes stretching
around in every direction. The cathedral is in the grounds.
'8 *June.* Mama and I were called late this morning and in
consequence crept down late to prayers in the great oak hall
feeling that we were being stared at by everyone. After prayers
came breakfast which was right good. Still neither I nor the two
girls have made any advances of friendship beyond wishing each
other good morning. Nannie Darley is awfully kind but has got
the Plunkett* trick of sighing deeply on every occasion, which
after a while gets monotonous and in the long run is aggravating
to an extent. The old Bishop would be delightful but for a trick
of snorting which at meal times is intolerable, and in society is,
to say the least of it, unpleasant. I worked in the morning whilst
the girls were at their lessons with their Frau. When they had
done we made a tour of the pleasure grounds and garden which

* Plunkett was the family name of the Barons Dunsany. The Plunketts were
connections of the Martins.

are the most beautiful things I ever saw. I got on very well with
the girls who are not at all a bad sort. After lunch I worked and
read during lesson-times and afterwards strolled about with
the girls and Frau till tea which we had in the schoolroom. We
then dressed and went down.

'*Friday, 9 June.* To avoid being late for prayers again I got up
at an unearthly hour and of course was down hours before
breakfast. At breakfast one of the candidates for deacon's
ordination slunk in and in a terrible fright meekly swallowed "an
'asty snack". After this cheerful meal I read and then went out
with the little Darleys and amused myself. More candidates for
ordination were arriving all the morning and were imprisoned
in the Bishop's study till lunch time. And no sooner had they sat
down to eat than more arrived, almost all of them young
curates and everyone of them without an exception positively
clammy with terror. We were huddled over to the side table to
make room, where the old butler fed us royally. After lunch we
sallied forth and played croquet till interrupted by the arrival of
a "nice companion" and we had to take a ghastly walk round the
gardens with her. When she went off we returned to croquet and
played in a desultory way till teatime. Both the girls are very
jolly but rather "fall off in the profile". We dressed in the
evening and went down, I attired in a beautious white dress with
a white rose in my buzzim. The room was full of young curates
sitting by fours and fives on the corners of chairs. Not one of
them opened their lips once.

'*Saturday, 10 June.* This morning I was down at an unearthly
hour whilst Mama slept it out till she missed prayers. After
breakfast I read for a while and practised, and then went and
banged about the balls on the croquet ground. As soon as the
girls came out we took a fine walk about the place encountering
several of the wretched candidates on the way. Poor creatures,
they were just going up for their final examination. They all
came trooping in to lunch and were promptly placed at the side
table to our great relief. After lunch I pottered about with
Darley and made an awful effort to play croquet with one of the

curates, which turned out rather a failure as the wretched man was so nervous about the result of his exam that he invariably hit his own feet instead of the ball. Just then to my great relief the girls came out from lessons and we set to and had grand games of croquet till teatime. Immediately after late dinner all the curates departed in flocks on outside cars, and the house was rid of their unwholesome presence. I must say I was not sorry to see them off as I was always coming suddenly on them wandering helplessly round the garden, and we could never play croquet or amuse ourselves in any way without being conscious that they were watching us from behind trees and round corners. We strummed the piano all the evening in commemoration of it all being over.

'*Sunday, 11 June.* We were awakened this morning by hearing the prayer gong. Consequently we were rather late for breakfast. Mama went off with the Bishop to church in Cavan to see the ordination service. All the rest of us went to church here in the cathedral. It is a very nice church with the usual smell of frieze coats,* which is at first rather overpowering.'

The entries in Violet's diary for the next few years are short and have to do with her studies. She was given lessons in French, German and Greek, drawing, music and dancing, but having a taste for reading largely educated herself. She heads each year with a quotation from the English classics. In 1879, when she was seventeen, she read a paper at the law students' debating society. But though studious she was far from a recluse. With her mother she went out frequently into Dublin society. The names of well known members of the landed gentry often occur, such as the Persses, FitzGeralds, Guinesses, La Touches, etc. At eighteen we find her attending Augusta Persse's wedding to Sir William Gregory, the Augusta to become so famous later as Yeats's friend and supporter, and as an author in her own right.

In this same year, 1880, she records that she had tea with Colonel Kendal Coghill, who was the uncle of the girl who six

---

* The country people at this date wore frieze coats.

years later became her dearest friend. Colonel Coghill, an
Indian mutiny veteran, was forty-eight at this time. He will
appear again and again as this narrative proceeds and is always
referred to as Uncle Kendal. Brother of Edith Somerville's
mother, and grandson, as Violet's mother was granddaughter,
of Charles Kendal Bushe, the Chief Justice, he was Violet's
cousin, as was his niece Edith Somerville, her future friend. He
and his numerous relations, all cousins of the Martins, lived far
away from Galway and Dublin in the extreme west of the
County Cork at a place called Castle Townshend, of which a
great deal more hereafter. Except for her meeting in 1880 with
Kendal Coghill in Dublin, it is not recorded that Violet had met
any of her Castle Townshend cousins. There is no hint that she
had thought of visiting them, no hint that the course of her life
would be determined there.

In 1882, when she was twenty, she made her first visit to
London, which lasted two months. By this time her brother,
Robert Martin of Ross, was thirty-six and was married. His
wife, Connie, has her place in the story. Violet, of course, either
stayed with them or saw them frequently. Her diary shows that
she went the round of the sights and theatres. Her brother was
well situated to introduce her in his circle. He was a gifted
charming man, who found it amused his friends for him to pose as
a stage Irishman. He had begun to publish in *The Globe* and other
papers verses and stories of Irish life, including the song Ballyhooley which was such a hit in the halls that it alone made him
famous. Though there are no surviving records to prove that
Violet already had literary ambitions, there can be no doubt that
her brother's success in London was rather dazzling for her, a
girl sixteen years his junior. In 1899 he was to publish a collection of his best stories and verses in a volume called *Bits of
Blarney* under the pseudonym of Ballyhooley. Many of these
had appeared in previous years in the London press and had
been read by Violet. *Some Experiences of an Irish R.M.*, to be
published by Violet and her friend Edith Somerville, also in
1899, were very much better stories of the Irish country scene

than he achieved, yet his success facilitated their publication and created a brisk market for them. How the editor of the *Badminton Magazine* commissioned them will be related in its place. Backed, as her brother was, not only by London's popular opinion but also by the admiration of the several houses in high London society which his birth, charm and talents enabled him to frequent, she looked up to him for years until she found that she was vastly his superior as a writer.

In 1883 and 1884 Violet was out of Dublin a good deal. In the former year she was again in London for two months and in the latter stayed three weeks with friends in Devonshire. It is unfortunate that her diary contains no descriptions of the prominent persons she met to be compared with the delicious picture of her visit to the Bishop of Cavan nine years before. By 1886 her acquaintances in Dublin and London were quite numerous. There is no record of her having received offers of marriage, nor of her having fallen in love with anyone, which might have been expected in the circumstances. A fragment in the MSS. however suggests that in 1885/86 she saw a lot of a man called Willie Wills, a Bohemian friend of her brother Robert, who lived in London and had a position as a playwright as he wrote dramas for Irving. He also painted portraits in society. Extant letters of his show that he was very fond of her, but give the impression that he was a very silly man. He was sixty years of age and a distant cousin. She seems to have liked him enough to write to him and see him often when staying with her brother in London. No doubt his position in the literary world, such as it was, impressed her.

This is as much as we know of Violet Martin on the eve of her meeting with Edith Somerville, which took place in January 1886. By then she had, it seems, written articles, but had published nothing of importance, though she must have been aware of latent powers. There is reason to think that she wrote poetry, but none of such compositions have survived.

The meeting of the two protagonists of this book came about in the most natural way, as will appear in the next chapter.

2

*Edith Somerville's youth and meeting with
Violet Martin*

In January 1886 Mrs Martin (Mama as she is always called in
the Martin papers) left Dublin to stay at the village of Castle
Townshend, accompanied by two of her daughters, Violet aged
twenty-four and Selina a year older. The other three daughters
who had come with her to Dublin were now married. Castle
Townshend was an unusual sort of place, because half a dozen
families of the Cork landed gentry were settled there, instead
of living, as the Irish landed gentry generally did, on estates
dotted about the counties, miles apart from each other, as at
Ross. Here their houses clustered round the village of Castle
Townshend, occupying a square mile of ground or less. The
sketch map and the aerial view give the general impression.
The site was high ground which shelved steeply to the sea, a
deep inlet or haven from the Atlantic like many others in
western Cork. The view from the houses down to the haven
and out to its mouth on the ocean was very fine. Near the west
entrance to the village, a high point on the site, stood Drishane,
the seat of the Somerville family. The avenue gate to Glen
Barrahane, the seat of the Coghills, was just below. Standing
on the shore of the haven to the eastward was the Castle, the
seat of the Townshends. These were the leading families, heads
of which had held at times the office of High Sheriff of the

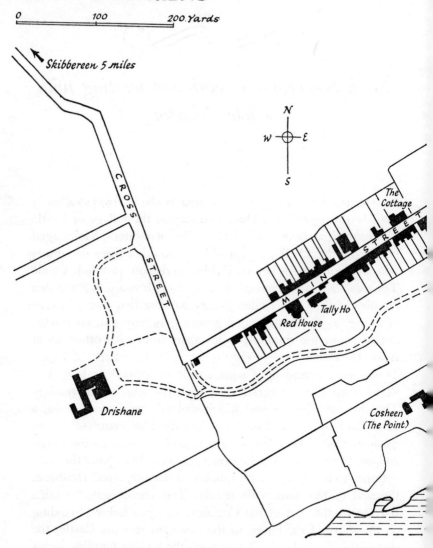

CASTLE TOWNSHEND

0   100   200 Yards

Skibbereen 5 miles

N
W E
S

CROSS STREET

MAIN STREET

The Cottage

Tally Ho

Red House

Drishane

Cosheen
(The Point)

St. Barrahane Church

Castle Townshend

Quay

Quay

Two Trees

Malmaison

Mall House

Seafield

Glen Barrahane

THE MALL

Coastguard Station

The Harbour

(Castle Haven)

County of Cork and also high rank in the British army and navy. During the eighteenth and nineteenth centuries they inter-married. At the time of the Martins' visit, the mother of Colonel Thomas Somerville, the owner of Drishane, was a Townshend, and his wife was the daughter of a Coghill. Castle Townshend was a nest of cousins.

To get there from Dublin Mrs Martin and her two daughters had to take the train to Cork, change and catch another to Skibbereen where a Somerville carriage would be waiting to drive them the five miles to Castle Townshend. It appears that the Townshends had offered to lend them or lease them for a while Tally Ho, one of several houses which belonged to them at that time. It backed onto the main street of the village and faced down the hill to the haven, a long low house standing in its garden.

Violet thus found herself among a crowd of people related to each other, and also related to her through a common descent from Charles Bushe, the Lord Chief Justice, none of whom, however, she is said to have met hitherto, except Colonel Kendal Coghill, uncle of Colonel Thomas Somerville's numerous family of five sons and two daughters. These young people, the eldest four years Violet's senior and the youngest eleven years her junior, were to become her closest friends. Her love for the eldest, Edith, aged twenty-eight, grew to be the central emotion of her life. Her first mention of Edith in her diary is dated 27 February 1886, over a month after her arrival, where she records that 'Edith is beginning my portrait', the portrait which is reproduced here. This event marked the beginning of Edith and Violet's friendship.

What Edith's life had been up to this may be gathered from her diary and correspondence. When she was born in 1858 her father, Colonel Thomas Somerville, was stationed at Corfu, where he commanded the 3rd Buffs. Influenced, no doubt, by his Greek surroundings, he chose Œnone for her second name (Œnone was the daughter of the river god Cabren, and the wife of Paris till he deserted her for Helen of Troy). In due course

Thomas Somerville came to live at Drishane, being now sixty-two. The 1873 entries of Edith's diary reveal her as an outdoor girl of fifteen who loves horses and dogs, reads little but has a taste for music and painting. She is more childish for her age than was Violet. Her great friend is Ethel Coghill, her cousin. In 1874 she and Ethel write and produce family theatricals, and design the scenery and costumes. She did some illuminated texts, which a Glasgow firm bought. And she dabbled in spiritualism; in August of this year she records that Cameron, her eldest brother, assisted by two other boys 'actually made a small round table turn and rap out some questions, when Mother put a stop to it, being a *questionable* amusement.' Her mother's objection was that table turning should not be treated as an amusement because it was a real and serious thing.

Edith's devotion for Ethel Coghill grew deeper. They saw each other every day and wrote long letters when parted. In 1877 they produced another family play which they had written. This year Edith, now nineteen, made her first trip to London, stayed with relations and took drawing lessons in South Kensington. Ethel had been taken by her family to Switzerland. The entries in Edith's diary are now maturer and have more bite. Her sense of the ridiculous is developing. Of a Wagner concert she attended in London she has: 'Poor old Wagner was overcome (by the applause) and unable to reply, so he kissed all the other old men and the hall floated in German tears.'

Back at Drishane in June she joined enthusiastically, though Ethel was still absent, in the summer amusements, dancing, bathing, tennis, boating; and practised her drawing. The brothers had to act as models. 'The Chimp (her eldest brother, Cameron's, nickname) attired in bathing drawers and native worth, stood alternatively as Esau and Jacob.' Aylmer, the third brother, similarly attired, was made to pose for a picture of Orpheus, and Boyle, the second brother (the future Vice-Admiral) posed as Ishmael (in bathing costume too). He was fourteen and Aylmer twelve. The two youngest boys, Jack and Hugh, aged five and four, were obliged to pose in the nude.

During the sitting 'it was difficult to prevent them from fighting each other'. Hugh's big success was as the infant Hercules, strangling two snakes made of flannel. (Eventually he became, like Boyle, a Vice-Admiral.) Her Coghill uncles Joscelyn and Kendal thrilled her by their psychic feats. On 3 April 1878 she records: 'Mother heard from Uncle Jos (Sir Joscelyn Coghill Bart, the head of the family) who was at a grand seance and was levitated, chair and all, until he could touch the ceiling.' Professor Nevill Coghill, his grandson, has informed me of the tradition that the baronet signed his name on the ceiling in pencil.

Edith now acquires a habit of dropping into her diary amusing anecdotes or country sayings. Many of these later were woven into her books to enliven the narrative and give it authenticity. Her entry on 21 April 1878 is: 'A child at Sunday school, asked why Joseph left Bethlehem in such a hurry, replied "Becaz it didn't agree with him, Miss".'

Drishane was a cold damp house; worse, it was infested with rats. If poison was put down they died under the floors. The smell of dead rats was so bad on 20 November 1878 that the drawing room could not be used. But the young people did not mind things of that kind. They knew how to keep the house lively. On 3 February 1879 Edith has: 'I dressed up the Chimp (Cameron was then nineteen) in Mother's clothes and we trotted him down to Glen Barrahane (the Coghills' house) and introduced him to Lady Avonmore as a Miss Fleming. She was utterly taken in. They asked him to sing, so Cam in a high falsetto squawked "Home they brought her warrior dead". The effect was splendid.' Cameron was to the end her favourite brother.

That month Lieutenant Nevill Coghill, heir to the Coghill baronetcy, won the V.C. for gallantry at the Zulu battle of Isandhlwana where he was killed, and was succeeded as heir by his brother, Egerton, the artist, whose influence on Edith's style of painting will later be discussed. When the news of Nevill Coghill's death was received, a seance was held and a spirit declared he was not dead, but a prisoner. Impressed and delighted, Edith recorded in her diary: 'If it is true I shall believe in spiritualism ever after. If not . . .' It was not true, for six days later Nevill's death was confirmed. But Edith's faith was not shaken. As will appear, she continued all her life to communicate, as she believed, with the dead. An essay in her book *Stray-aways*, published in 1920, forty-one years after Nevill Coghill's death, discloses her views at length and explains that though her mother once forbade tableturning, she was a keen spiritualist, as was her brother Kendal. 'My mother had' she writes 'a special flair for the occult.' In *Stray-aways* she declares, too, that when twenty-one she and her brother Boyle were obliged by Uncle Kendal to attend seances as he thought they had some mediumistic powers. 'We accepted the role of mouthpiece of the Oracle. Messages flowed over sheet after sheet of paper.' She remembers in particular the calling up of the shade of a Coghill ancestress of the seventeenth century. But a great deal more of this will be found in its place.

On 6 June 1879 something happened which disclosed an aspect of Edith's character which was fundamental. Her great friend, Ethel Coghill, the girl she loved so much that she thought of her as a twin spirit with whom she shared everything, shocked her profoundly. The entry in the diary is as follows: 'That unprincipled woman, the Twin, has been and gone and engaged herself to Jimmy Penrose. She had to come up and 'fess to her injured Twin. She ought to be ashamed of herself. The Twin came up bringing her sheaf with her. I only wonder that I didn't have a relapse at the sight of them. She can't go shares in her own mean Beast. Moreover she exposes me to public obloquy as the remaining Twin and deprived me of two nights sleep.' (Evidently the entry was written two days after the disclosure.) Next day she has: 'Crawled like a moribund caterpillar downstairs.' Ethel Coghill's marriage with James Penrose took place the following year, 1880, on 30 December. The account of it in the diary is headed 'The hideous day' and goes on: 'Got to church early. Jack and Hugh (now aged eight and seven) carried her tail from the carriage, the coastguards having made a sail-walk right up to the door.' She herself played the wedding march on the organ, for she had already become the regular organist in St Barrahane's, as the Castle Townshend church was called, which had something of a family chapel about it, though the congregation included a few Protestant farmers and coast-guards. There followed the breakfast and the departure of the couple. Edith makes it clear that the evening's festivities—music, songs, impersonations—made her think of animals in a menagerie going through their tricks. She was very sick in the night and stayed in bed all next day. However in the evening she got up and went to a dance given by The O'Donovan. 'One needed something to take the taste of that wedding out of our mouths. It felt like an aggravated nightmare.'

Now what is one to make of this episode? It seems to turn partly on the fact that Ethel's engagement was a complete sur-prise to Edith. Ethel had given no hint of the way things were going. As a general rule a favourite topic of conversation between young girls is their boy friends. It is a happy day when one of them marries. The more affectionate the terms on which the girls stand to each other, the freer the confidences they make. Ethel had not done this. She had said not a word; there was something about Edith which warned her not to do so. Without perhaps defining the difference between them, she intuitively knew that they were not twin souls; there was a fundamental difference in the view they held of their relationship. For Ethel there was no incompatability between love for a woman and marriage with a man. For Edith the incompatibility was abso-lute. The kind of feeling she had for Ethel gave Ethel no licence to fall in love with a man. Any sexual union with a man had something revolting about it for Edith. Deep in her was a pro-found distaste for the opposite sex. Ethel did not suffer from this disability. Her love for Edith had no trace of homosexuality in it. Edith's deepest feelings, however, were entirely concen-trated on her own sex. The emotion, however, was sublimated. It did not include what she would have termed its grosser manifestations. Nevertheless, as any psychiatrist will declare,

Grandpa Somerville and Edith, aged twelve (1870)

Drishane (1900)

it was the same emotion. Edith was a just woman. When she got over the shock of discovering that Ethel liked men well enough to marry, she could not justly blame her. They continued friends, but how differently! All the difference between a genial relationship and a deep overwhelming obsession.

It is essential to understand this aspect of Edith's character if what follows later is to be fully intelligible.

There was some distress in Ireland at this time. Harvests had been poor, prices for agricultural produce had fallen, the peasantry, incited to violence by a body known as the Land League, turned on unpopular landlords. The countryside was a good deal disturbed. Cork was not as affected as some other counties, but a distress committee was set up, and the leading people took their part in organizing relief. Mrs Somerville was one of those who helped. 'Troops of women,' noted Edith, 'came for relief. Mother lectured them on the necessity of not eating their seed potatoes. To all her instructive remarks they replied unanimously "May the Lord spare ye long." ' But on one occasion the carriage was stoned when she and her mother were returning home. In another entry her dawning literary power is in evidence. 'A woman who came for relief informed me that she was "the most disthressful poor person and had not the good luck nor misfortune to be in the Misthress's division." On asking her where she lived, she said "I do be like a wild goose over on the side of Myross Wood", which is, I think, a noble way of expressing that you have no fixed habitation.' All her life Edith listened for and collected such nobilities of country talk. She commands a neat turn of phrase herself. Thus on 2 October 1880 she comments on Harry Donovan, a new servant: 'He is one of whom it is extenuatingly said "He is slow and sure". This means that he is sure to be slow. His chief virtue is that he doesn't drink. But this self-denial is unnecessary. Nothing could affect his head.'

One of the characteristics of her diary is the great interest she shows in her brothers. How Cameron, now in the Army and twenty-one, returned from the West Indies, she wrote: 'At 2.30

C   [33]

the Chimp accompanied by his tame ape—a small very gentle chestnut monkey—appeared. Both looking very well.' Cameron had from early days been known as the Chimp, though the reason for the nickname has not been handed down. Boyle, the naval brother, aged seventeen, was also just back from service overseas, the Pacific. She has: 'A Skibbereen man, very screwed, pointed out Papa as he drove off and said: "Never shaw him so dhrunk before." Boyle knocked him down.' Thomas Somerville became High Sheriff of Cork in 1888.

So the diary goes on, full of amusing bits. 'We went down to see Aunt Bessie who never changes and is always like a healthy, rather withered but ladylike radish.' Cameron's monkey gives trouble. It spills the soup being handed round at dinner and 'alarms the household by having a fit'. Which reminds one of what Juliana, one of the maids, said when Edith's pet dog, sitting on her knee at dessert, made a snap as Juliana was changing the plates: 'For all he's so cross to me in the parlour, he's very favourable to me in the kitchen.' The said Juliana also observed of one of the stable hands: 'Ah! poor Mick! Twas he was the nice kind boy. He was very dhrunk the night he died.'

So the days passed. Edith is fully occupied with her music and painting. It has been said of her that she never read anything, but in 1882 she records that she got through the Brontës and George Eliot and even one of Henry James's novels. Occasionally she tried her hand at writing short pieces intended to amuse the family, who all had literary and artistic tastes of sorts. 'The Chimp intends to publish some waltzes he wrote while abroad.' This was recorded the day his monkey upset the soup at dinner.

Edith's sister Hildegarde, a reliable and sensible girl, nine years her junior, is not often mentioned in these early diaries, though in the end she turned out Edith's trusted friend and companion. In April 1882, when Edith in her twenty-fourth year went to Germany to continue her art training, Hildegarde was with her. On her return her paintings were good enough for exhibition at a mixed exhibition in Cork. She sold one painting, but was not so lucky in Dublin. 'A picture of the Chimp as an art critic was rejected by the Dublin Art Society, though they like Aylmer (the third brother) done up as a Zouave.'

These various extracts from Edith's diary allow the conclusion that she saw herself a painter rather than a writer. By twenty-four she had studied art in London and abroad, and exhibited in Cork and Dublin; and she had compiled a book called *The Mark Twain Birthday Book*, which consisted of passages from his works. The cover was designed by her. In writing she had attempted nothing beyond a few articles. Her intention clearly was to become a painter. Her cousin, Egerton Coghill, painted very well and had a studio in Paris. On Violet's arrival at Castle Townshend the friendship begins by her painting her portrait. But painting was not to be her career, though she learnt to paint well and illustrated many of her books. Violet did not paint, but was already showing signs of becoming a writer. Very soon she and Edith got to like each other, and Edith saw that writing, not painting, was to be her main career.

3

Edith and Martin become intimate friends

Five years had now elapsed since Edith lost Ethel. They corresponded, they met occasionally in Dublin. But Edith had been
deprived of what she required, association with a woman who
had no desire to marry or go with a man, a woman who would
be all in all to her and to whom she would be all in all. Could
Violet be such a woman, fulfil such conditions? She was already
attracted to her. By a coincidence, Violet looked a little like
Ethel. She had, it is said, something of Ethel in her air, particularly when riding and singing. She was clearly Ethel's superior
as a personality. There was a depth in her quite lacking in the
other. As an intellectual she was far superior. Indeed, Edith as
she studied her for the portrait perceived in her qualities to
which she herself could only look up, a fastidious taste, an
enlightenment that belongs to the poet, a sensitivity which was
mysteriously withdrawn. With all that she was an out-of-door
girl too, rode well and played all games. But she was not a
painter; their interests differed in that important respect.
Moreover, she lived in Ross, so far away. When her visit to
Castle Townshend ended, she might disappear. At first Edith
felt that to pursue the matter would lead nowhere. So three
weeks after starting the portrait she decided to go to Paris and
continue her art studies; her cousin Egerton Coghill had a
studio there. She was away during March, April and half May
of 1886. Meanwhile, Violet, her mother and sister Selina, who

was an eccentric, moved from Tally Ho to another house nearby, The Mall House, which belonged to the Somervilles. When Edith came back on 16 June, Violet found her, as she records that day, 'pale and dwindled but a fashionable lady'. She had bought some Parisian clothes, which looked wonderfully smart in a place like Castle Townshend. The 'pale and dwindled' look may have been due to the fatigues of the journey or a bad crossing from England. She says Violet gave her 'a great welcome'. The separation seems to have brought the two closer together, for Violet is now mentioned nearly every day as Edith's particular companion. She is in and out of Drishane at all hours and often sleeps the night there in Edith's room. They have become intimate friends. Violet was much liked by all Edith's family and relatives. She was treated as one of them, though, indeed, as a cousin no one would have thought of treating her otherwise. Edith no longer called her Violet. There was a Violet already in the circle of cousins, and to avoid confusion, particularly in the diary, she decided to call Violet by her surname, Martin, preferring this to using her second name, Florence, as there was an aunt Florence. (From this on I must follow suit, so as to avoid discrepancy in quotations from the MSS.)

So in 1886 a close friendship between the two young women was developing, though there was a difference in their approach to each other. Unlike Edith, Martin might have married. That she had not done so may be ascribed to her not having met a man who roused her in that way. But she was capable of falling in love with a man, while Edith was not. Edith could only fall in love with a woman. In falling in love with Martin she was taking the same risk that she took with her cousin, Ethel, who married Jim Penrose. Martin might be seduced from her by a member of the other sex. But though this could happen, it was not so likely as in Ethel's case. Martin was a literary genius in embryo. Such women may, of course, marry, but that state is not essential for their happiness; the development of their talents comes first. To be fully satisfied, Martin must find an outlet for her genius. She was to find it in collaboration with

Edith, whose love she could return with the tenderest affection. Edith's feeling for Martin, however, was something more over-whelming than tenderness and the development of a common talent. It was a passion, an obsession from the depths of her being.

How the friendship ripened and how a base for the coming collaboration was laid may be gleaned from the entries in the two women's diaries.

During the summer months of 1886, always the gayest at Castle Townshend, with picnics, dances, tournaments, boating, the two friends were close companions, though Edith paid a week's visit on 9 September to cousins at Lismore, a town in Waterford. Martin's diary has: 14 September 'Wrote to Edith.' 18 September 'Did nothing particular, being too excited by the return of Edith. At 6.30 walked up the Skibbereen road in tor-rents of rain and met Edith.' They go for rides together and to view points which might make a good picture. Edith would get out her paints, Martin her writing pad, for she was trying her hand at articles for the London press, encouraged thereto by her brother Robert's success. To begin with, the idea was that they might collaborate in such articles, the text to be by Martin, the illustrations by Edith. The first such collaboration was an article for the *Graphic* on palmistry dated 11 October 1886.

Mama and Selina now departed for Dublin, but Edith per-suaded Martin to stay on for a while, and she moved into Drishane. But on 13 December she had to go and rejoin her mother. There is a letter of 14 December to Edith in which she describes her journey to Dublin. She had the portrait with her and reports how much her mother liked it. 'Mama is an un-reliable art critic but I cannot say how pleased I am at her liking the portrait.' She wished she had not had to say goodbye to Edith. 'I don't know when I have been more depressed than at leaving Castle Townshend, and more especially Drishane, and more especially you.' But she was cheerful enough to append a little story she was sure would amuse Edith about 'what a woman said to Mama about another woman who had lost her

husband. "Oh, indeed, yes, madam, there she is the crayture
and he having left her with one child and the invoice of another."
Is it very improper? I feel it is but am not sure,' she concludes
with a laugh; Martin had so keen a sense of the ridiculous that
she used to laugh uncontrollably to the embarrassment of staid
people.

She felt the separation from Edith badly. On 16 January 1887
she has in her diary: 'Just a year today since I went to Castle
Townshend. Wrote to Edith today to wish her many happy
returns of the day,' as if their first meeting was a sort of birthday, an entry into life. Unable to bear the separation longer,
Edith goes to Dublin on 4 February. Martin has: 'Went to the
station to meet Edith who arrived with her little dog (an engag-
ing but ill mannered little thing).' This was Patsy, of which
Edith had written in her diary of 4 January 1887: 'My little dog
Patsy came. A fox terrier, 3 months old, small wizened, well
bred and bursting with intelligence.' On 9 January 'Patsy fear-
fully sick' and on 12 January: 'My little dog all right and learn-
ing manners and deportment such as would grace a court.' When
she got off the train in Dublin she had Patsy hidden in a carpet
bag, so as not to have to pay for a dog ticket. Patsy was the first
mentioned of the long line of beloved dogs, the most delightful
of which are immortalized in *Maria*, published by Edith in 1949,
the year of her death.

In one of the many letters written by Edith to Martin between
13 December 1886 when Martin left Drishane and 5 February
1887 when Edith rejoined her in Dublin, Edith wrote a very full
description of a hunt on 1 January 1887. As it is the first description of a hunt in the papers and presages so many more, the
greater part of it is quoted here: 'Of all the foul coverts to get
a fox out of, Manch takes the cake. Lissard isn't in it, and it is
worse than Lissard in being *absolutely* impassible so that if the
fox breaks covert on the wrong side you are done for, and it is
nearly a mile long. Well. We were fooling up and down, waiting, to the south in the field, when I saw the fox,—a crool brute,
as big as a calf—steal along to the east and in a minute the whole

pack helter-skelter after him. We waited to let him break when suddenly there was silence. They had overrun the scent in some mysterious manner and some blug had headed back the fox. Then ensued long waiting and trying back. Mr Beamish (M.F.H.) creeping on foot among the jungle, and no one knowing where the fox wd break, but the wind being west we all hoped he wd break east and run down the wind. At last after about $\frac{1}{2}$ an hour, we heard very faint shrieks the *far* side of the hill to the west. We belted round and found the fox had broke and the whole pack got away a mile ahead of old Beamish, who had however slipped off after them without giving a word of warning to the field. We could see no sign of anything, but little fringes of country fellows along the hill waved to us the way. It was a horrible country, rotten fences and very high stone gaps. Our horses went splendidly over horrible ground till we came to a boreen with a low wall across it, on the other side a stream full of huge stones and a sort of bank. Sorcerer (her horse) jumped it in the most able way but the mare wouldn't have it. It certainly was a very ugly place. Aylmer (her brother) licked and spurred in vain. Then he shouted to me to go on, so as we had made an agreement to that effect I did so, following some other people up a road for about $\frac{1}{2}$ a mile. Then I saw Jack Burgh and Mr Maxwell going away to the north. I was just going after them when I thought it was hard luck on Aylmer to leave him, so I waited and in about 5 or 6 minutes he came up, having lifted her over with the spurs. She refused no more. Just then, on a hill about a mile away to the north, going like blazes, we saw the hounds and Mr Beamish. Between us and them was a big turf bog with no sort of passage. So A and I made a hurried guess by the look of things at the way he was running, and set off as hard as we could lick round the bog, on a bog road. One local genius was with us but after we got round the bog he turned off to the east and we saw him no more. We had a moment of agony as to whether we would follow him but decided to go our own way. And it was well for us. We went on for about 5 minutes, best pace, when a country boy began to

[40]

roar at us, something about going to the west (we were riding NW) over the bog. We turned sharp off, Sorcerer nearly pulling my arms out, he was so excited, when we heard something. My dear, about 100 yards back to the south we saw the *whole pack* come streaming down the hill, without a man within a mile of them. It was the fox only who had gone across to the west. When they got to the road we had just left, they checked. Then was our time. We rode down like mad, whipped them onto the line the fox had gone, and off they went again, full cry, with A and I *alone* after them. It was almost too supreme a moment. I could not have spoken, except in a sort of mad howl to the hounds, to save my life and I could hardly see. However they ran over a country where you had to see. We were just going about as hard as the horses could leg it, but the hounds were racing with their heads up and the scent red hot. It was all we could do to keep them in sight over that breakneck place, but we did somehow and in about 20 minutes they checked round a huge cairn of stones. A nipped off and climbed round to get the fox out, when suddenly before you could say knife out jumped the fox into the very jaws of the whole pack. He had been in a tunnel and A had started him out. The hounds were so taken by surprise that they hadn't time to nail him and out, *literally*, between their legs he slipped and away with him with the hounds, A and me, all blue with passion, after him. But he knew what he was up to. In about 1 or 2 hundred yards there was a big rock and he just wriggled into it as the leading hound made a snap at his brush. I couldn't have believed anything could have got away as he did. I am generally glad when a game fox gets off, but I must admit that A and I could have cried. We thought we were sure of the brush. There we stood and stared at each other.'

A sentence to notice is: 'I am generally glad when a game fox gets off.' Edith was humane beyond her period. She had immense compassion for animals, but living in the atmosphere of a hunting county, sport took precedence in her mind over compassion, though her conscience was a little pricked.

It seems that Edith had some time back booked another session at her Paris art school and now tried to get Martin to accompany her. But Mama was against it; she thought Martin too young to go off to Paris without a chaperon. However in March 1887 the two of them went as far as London together. There Martin stayed with her brother, Robert, and his wife, Connie, and began writing an article on the Dublin season for the *Graphic*, to be illustrated by Edith.

Edith went to Paris alone, her only companion the little dog Patsy, which travelled at the bottom of a carpet bag. Settled to *atelier* routine, she wrote to Martin at length several times a week. In due course the article for the *Graphic* arrived and she set to work to illustrate it. Patsy had behaved well at first but on 20 March was 'seedy with a sort of snorting disease'. Later he had hysterics 'and shrieked for nearly ten minutes till I gave him cognac and sal volatile'.

Martin's reply of 27 March, after condolence about the dog, has the following: 'A dog that I once had was taken in that way one night on seeing me in my (hip) bath for the first time and frightened me awfully—half flew at me and then fled to the door and yelled till everyone in the house came to the rescue, while I naked and dripping in safety under the bedclothes adjured them to stay outside till the paroxysm was over, which it soon was. This animal was a large harrier and it was most alarming. I may add that when I did succeed in getting her out of the room she immediately proceeded to the kitchen and drank about 2 quarts of milk which had been set for cream and then perambulated the house all night uttering faint injured cries, and clattering on the oilcloth with long nails, and decorating the various landings with a patent kind of fluid outline map.'

During April she came across the ridiculous cousin of her mother's, Willie Wills, who has been mentioned before as being fond of her. 'I met him today in an unexpected way. He was skulking à la conspirateur and was dressed in *the* coat. This has an immense coachman's collar and cape. The former was turned up till it touched his hat, the latter hung freely back from his shoulders like a hood. He was covered with white smudges, and in this guise did I, in my very best bonnet, white veil and all the rest of it, wander with him down High Street to Gloucester Road, while he affected not to know the way except by the spires of churches and distant trees and the stars and such things. I am so accustomed to this nonsense and so wearied of combating it that I pretend to believe in it now and follow him when he deliberately takes the wrong turn. No one would believe that a man of his age and ability would be so perverse and foolish, but no matter.'

Under further pressure Mama consented at the end of April to Martin joining Edith in Paris for a short stay. She arrived on 1 May 1887, was met by Edith, taken to her room in the Hotel Haute Loire, Boulevard d'Enfer, near the Luxembourg, which they shared. For the next ten days she saw the sights, visited the galleries, went to a music hall and much enjoyed herself. On the 10th Edith and she returned to London. They had to smuggle Patsy through the English customs. Edith's diary reads: 'At Newhaven had a moment of terror, all small bags examined.' (Patsy was in the carpet bag.) 'Martin crammed Patsy up her sleeve and he escaped.' Edith crossed to Ireland, leaving Martin who went to Portsmouth on a visit to one of her three married sisters, whose husband was in the Navy. From there in June she went up to London for the Jubilee celebrations, after getting an invitation from Lady Waterford to view the procession on 26 June from the balcony of her house in Pall Mall. There is an excited letter in which she describes what she saw. She and her sister, after a walk through Charles Street and the Park where the crowds were enormous, reached the Waterfords at 9 a.m. 'There we found peace and calm, the best of good seats on the balcony and a breakfast of the most inviting and comprehensive kind. There were about 15 other people there. We had a perfect view of the procession as it came towards us. There were some entrancing fights at the corners (of Pall Mall and Waterloo Place) between the police and people. What struck me most were the Indian people, who looked like the real fine old stage princes, sparkling fit to blind you. . . . The Queen herself was the finest of the whole show. You could not believe what a great lady she looked.'

After the procession had passed, Martin and her sister went up St James's Street to watch it return. 'We wrestled with the filthy mob. A drunken man steadied himself against me to cheer as they passed, and though I could see nothing but the coachmen's heads, I bellowed and screamed too. Most refreshing it was after the ladylike reserve of the Waterfords' balcony. . . . It is something to remember to have seen London off its head.'

The *Irish Times* brought out a book of fifty Irish poems celebrating the occasion for presentation to the Queen. Martin was delighted to find a poem of hers included, which she had sent in on the chance. In high spirits, she ends the letter with a ludicrous story of a cousin who was obliged 'to visit some relations with discouraging manners and an awe-inspiring house. To show that he was quite unembarrassed he began to play with the favourite pug, finally dancing it round on its hind legs. It immediately threw up and that I think ends the story.'

Martin remained in England till August 1887 when she rejoined Edith at Drishane. The idea of a literary collaboration had not as yet come to anything much, though they had been in frequent correspondence about its possibility. Now was the opportunity to try to write something more solid and ambitious than miscellaneous articles. But what they should do or could do together remained in question. Edith knew she had literary talent, but had put her painting first. But if she were to have the close association with Martin she so desired, she must put painting second and develop her writing. Actually she had more literary than artistic talent, though she did not know it. She was a most gifted woman, but of all her gifts writing was the greatest.

Throughout September 1887 the diaries show them experimenting. 'Various literary labours till tea time' as Martin puts it on 26 September. In October it is reported for the first time that they are writing a novel together, the novel which was ultimately call *An Irish Cousin*. On 4 October Edith has: 'We began to invent a plot for a penny thriller.' The intention was to write a novel with an exciting plot which would sell widely. They wanted to make money. Except for what their mothers let them have, they hadn't a penny. 'Discussed the *Shockerawn*' (Edith, 19 October); 'We stayed in and worried over the *Shockerawn*, an Irish tale of love and gore' (Martin, 21 October). The future *An Irish Cousin* was so-called because Mrs Somerville used to say with a laugh 'How's the shocker going?' or 'At the shocker again, I see.' The rest of the family joined in laughing at 'that nonsense of the girls'. In her *Irish Memories* (published in 1917) Edith, recalling that time, writes of the sniffyness of her brothers and uncles. 'When not actually reviled, we were treated with much the same disapproving sufferance that is shown to an outside dog that sneaks into the house on a wet day.' They 'reached chapter XI with great labour' on 10 December 1887. And on 2 January 1888 Martin has: 'Terrible stress of the Shocker. At it all day, except when we went down to help at the Christmas tree. Shockered far into the night.' In *Irish Memories* Edith explains the method of the collaboration. 'Our work was done conversationally. One or other—not infrequently both simultaneously—would state a proposition. This would be argued, combated perhaps, approved or modified; it would then be written down by the (wholly fortuitous) holder of the pen, would be scratched out, scribbled in again.' Only two people marvellously suited to each other could compose successfully in such a way.

By 3 January 1888 they had finished the first half. Edith notes: 'Gave it to mother to read. She loathes it.' As the authors developed their story, their first idea of writing a 'penny thriller' was seen to be nonsense. They could not write that sort of stuff anyway. 'The faked thrills that were to make our fortunes were repudiated,' wrote Edith, and ascribes their change of mood to a curious experience. They had gone to visit a cousin, one of the Townshends, who lived in an old house called Whitehall twelve miles from Drishane, a lonely spot over the sea. When their horses were at the door for their return at sunset, 'in the darkened façade of the long grey house, a window, just over the hall door, caught our attention. In it, for an instant, was a white face. Trails of ivy hung over the panes, but we saw the face glimmer there for a minute and vanish.' They believed it to be the face of some half-witted relative, a living ghost that haunted the house. It was this experience, says Edith, that turned them aside from silly thrills to realities which were far more thrilling.

But Martin was now recalled to Dublin by Mama. She left the MS. with Edith to work on. 'Found Mama at Ball's Bridge (a south Dublin suburb) and went over to see Jim and Amy (her brother and sister-in-law who were back from planting in Ceylon). Jim scarcely a bit altered. We dined and went to see "Dorothy" at the Leinster Hall and back to have oysters with Jim.' Martin, delighted at the change of scene and eager to see her Dublin friends and relatives, made a round of visits, went drives and shopping. Soon, however, she heard from Edith, asking her to return and go on with the novel. Before doing so she rushed down to Kildare to stay with her married sister Geraldine. A clean copy of the novel reached her there. Edith had made 'many improvements'. Martin read it to Geraldine and worked on it a little. More invitations came in and she went on to Kilkenny. One has to remember that aspect of her character; she was a very popular and delightful person. On 30 January she got another letter from Edith begging her to come back. On 3 February 1888 she was at Drishane again and the collaboration recommenced.

All February they were working so hard at the book that they hardly got out at all, for them a most unusual state of affairs. On 14 March: 'Martin and I now inhabit the study and feed in the ante-room.' On 21 March 'worked more feverishly than ever.'

At the end of March they decided to go over to London, partly because Martin's brother Jim, who was now staying in London, wanted to see his sister before he left for Ceylon, and

ROSS AND NEIGHBOURHOOD

0   1 MILE

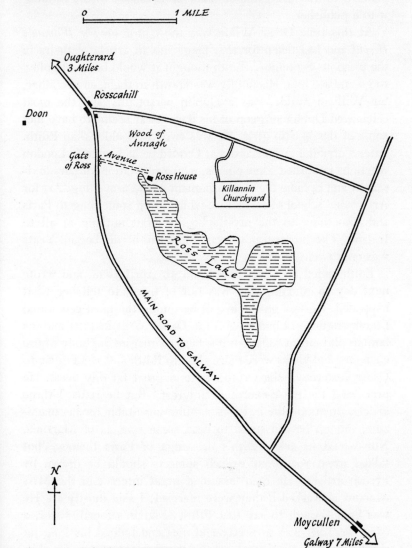

Oughterard
3 Miles

Rosscahill

Doon

Wood of
Annagh

Gate
of Ross

Avenue

Ross House

Killannin
Churchyard

Ross Lake

MAIN ROAD TO GALWAY

N

Moycullen

Galway 7 Miles

partly to make inquiries in the literary field. Their novel was largely written but drastic revision was required, which they planned to do during the summer at Drishane before sending it to a publisher.

At this time Oscar Wilde was the editor of *The Woman's World* and had taken for that magazine an article of theirs in the previous September. Edith thought it would be good policy to go and see him. His family was known to them, as his father, Sir William Wilde, was a Dublin personality and the most celebrated Dublin surgeon of his day. Oscar seems to have met some of the Martin girls. He was two years older than Edith. After a double first in classics at Oxford he had come to London where he published some poems, won a reputation for paradoxical wit and become the chief ornament of the prevailing 'Art for Art's sake' school of aesthetics, which owed something to Paris and something to the pre-Raphaelites, but nothing at all to Ireland. The literary movement there had hardly begun. Yeats was only twenty-three in 1888.

Edith called on Oscar Wilde on 10 April 1888, and wrote next day to Martin, who was out of town, to tell her what happened. He was on the eve of becoming the most celebrated literary figure in London with his *Dorian Gray* in 1891 and his famous plays from 1892, but it is hard to imagine anybody whose character and views were more alien to Edith's. 'I went down to Oscar yesterday,' she wrote; 'he is a great fat oily beast. He pretended the most enormous interest.' But he refused three articles on studio life in Paris as quite unsuitable for his magazine, though he consented to read some sonnets of Martin's. Nor would he take Edith's drawings of Paris themes, 'but talked great rot about French subjects should be drawn by French artists'. He then 'assumed great interest in the Miss Martins and asked if they were married; I said mostly all. He was kind enough to say that Edith (Martin's fourth sister, a Mrs Dawson) was so pretty and nice and bulged his long fat cheeks into an affectionate grin at the thought of her. He then showed me a book of very indifferent French sketches, was

Edith's portrait in oils of Martin (aged twenty-four) (1886)

Aerial view of Castle Townshend

foully civil, and so goodbye.' The fact was that Edith could hardly have gone to anyone in London less likely to be of use to her and Martin. There are angels and angels; he was the wrong sort of angel. Under no circumstances could she have appreciated at its proper value his future oeuvre, any better than he could have appreciated hers and Martin's. That the meeting was good comedy neither perceived, great humorists though both were.

This interview was on 10 April. On 22 April comes Edith's diary entry: 'Nanny (Martin's mother) insists on going to Ross for the summer. Infernal.' Martin's entry of corresponding date is: 'Mama intends to stay the summer at Ross and bang goes Castle Townshend.' This meant that the revision of the book would have to be postponed. Why Mama insisted on returning to Ross with Martin, which they had abandoned sixteen years before, and what happened when they got there, is the subject of the next chapter. Edith was back in Castle Townshend by 26 May. Martin remained a further month in London writing a précis of the book for an agent and left for Ross on 23 June 1888.

4

The Martins return to Ross

When Mama and her five daughters left Ross House in 1872 to
live in Dublin, and Robert Martin chose to stay in London, the
property was put in charge of an agent from Galway, a man
known and trusted by the family. The agent's duty, as usual in
such cases, was to collect the rents from the tenants on the
estate, oversee the property which contained valuable timber
and good woodcock shooting, and account to Robert Martin in
London, who thus became an absentee landlord. Ross House had
also to be let. This was arranged in due course. The estate and
house rents were at first duly remitted. During the woodcock
season Robert Martin sometimes came over to shoot. Things
went on like this for some years, but in the eighties the agent
sent less and less rent, alleging bad crops, which was true in
part. It was not difficult to convince Robert Martin that the
tenants must be allowed time to pay. He believed the agent's
excuses, made no enquiries, for he couldn't be bothered with
accounts. The truth was that the rents were being embezzled.
There was some distress at this time, but not nearly as much as
the agent pretended. He seems also to have been in league with
the lessee of Ross House, who was debiting against his rent
expenses for keeping the place in repair, when in fact he was
letting it go to ruin. As no check was made by Robert Martin,
the agent's depredations became worse. Finally he and the
lessee of Ross absconded to Canada, the latter having cut

down and sold a quantity of valuable timber on the estate.

What was to be done? Clearly somebody had to go to Ross. One would have thought that Robert Martin's duty to his mother and two unmarried sisters was to make a stay there and examine things on the spot. It seems, however, that his mother, sympathizing with his disinclination to abandon his London career when he was doing so brilliantly, offered to go herself. She was about sixty at the time, a woman of immense vitality and sense. She had brought up five daughters and married off three of them. There was no longer necessity to remain in Dublin. She loved Ross and had happy memories of the years she had spent there with her husband, the greatest figure in those parts. Moreover, the estate was her chief source of income. Failing its rents, or that part of them she enjoyed under her late husband's will, she and her two remaining daughters would be largely dependent on her son Robert and on what her other two sons, one a planter in Ceylon and the other in the army, could contribute. Such were her main reasons for returning to Ross. Having come to that decision, she wrote to her two unmarried daughters, who were away on visits, asking them to join her there, and herself set off in the early spring of 1888, leaving them to follow.

Some letters written by Martin to Edith about the return to Ross have survived. They are of particular interest. Besides providing a most vivid impression of events, they reveal Martin's power as a writer. Most of her writing outside the collaboration with Edith is lost; these letters show what a loss that is.

One of the letters, an undated fragment, begins: 'Mama told me in her magnificently unconscious way of her drive from Galway last March, when she first came.' She had ordered an outside car to take her the sixteen miles to Oughterard, five miles beyond Ross, where she stayed till she could move into Ross House. 'She said that a *monstrous* horse drew up at the door in Galway, of great height and portentous girth. Before she was far on the road the animal seemed inclined to stand still.

The man then explained that she might have a foal at any minute, and expressed many times in good Saxon English his regret at the matrimonial schemes of her guardians. So they went along in sweet converse, and this man, a stranger to her, asked her how "Miss Edit"* was, and said "God be with the times she used to be playing cards with me in the servants hall." By the time they got to Moycullen† Mama was *frozen* and went into a little public house sort of place, and there sat down by the fire and partook of whiskey and water. Crowds were outside, it being market, or a funeral or something—and she heard a woman's voice bawling outside "Is thaht Rahbert's wife?" thinking she, Mama, was Connie. I don't know how she escaped from there, but she did get to Oughterard that night somehow, having taken several hours on the road.'

On 23 June 1888 Martin's diary has: 'Left for Ross with Selina by 9 a.m. train from Dublin, arriving Galway at 2.15. Came out on the mail car to Ross. House much delapidated. Mama and Nurse Barrett the only occupiers.' Nurse Barrett was an old retainer of the Martin family, who had been wet-nurse to one of Mama's children, and rejoined the household now as general maid, though keeping her title of Nurse, as was the custom of the country. She has been immortalized in Edith's later book *Irish Memories* in a passage of singular felicity. She and Martin one time were discussing nursery days of long ago when Nurse Barrett recalled how once she intervened to stop the correction which the under nursemaid, Kit Sal, was inflicting on Miss Wilet (the way her name Violet was pronounced).

'Sure didn't I ketch Kit Sal one time an' she bating and kicking yerself on the avenue!' Nurse Barrett began. She then went on to describe how she had fallen on Kit Sal, torn her hair and 'shtuck her teeth in her.' 'The Misthress seen me afthewards, and she axed me what was on me, for sure I was cryin' with the rage. "Nothin' Ma'am!" says I. But I told her two days afther,

---

* Mama's fourth daughter, married a Mr Dawson who lived at Oughterard.
† Village half way from Galway to Oughterard.

an' she goes to Kit Sal an' says she, "What call had you to bate Miss Wilet?" says she, "Ye big shtump." "She wouldn't folly me," says Kit. "Well, indeed," says the Misthress, "I believe ye got a bigger batin' yerself from Nurse, and as far as that goes," says she, "I declare to God," says she, "I wish she dhrank yer blood!" says she.'*

The tenantry were pleased to see the mistress of Ross House back, as their personal liking for her was great, and it was not forgotten what her husband, James Martin, had done for them in the terrible years of the famine. Nevertheless, things were not quite what they had been sixteen years before. The Home Rule movement had gained considerable momentum; agrarian unrest had been fomented by the Land League. The landed gentry stood for a regime that was passing away. As will appear from letters shortly to be quoted, the Martins were still paid the respect due to The Family, a respect belonging to a past order, but it could not be hidden that times had changed. Every politeness was extended to them, every old style of affectionate endearment uttered, but it was not the same, could not be the same.

In the evening of 24 June, the day after Martin and Selina's arrival, Paddy Griffy, a tenant who had held some position of authority, such as bailiff, on the estate, called. Martin's description of the scene in a letter to Edith written soon afterwards is very vivid; it lifts the curtain on the old world of Ireland. 'I wish you had seen Paddy Griffy on Sunday night when he came down to welcome Selina and me. After the usual hand-kissings on the steps, he put his hands over his head and stood in the doorway, I suppose invoking his saint. He then rushed into the hall. "Dance Paddy" screamed Nurse Barrett, our maid-of-all-work. And he did dance, and awfully well too, to his own singing. Mama, who was attired in a flowing pink dressing gown and a black hat trimmed with lilac, became suddenly emulous, and with her spade under her arm joined in the jig. This lasted

* This is recorded in Martin's own handwriting in the hereafter to be mentioned Notebook 10.

for about a minute, and was a never-to-be-forgotten sight. They skipped round the hall, they changed sides, they swept up to each other and back again, and finished with the deepest curtseys. Mama is indeed a wonderful woman.'

This is one of the finest passages from Martin's letters. Mama comes marvellously to life, a grande dame who knew how to respond with abandon to the salutations of the old singing and dancing rustic. To do that as naturally as she did you have to be a wonderful woman.

In this same letter Martin describes her feelings at being back in the ancestral home: 'It is a curious thing to be at Ross —but it does not seem as if we were—not yet. It takes a long time to patch the present Ross and the one I remember into each other. It is deeply interesting and also heartrending.'

She goes on to describe the state of Ross. One has to picture the house on rising ground above the rock-strewn margin of a reedy mere, a solitary, gaunt, stone pile, immense, rectangular, its frontage facing south down a vista through the encircling woods. Surrounding it was an area, like a moat, and a terrace with balustrades. Behind and to the eastward lay the Wood of Annagh, where long ago reigned a rustic goddess of that name. Of it Martin has the sentence: 'The lovely Wood of Annagh, lovely always but loveliest when primroses like faint sunlight illumine every glade.' On the far side of it, half a mile from the house, was Kilannin, the Martins' graveyard, in which stood their burial vault, covered with memorial inscriptions, where among many generations of ancestors James Martin, Mama's husband, was buried in 1872, carried to the grave by his tenants, while the Irish cry, barbaric and terrible, burst from the women. The entrance to the Ross demesne was through a stone gateway on the Galway-Oughterard road. From it to the house was half a mile of avenue. In her letter of 27 June Martin describes the general dilapidation. The ground about the house was a jungle of weeds. She immediately got to work. 'There is literally every-thing to do except what Mama got done in the garden, which was, as the people told me, "the height of yourself in weeds".

The stable yard is a meadow. We inhabit 5 rooms in the house.'
The drawing room was made the kitchen. The whole interior
required repainting, repapering. For getting about there was a
farmer's outside car drawn by an old mare taken in from grass.
Martin turned her hand to everything, even clipping the laurels,
whose branches nearly blocked the avenue, half a mile of clipping, four furlongs up one side and four down the other. '25
June, began to work on the avenue. 26 June, up and to work. 29
June, worked at the avenue. 30 June, cleaned the terrace.' Thus
the diary. When the tenants saw her working like this, they
came to help without being asked. In the same letter she has:
'The tenants have been very good at coming and working here
for nothing except their dinners, and a great deal has been done
by them. It is, of course, gratifying, but in a way painful.' The
Martins had not the money to engage labour. And she goes on:
'We have had many visits from the poor people about, and
compliments and lamentations and finding of likenesses go on.
This takes some time and exhausts one's powers of rejoinder.
Added to this I don't yet know what to make of the people. I
know that they are many of them blackguards, but they are the
divil to talk and jackact. Of course some are really devoted, but
there is a change and I can feel it.' In a subsequent letter she
gives Edith examples of the kind of blarney to which she finds
it difficult to reply. 'I have been much harassed by trying to give
presents to the poor people, and today have had a long walk
with tea and tobacco—but was repaid by the Leonards (my
admirers) saying many precious things during a visit to them.
I had to drink first a glass of excellent sherry and then a
tumblerful of negus. There was no way out of it, but I had the
negus made very weak and escaped without being very drunk.
I was as usual told I was lovely in a sort of chorus "and its not
that you're lovely, but so commanding, indeed you have an
imprettive (imperative) look. Sure we're all enamoured by you".
This and much more, and I just sat and laughed weakly and
drunkenly.'

Martin also writes amusingly about their reception by the

local gentry. They had an indifferent one by the Bradys, whose social standing, however, was hardly that of gentry despite Mr Brady's official position of R.M. at Oughterard. This is the first mention by Martin or Edith of an R.M. or Resident Magistrate, a term to be so closely associated with them later on. Men appointed to that judicial post were as a rule officers retired from the army and posted to civil duties, but not in this case. Introducing what was a disagreeable encounter, Martin tells Edith: 'Brady and his large family have been for some time in the habit of sitting in our seat in church.' The Martin family had occupied a certain pew in Oughterard church for generations. Now that they were back again, it was expected, in spite of the long absence, that the Bradys would vacate it. This, however, did not happen. The diary for Sunday 24 June, the day after Martin's arrival, has: 'Jostled as to our seat by Brady R.M. Consequent indignation of Hodgsons' (landed gentry living three miles north of Oughterard). The letter gives full details of the comedy: 'Brady accompanied by Mrs Brady and a number of his children crowded us to suffocation and looking like thunder.' The matter was referred to the churchwardens, who enquired and confirmed that the Martins had from time immemorial occupied the pew. They called on Mr Brady 'and asked him to cease from troubling'. He, however, refused to transfer to another pew. Mama, feeling it would be undignified for her to have an altercation with a man like Brady, offered to sit elsewhere. The churchwardens, however, would not have this, and ruled that Brady was to take another seat. He refused. 'The congregation was furious, Mama indifferent.' At a tennis party next day he was cut 'but not by Mama, who shook hands with everyone with the greatest urbanity'. Feeling increased against Brady, whose insistence was held to be the height of bad taste. Martin adds: 'I hate a row and especially this sort of row. Mama never contemplated the possibility of anyone disputing her seat.' But in came the Bradys jostling and angry. The end of it was that Brady, alarmed by the feeling he had aroused, gave in. 'Last Sunday we resumed our old seat and all is well, except that Mama is rather implacable about the Bradys.'

Martin's letters from Ross to Edith continue to give glimpses of the return. Martin writes like a master. No wonder Edith worshipped her. Take her description of how her married sister, Geraldine Hewson, was received by the people when she and her husband, Edward, came on a visit to Ross House in August. She had not been to Ross for the full sixteen years since the family's departure in 1872. 'She felt the place more of a nightmare than I did. I pitied her when she came up the steps, she couldn't say a word for a long time. There was a bonfire at the gate in her honour in the evening, a moderate one only, a heap of turf, glowing all through, the sticks on the top.'

The tenants had crowded to it and expected her to come down the avenue and speak to them. 'Poor Geraldine was so tired that I had to drive her down to it, but she went very gallant and remembered the people very well. There was no cheering or any demonstrativeness, and owing to a mistake many of them had gone away thinking she was not coming, but there was a great deal of conversation, and subsequent drinking of porter. Edward was wonderful, in a trying position. In about two minutes he was holding a group of men in deep converse, without any apparent effort, and he was much approved of. "A fine respectable gentleman," "the tallest man on the property," such were the comments. In the strictest privacy I may say that I felt all of a heap to see the bonfire blazing there just as it used to in my father's time, when he and the boys used to come down and all of us, and it was all the most natural thing in the world. It was very different to see Geraldine walk in front of us through the gates, with her white face and shabby clothes. Thady Connor (who is the bailiff and was the steward) met her at the gate, and not in any vice-regal circles could be surpassed the way he took off his hat and came silently forward to her, while everyone else kept back in dead silence too. I know Thady is not what he ought to be, or any of them for the matter of that, but I think they felt seeing her; of course they had all known her so well. What with the glare of the bonfire and the welcome, killed with memories for her, I wonder how she stood it. It was the attempt at the old times that was painful and wretched, at least I thought it so.'

It is such quotations as this from Martin's letters to Edith that let one guess what passages in the books to come were hers alone and, when she died, why the subsequent books lost in intensity and elevation. Geraldine advancing to the bonfire with her pale face. The country people, though somewhat alienated by echoes of their political leaders' fulminations, still felt that a daughter of Ross must be welcomed or given a show of welcome. But the wise women from the mountains were not there. It was not the same, not the same.

The Hodgsons, who were the first to show indignation at the slight put upon Mama in church, gave a dance on 28 August at their house, Currarevagh, three miles north of Oughterard, a lovely situation of the shore of Lake Corrib, a lake like an inland sea. Martin with Geraldine set out for it after dark, a journey of eight miles on their outside car, the groom, Jim Connor, driving the old mare. The letter portrays in detail what a drive at night in the Galway of 1888 could be like for two young women in evening dress. 'We started at 9 in pitch darkness just before moonrise and as soon as we got into the road remembered with some apprehension that it was the night of the Oughterard Races, and the roads would be full of carts with drunken drivers. We were scarcely $\frac{1}{4}$ of a mile from the gate, when something came lumbering along with shoutings. We shouted too, all we knew, and drew into the wall, and the next moment there was a thump and a crash. Up went the car on my side, the mare backed, and I found myself clawing at the coping stones on the top of the wall, in fact on my hands and knees on it. Looking round I saw Geraldine and Jim safely in the road; how they got there, they don't know, but they were all right and the cart had passed on. We got the car down the bank without any trouble, and nothing daunted Geraldine and I got up, on the same side this time, giving Jim the brunt of everything we passed. With the dint of shouting and hiding in the ditch, we passed innumerable other carts and cars, and were nearing Oughterard, on the top of a big hill, when we heard the rattle of a heavy cart trotting towards us. We as usual made for the ditch which in this instance was a bank with a very high wall on top, but before we could look crooked that cart just dashed straight into us. The car and mare spun completely round. Geraldine somehow jumped off, so did Jim, and I not seeing exactly where to jump got onto the wall, the car all the time tilting forward, and my ears full of drunken screeches. I finally managed to precipitate myself onto the muddy bank and got clear. In the shouting and darkness we could just make out that the mare had fallen partly on her side, and was somehow caught in the cart. Then followed indescribable vituperation, and we got the cart clear after much difficulty, and talking ourselves hoarse. There lay the mare apparently stone dead. It was too dark to see a thing—and in the height of the confusion there came along an awful gang of roaring pedestrians. On this Geraldine and I applied ourselves to the task of climbing the wall in our ball dresses and wraps. We were not so much afraid of the drunkards as of their language, and having got up, hid behind the wall till they had passed. Emerging we found the mare on her feet, without a scratch apparently, the relief of which was enormous. The harness was in pieces, and no wonder. The shafts of the cart had gone between the bellyband and the mare's body, so that she was lifted and swung round, astride of the shaft. When the band broke, down she fell. How she was not killed is a miracle. We then made up our minds to walk on into Oughterard about ½ a mile, and get fresh harness, leaving Jim to follow with the mare. We got hold of a Ross man who was passing and made him protect us, but even with him we had a fearsome time from the drunken brutes we met—and from hobbling in thin shoes through the mud. It was a horrible walk, but once we got to Miss Murphy's hotel all was well. Jim brought in the car and mare, both perfectly uninjured! And the fresh harness was jammed on and away we went for Currarevagh, feeling I must say a good deal battered but still undefeated. I cannot say how the whole situation was complicated by the darkness, and by my having on Mama's sealskin with a mackintosh on top of it. The feeling of suffocation when trying to climb that wall was near nightmare. We were of course very late at the dance, arriving about no. 7, but I had quite enough of it. Somehow being knocked about tells on one, and I felt ready to subside into any corner available, instead of which I dragged my weary bones through about seven dances and enjoyed my supper extremely. And we left as early as possible. The drive home was long and chilly but the dawn on Lough Corrib was worth looking at. I have discovered an inky bruise on my knee, another on my foot, and am generally stiff.'

Martin's letters written this summer of 1888 to the absent Edith are so full of poignant beauty, so self revelatory that one cannot leave them. They show so vividly how she stood with the people, what an Irishwoman she was, how open her heart was, how right Edith was to love her. In August she wrote: 'Here things have been rather melancholy on account of the death of our carpenter, Tom Walsh, a man of about sixty, as clever and even brilliant a man as ever lived, with a face very like Carlyle, white hair, black eyebrows, and a delightful swinging walk. He has been ill for some months and Mama and I have been with him a good deal, and small trouble it was, it being a treat to talk to him. He died rather unexpectedly and on Friday last did not know anyone, not his own children, till Mama went in. "Do you know me, Tom" she said, stooping over him. "Mrs Martin" he said with a smile of the gentlest kind and then relapsed into muttering to himself. He died early next morning and I went up to see his wife, who was dreadfully quiet, and took me in to look at Tom, through a kitchenful of neighbours squatting about. There indeed was Tom, and such a sight as I shall not forget. I had not seen anyone dead since my grandfather and I forget that. I will only say that his expression was that of a person alive, not dead, a person who could speak if he liked, but deliberately shut up his mouth. And the stillness gave the feeling of living tension and not dead inertness. That was

[60]

the frightful feeling, and I made up my mind that if I have the
misfortune to outlive the people that make life pleasant I shall
not see them after they die. It is only running your head into a
suffocating intolerable mystery. On Monday he was buried and
we all went to his funeral, despite the fact that he was a delegate
of the League. At least we went a bit of the way. The funeral
passed our gate and I waited there with a cross of white asters
and ferns, while the others drove up to meet it. It was horrible
when it did come, two or three hundred people straggling
along, lots of them drunk, the coffin in a cart, and Tom's
daughters sitting on the coffin, as is always done here. One of
them was nearly distraught, with red hair flying about her.
There was a sort of howl when the cart stopped at the gate, but
the Irish Cry was mostly done with by that time. I put the cross
on the coffin and walked half a mile or so with Tom's son and
then we all came back and visitors descended and your letter
came and I thought no more of it.'

One has to keep in mind that when Martin wrote this
passage, so charged with emotion, she was only twenty-six.

A cousin who had emigrated to Canada, Archer Martin by
name, belonging to that branch of the family whose seat had
been at Dangan, near Galway, came over at this time to visit
the old country and stayed at Ross. Mama could hardly stand
him on account of his 'American or Canadian vulgarisms'. But
Martin was less severe. 'He was a gentleman somewhere or
other in spite of them. I walked over to Kilannin with him on
Saturday morning to see the tomb of the Dangan Martins
there.' It was under the altar of a ruined chapel in the graveyard. Archer Martin had just completed its restoration and his
workmen were waiting to be paid off. Martin watched him make
them a speech through the window of the old chapel. 'I sat on a
tombstone and thought that he wasn't quite good enough somehow. For all his talk he did not know how to talk to them. He
only knew how to deal with them.'

It is worth pointing out that the leading figure in *An Irish
Cousin*, for which at the moment the authors were struggling to

find a publisher, was a Canadian girl on a visit from Canada to her ancestral home.

There remain a few Martin fragments over which oblivion should not be allowed to scatter her poppy. One of them, dated 8 August, concerns a dog. That Martin had the same tenderness for dogs as Edith was another tie between them. Both of them had received the enlightenment which dogs can give to man. A little white cur dog, strayed or lost and hungry, scrambled down one night into the area surrounding Ross House and was caught in a rat trap. 'He endured what way he could till the people got up.' Martin's window was over the area where he suffered, but not till dawn was she aware of his predicament. She hastened down fifty-two steps to succour him, but she was too late. The servants had put him to death and were laughing.

It was at this time that she wrote the short story called 'The Dog from Doone' which Edith some thirty years later included in a book of essays called *Stray-aways*. It concerns a dog which its owner had tried to drown. It escaped and came to her. The story ends: 'The Dog from Doone was lying on my bed. I looked at him and he at me, as man to man. He was at peace in an understanding' which was quite other than what he had had with his master.

In the lofty and grand mood, which Edith admired in her so much, Martin ends a letter which she had been writing far into the night: 'I may as well finish for once with a quotation. It is appropriate to the hour, perhaps you know it. "The night was even now: but that name is lost; it is not now late but early. Mine eyes begin to discharge their watch, and compound with this fleshly weakness for a time of perpetual rest; and I shall presently be as happy for a few hours as I had died the first hour I was born." Beware of dogs, as St Paul saith.' (Or as St John, the Divine, hath: "Without are dogs and sorcerers.")

While Martin was putting Ross House to rights, Edith at Drishane was trying her hand at short stories. In June 1888 the *Graphic* printed a sort of comic strip of hers, called 'A Mule

The Martins return to Ross

Ride in Trinidad'. The same month she began 'a story of moderate length'. On 27 June she received the depressing news that *An Irish Cousin* had been rejected by the publishers Sampson & Co. It was then sent to Richard Bentley & Son. On 20 August she wrote urging Martin to come back to Drishane, but Martin replied that there was still so much to do at Ross that she could not leave Mama. Edith, always immensely industrious, struggled on with her story alone. At the end of September she again asked Martin to come, and on 9 October she arrived at Drishane for a short stay. They at once got to work on the story which Edith had begun and which eventually, after being enlarged and re-written by Martin, was published as a full-length novel called *Naboth's Vineyard* in 1891.

On 2 December 1888 came the glorious news that R. Bentley & Son offered to publish *An Irish Cousin*. The diary entries are indicative of the authors' excitement. Edith's: 'Wrote a dizzy letter of acceptance. Went to church twice in a glorified trance.' Martin's: 'Got a letter from Richard Bentley & Son announcing that the birthday of our lives has come and that he was prepared to publish the Shocker giving us £25 on publication and £25 on sale of 500 copies. All comment is inadequate. Went dizzily to church twice. Wrote accepting terms with dignity.'

On 5 December 1888 Martin returned to Ross. Her mother urgently required her help. Selina was quite incompetent to take her place.

5

The Somerville-Martin Ross collaboration begins

Edith and Martin now saw themselves launched on a literary career. In a fortnight proofs arrived from the printers, better than nowadays when six months is more the rule. Martin at Ross and Edith at Drishane set to work to correct them independently. Mrs Somerville, who had disliked the novel from the first, forbade Edith to subscribe her own name. As *nom de plume*, Geilles Herring, the name of some ancestor, was finally chosen. Mama, on the other hand, liked the book, but it was decided that the style, Martin Ross, rather than Violet Martin, should be used. The plot was a simple one. A younger son of the Sarsfield family of Durrus, an estate on the west coast of Cork, had emigrated to Canada and in due course his daughter came over to stay at Durrus with her uncle and his son, her first cousin. Durrus, deep in the Irish countryside, is more like Ross than Drishane, though it partakes of both. A love story evolves along Victorian lines, professionally handled to a happy ending for the heroine. But below is a brooding air of calamity. One perceives here Martin's touch. Take the following passage. The niece from Canada finds herself one day at a cove called Tra-na-morruf, the Strand of the Dead, a place where funerals coming by water landed the coffin for burial in an old graveyard above the sea. She hears the sound of oars. The waiting crowd was quite silent as 'the boats slowly advanced to the shore; but directly the keel of the first touched the shingle, the women in the others raised a sustained, penetrating wail, which rose and fell in the sunny air and made me shiver. I thought I had never heard so terrible a cry. I had often been told of the Irish custom of "keening" at funerals, but I was not prepared for anything so barbaric and despairing. It broke out with increasing volume and intensity while the coffin was being lifted from the boat . . . the women clapping their hands and beating their breasts, their chant rising and swelling like the howl of the wind on a wild night. . . . Behind the ruined chapel I now noticed for the first time an open grave. The dark crowd closed in around it, and after a few stifled sobs and exclamations I heard nothing but the shovelling of the earth upon the coffin.'

The Irish Cry was a phenomenon which captivated Martin. It comes again and again into her writings. In the year when she and Edith were working on *An Irish Cousin*, Martin wrote an article on her own called 'From Olympia to Connemara' and had it published in the *World* magazine. In it she writes of 'a dolorous wailing sound, a howling and lamentation of women's voices. . . . This is indeed the Irish cry, a burial custom belonging to another age and full of barbaric echoes.' It does not merely express sorrow for the departed, but hails the omnipotence of death. In this sort of diction we hear Martin's voice alone. Their sense of humour, however, was so much alike that where humour predominates in the narrative, it is impossible to pronounce which of the two authors was responsible. Their collaboration achieves such an identity of mood that to disentangle their individual contributions is not feasible.

Edith, accompanied by her pet dog Patsy (now called the Puppet), paid her first visit to Ross on 5 February 1889; Martin had been struggling with the proofs since December. Now they were able to compare their corrections and discuss further literary projects. One of the rooms in Ross House was made a study, which Edith also used as a studio. She stayed till 9 March, but is back again on 5 April. On 7 May the Puppet died which

E

for Edith was a profound grief, since her dogs stood to her in as close a relation as members of her family. 'Edith took it to heart awfully,' is Martin's comment in her diary. Edith poured out her feelings, not only to Martin, but in a letter to her sister Hildegarde, dated the same day as the tragedy.

'I have to tell you a thing that you will be almost as sorry for as I am. My little Puppet is dead. The keeper here laid poison in the woods yesterday and told his wife to tell me. She never did so till about 11.30 today, after Patsy had gone out (with Martin's niece and another child) to the post. They came home without him. I ran out and in a few minutes he came tearing up looking all right. But in a minute or two I saw blood on his throat. He looked as if he had eaten a lot. We took him down at once and gave him mustard and salt and hot water. It was hardly down his throat when the usual signs of a fit came on, only not a bit violent. At last he fell and stiffened and gasped. We got him into a hot bath with mustard. All the stiffness went out of him. I thought he was coming round. It was very long before I could believe he was dead. There are so many things that make it much worse. If I had gone last week. If I hadn't sent him out with Muriel, and if only I had been told of the poison. I am too miserable to write any more. I can't help it if people laugh at me for being a fool. I had got so very fond of that little thing. That he is dead is a thing I can't believe. It takes away all my pleasure in going home. I know Papa and Mother will be so sorry. I hope they won't reproach me. After all it is worst of all for me. He was always with me. No one could be as sorry as I am. My little Puppet one. If that woman had come in an hour earlier it would have been all right. Martin is nearly as sorry as I am. She was always fond of him.'

And two days later she continued: 'I was very glad to get your letter this morning tho' it only brought me a little more vividly the fact that the little Puppet is really gone from me. I won't say any more, it only makes me cry and I am trying not to, as much for Martin's sake as anything else. We were both awake for such a long time last night, feeling thoroughly miserable, and one after another of his little tricks and plays comes into my mind, and I break down again. The keeper, who is a decent chap, met me today and made me a long apology which was very hard to bear. He said "I'm a poor man, but for £5 I wouldn't it should happen. I was like a man in a stound when I heard it".' In her diary Edith adds: 'Martin without telling me took my little Thing and buried him. I was glad of it.'

Edith left for Drishane a few days later. That meant starting from Ross at 2.45 a.m. by the mail cart to catch the 6 a.m. train at Galway. Martin saw her off there. As it was so early in the morning she had to wait some hours before the mail cart returned to Ross, a weary wait. She was feeling sad at saying goodbye to Edith, and sad too because Edith was sad over the Puppet's death. In a letter to her written that same evening on her return home, Martin has: 'I can't forget the unhappy look you have had all the time lately.' The letter describes her wait at Galway and tells how she tried the ladies waiting room at the station. 'After five minutes there I became aware that my brain was giving way', and she wandered out into the street. Galway was a depressing place at 6 a.m. 'I discovered that the outer door of a filthy hotel called the Imperial was open and I boldly effected an entrance. There was a grimy hall with the sunshine blazing in on the dust and frowst, and not a creature to be seen, but apparently from the little parlour alongside came the most deep and manly snores. I crept in and found the snores were from overhead, and could have wept for joy at seeing the *Family Herald* and *Tit-bits* on the table. I read for at least an hour. At last the postman came and banged till he got the boots up. Then I made myself known and demanded tea and was whisked upstairs to a foul coffee room and got good tea and bread and butter and a dirty knife.'

She started for home at ten o'clock. 'This is market day and I have seldom had a more interesting drive from Galway. Nurse* sat beside me and expounded the history of every cart we met. Endless were the varieties of salutation as apparently

* Nurse Barrett had accompanied her to Galway and gone to the market.

every tenant in Ross was on the road, and I would have given anything for you to have seen them. Such fiery skulls, such old women, such screamings of Irish by Nurse and to Nurse. . . . Do try not to be so sorry. My heart aches for you when I think of you arriving at Drishane. Goodbye Edith my dear—not for too long I hope.'

Edith had promised to come back soon, which did not prevent Martin from writing two or three times a week to her, letters which contain autobiographical fragments, so carefully phrased as almost to equal her published writings. Thus on 13 May 1889, after saying how she wished she had taken Edith to Tully, a village a few miles from Ross, near Doone, she describes a walk back alone by a short cut over the bog. 'I had one or two perilous crossings on little trees laid over the awful black profundities underneath,' bog holes that would swallow a horse if it blundered into one, tempted suicides, and invited a murderer to pitch in his victim's corpse, which would never be seen again. In the strange story, 'The Dog from Doone', written at this time, Martin describes such a bog hole; and also in *An Irish Cousin*, for bog holes appealed to her sense of mystery. Tully, she goes on, was very different in mood. 'It is beautiful past telling,' yet like the bog holes it too has a weird quality, with 'very big pines and a soft dark walk winding in obscurity among them. There is nothing like it in Ross, or scarcely anywhere that I have seen. I was frightened by the solitude and stillness and the strength of everything. There are strange little glades of pallid sedge with little old fir trees in them; and I came on a perfect place for you to have painted. A little lake surrounded by trees, except on one side, that opened beautifully to that hill behind Doone and to the sunset.'

The letters contain laments at Edith's absence. She missed her at all hours. 'I dined alone, a dinner you would have liked, only too long for a solitary creature—nice soup, pike, an excellent fish like haddock, hot beef, stewed gooseberries and cream.' Yet she feels that Edith's more down-to-earth mind puts a brake on her at times. 'I believed in things more after that long summer here last year than I do now. You take the high falutin out of me, I think.' Thus on 18 May 1889. And she adds: 'I feel you saying "Well, but I don't see—" and then I don't see either. But it is very good for me.' She is referring here to their collaboration. Was Martin, one wonders, over generous in this view? Did Martin's vision, her absorption in the darker moods of the remote countryside, so different from the straight comedy of Irish life which was Edith's speciality, actually require a check? Was Edith doing her a disservice? Or was it good for her, as she alleges. One can give no answer here to so searching a question; can only read on and hope that as the story unfolds an answer will come. If there was to be a collaboration between these two gifted women, there had to be compromise. Without the collaboration, could either alone have effected as much? One cannot forget, too, that the collaboration was not merely a literary one. That they loved each other figured in it. But if Martin lost something of herself, did Edith lose anything, or was it for her all gain? As I say, one can only hope that the answer to these baffling questions will gradually take shape. The problem of their personalities becomes more complicated when one recalls that Martin's delight in the droll was as keen as Edith's. In these very letters of mid-1889 are delicious examples of how she put on paper anything that amused her. Take the sweep's remark, which she rescued from oblivion. He had found a jackdaw's nest in a chimney and said: 'Damn the bit, but the jackdaws had the hair off o' the cows down in the nest undher the young ones.' She did not know what 'damn the bit' signified, but liked it, and would use it herself, she wrote.

Another entertaining anecdote concerns a brooch of Edith's which disappeared a few days before she left for Drishane. It was supposed that one of the Ross servants had stolen it. 'I was reading your letter for the second time when Nurse Barrett came into the room and said with awful stillness "Is this Miss Somerville's brooch?" *It was.* One of the men had found it at the bottom of a boat and hung it on his watch chain. Nurse Barrett saw it on him as he came in and flew upon him. "Faith

I think he thought I was going to ate him, the grip I took of him." ' That was the kind of servitor Nurse Barrett was, very faithful but very rough for a housemaid.

And there is the account of the visit to The O'fflaherties an old Galway family, on whom she and Mama called. 'When we got there I knocked at the door. It was answered by a smart reddish-haired girl, who told me that Mrs O'fflahertie was at home.' This girl reminded Martin of Emma, one of The O'fflahertie daughters, but she thought no more of it at the moment. Two other visitors were there, strangers called Jackson. 'When the maid brought in tea the O'fflahertie who talked to me became very red. I guessed nothing till, as we drove away, May B (a friend with Martin) said "The parlour maid *was* Emma O'fflahertie." ' The explanation was that Mrs O'fflahertie did not want to let the Jacksons, whom she had invited, know she had no presentable maid. The Martins' call was unexpected. It made Mrs O'fflahertie blush to think of their amusement if they saw through her little strategem.

On 25 May 1889 Martin followed Edith to Drishane and stayed there till 12 August. On her return to Ross she immediately wrote that during her absence the place 'had become very ragged, frightfully overgrown with thistles and bracken and weeds. . . . The house and all therein have quietly slipped back into chaos, not quite as bad as last winter, but very discouraging.' Her mother did not keep the servants up to their work. The letter goes on: 'I have thought much and bitterly of the Puppet since I came back and last night more especially. When I was saying my prayers there was a most distinct scratch at my door—a little dog scratch—and only just before that I had been round the outside room to make sure there was no cat there and had shut the outer door tight.' (This is the first mention in the MSS. of the ghost of a dog. The subject comes up again often later on.) At the end of the letter she says how eagerly she looks forward to Edith's letters. 'I like to hear any little things about what you do and how the painting goes on.' It is only a few days since she left Drishane but 'it seems a long time since Monday morning and I miss the spoiling dreadfully.'

Her letter dated the next day, 15 August 1889, shows her still depressed. 'I do not feel in the least like writing anything more just yet. I suppose it will come, but at present I think of nothing but the atrocities of bad servants and the knavishness of hangers-on, and feel a profound and paralysing depression on these subjects. I feel tired of the whole show and find the machinery of life more trouble than it is worth.' However she sets to work on the thistles. 'I found it amusing swishing down 6 or 8 huge thistles at a sweep. I shall do lots of it, please goodness. I am rather handy with a scythe.' But melancholy returns: 'I must stop, my dear. What is the use of writing, after all. It is a very feeble thing, and conveys very little of what one would like to say and of what one would like to know.'

But on 21 August all depression flies at glorious news. The post brought a copy of the *World*, the magazine where sometimes she had an article, and she saw 'in large type, heading Bentley's (their publishers) list therein' *An Irish Cousin* advertised. Out at last, 'it really took the sight out of my eyes. I was not looking for Bentley's list even, but languidly reading the reviews when I saw it by chance.' And she gives all the credit to Edith for having started them on the novel by being first to catch sight 'of the old maniac's face at the window over the door' of the Townshend house called Whitehall, which in the book became Durrus, the seat of the Sarsefields. 'You were also the person who lifted us through the first chapters.' The letter ends in highest good spirits. 'Good night now whatever. Here's luck to the Shocker, and even if it doesn't do much towards making our fortunes, I do not think it was time wasted. It taught us a lot in a literary way, and I don't think we shall ever forget it. And the long time that we fought over it was my fault. Isn't that true? Yours ever, Martin.
Goodnight again. You were a nice woman to write with.'

By 24 August advance copies had arrived. She writes: 'I am delighted that your mother likes the book now. I think it does read a little better than I expected, though here and there I feel inclined to put the bedclothes over my head. Mama revels in it. I certainly should like most awfully to see you, but these things are not to be.' The next excitement will be the reviews. 'Mama is in the most *shining* good humour, the best I have ever seen her in. I think she really takes great delight out of the Shocker.'

The Ross household awaited the reviews with some trepidation. Martin had 'a hideous dream about one written by a kind of intellectual Jack the Ripper.' But all is well. '3 September. Wonderfully good review of *An Irish Cousin* in *Athenaeum*,' so Martin's diary. On 9 September: 'Enthusiastic review in the *Observer*.' On 16 September: 'Laudatory reviews still continue.' The book had space given it in all the leading papers, far longer notices than an unknown novelist of today would get. It was in a second edition by 8 October. By this time Edith had joined Martin at Ross. 'We have definitely established ourselves in my room with a good fire and find it a good place to work.' On 13 December they left Ross together for Drishane. So ended the year 1889, with flattering demands from publishers for more of their writings, and the editor of the *World* asking for articles 'in your own delightful style'. They were launched. Nearly four years had passed since they first met at Drishane in January 1886.

6

Doings at Ross

During the early part of 1890 Martin was either in residence at Drishane writing with Edith or visiting relations. The two friends managed to finish a novel called *Naboth's Vineyard*, written at the request of a literary clergyman, the Rev. Frederick Longbridge, who acquired from them all rights for £35. He had read a story of theirs, called 'Slide No 42', in the *Lady's Pictorial*, and persuaded them to expand it into a novel. The result was a minor work of Irish fiction, shortly to be over-shadowed by *The Real Charlotte*, considered by many to be their best book, over whose plot they were beginning to meditate. But they wanted something immediately that would bring them in cash and went over to London in June to see publishers and make inquiries from editors of magazines.

Martin's brother, Robert, and his wife Connie put them up. Robert was very qualified to give them advice as he knew everybody. What he did for them is not on record but it is certain that they discussed their problems with him. Though he had decided not to take up his residence at Ross House in 1888 when Mama returned there, he had made several visits. He was also on excellent terms with his cousins, the Somervilles; he and Connie had rented a house close to Drishane at Castle Townshend during part of the summer of 1889. Moreover, he had attended the tenants' New Year dance at Ross. There is a letter of Martin's to Edith describing the occasion, a thoroughly Irish one, old style. 'The poor people began to come at about 5 o'clock and were let in at about 6.30 and immediately began to dance. . . . We went out at about 10.30. The place was packed and there was terrific cheering when we came in. They made a little space for us and then Robert made a speech and every point was cheered with frenzy. I felt a little chokey at the allusions to papa and the reception they got. After the speech Jimmy Lee came forward and proceeded to sing the song about Robert's "lovely fatures" and "his honourable lady" etc. . . . When it came to the word Martin there was a yell you might have heard in Galway. After that Robert sang Bally-hooley and then there was a jig in which Robert and old Anne Connor and Andy Welsh and I were the performers. . . . I must say I never thought to see such a crowd and such enthusiasm at Ross again. Even with restricted numbers from each house there were about 300 people there. . . . It moved me a great deal that after Robert had sung his song and made his speech Reynolds came up and said to me "It would be a great consolation to the people if you'd play the piano." I granted them this mitigating circumstance. There was wonderfully little drunkenness, except one or two who *came* drunk. The first of these Robert had to kick off the hall door steps.' The second was driven out through the rockery with a stick; the third was put into an open drain in the yard. 'And that disposed of them all.' This was not too severe; they were fighting drunk. It is not certain that Connie was at Ross for the dance, but may have been there for a day or so. She had been married to Robert for over eight years. They had one child, a daughter called Barbara. Connie's family was said to have Jewish blood, and is reputed to have been well off. A degree of coolness existed between her and Mama, who thought her manner rude. Before marrying Robert she had been the wife of one, Roche, a marriage ended by his hanging himself. Whether this prejudiced her in Mama's opinion is not known. During the London visit something was said about her and Robert coming over to Ross and making a long stay later in the year.

For Martin and Edith the immediate concern was to find some London publisher or editor to commission them. A travel book was suggested to the *Lady's Pictorial*. The idea caught on. The magazine would publish a Connemara travelogue, in ten articles, which could be made into a book afterwards, the fee for each to be £4, including illustrations, not much of an offer but better than nothing. On 22 July 1890 they left London and started on their Connemara tour, subsequently entitled, when it appeared in book form, *Through Connemara in a Governess Cart*, an open trap with a jennet in the shafts, 'able to kill any horse on the road,' as its hirer assured them, though it was admitted 'she was a little giddy about the head, but if ye'll not touch the ears she's the quitest little thing at all.' A day to day account of what happened is contained in the diaries, of which the articles were an expansion. The amusing episode of the night in the cabin of the Widow Joyce is not mentioned in the diaries, and must be an invention, introduced to brighten the narrative when it threatened to become humdrum. Though departing in some degree from fact, *Through Connemara in a Governess Cart* can safely be considered largely autobiographical. It anticipates the lively style which was soon to make the authors famous, contains passages of high comedy and reports fresh from the lips of local inhabitants many examples of their vivid and original way of talking English. Thus, of the fleas in the bed at the Widow Joyce's it was said: 'It isn't the little bit they ates I begrudges, but 'tis the continial thramplin they keeps up.' In a subsequent note on the book Edith complains that her drawing of the 'Galway beggar dwarf, described in the text as the appalling presence of a seventy-year-old nightmare of two-foot-nothing, well known as Judy the Menlo, was vetoed by the Editor as being calculated to shock delicate ladies.' They themselves had a liking for this apparition She personified the Irish extravagant mixture of the macabre and the comic.

At the end of the tour Edith went back to Drishane, leaving Martin at Ross. Her brother Robert arrived from England the

[75]

same week; Connie was to follow shortly. The situation had its complications. In 1890 Robert was forty-four years of age. He had a London house, was, as we have seen, enjoying a successful London career as journalist, song writer, politician, a favourite in society, and a close friend of Arthur Balfour, at that time Chief Secretary for Ireland, and twelve years later Prime Minister. He had no intention of abandoning all this and burying himself at his ancestral seat as Martin of Ross. But it seems that at the moment he fancied the idea of a part time exercise of his rights and of spending at Ross some months, at least, of the year. He had political ambitions and thought of contesting a nationalist seat and getting into Parliament in the unionist interest. The New Year dance of 1889/90 had reminded him how popular he was with the tenants. His wife, Connie, would of course become Mistress of Ross. Mama would be Dowager and, if she continued to reside there, would not have the ordering of the place. It was true that for the last four years she had exercised all the powers of Mistress of Ross and with the help of her daughters had done much to rescue the property from imminent ruin. But now with Martin so often away at Drishane, it was really too much for her. Anyhow, as it would be impossible for Connie to be under her, she would have to step down. When Robert explained this, it was a great shock to Mama. In Martin's letters to Edith the crisis is described.

'11 August 1890. Broadly I may say that Mama says the only possible plan is a separate establishment in this house. Separate kitchen, meals, servants. It is loathsome, of course, but better than having Connie at the head of everything. And in fact makes it possible for Mama to stay on here. I did pity her when she heard that Connie was coming in a week; she was stunned into dead silence, on which Robert also fell into deepest gloom. However, they talked it out that night, after an evening when no one opened their lips. Now things are most friendly and Robert thinks that Mama and Connie will hit it off to a T. In the meantime Connie never makes the least allusion to Mama in her letters—never has from the first. However, I won't write myself into a fury over it; the great thing is to keep one's temper and sit tight.'

Thus Robert's charm had smoothed things over. The letter goes on to describe gaily how he read family prayers in a manner which was a mixture of Irving and Beerbohm Tree, broad in the lessons and low church in the prayers. 'If you had been there, you would have laughed, especially as on that solemn occasion the cat came down to lie on the sofa. At the kneeling down upheaval she stood and looked disgustedly about her for some time, and then exactly as Robert began to declaim the general confession she uttered a series of the most heartrending wails, seemingly of contrition, and did not stop till it was over, when she jumped on Mama's back.'

Two days later, 13 August, Martin is not so cheerful. She writes to Edith: 'It is a dreadful thought that this fuss and difficulty is to be thrust upon us, and here is a new slavey to be licked into shape, one Ann Davy, daughter of the flute player and of a whilome kitchen maid, an animal of about 17, whose only education has been two months in that Academy for Manners, Mrs Macreery's house. I hear that Mrs M spent her time in D.T. and was at the best of times "no better than one of ourselves, and a Catholic too," as the flute player's wife said with huge scorn. . . . Mama is stiffening her neck a bit, now that she has drawn her wind, and realized the state of affairs, and I tremble at the thought of Connie and her in opposition. She says that she will not give up her place and that if Connie doesn't like to live here as a boarder that she must hire her own servants and have her own establishment. I think that will be the end of it myself; certainly whatever happens Mama ought not to leave the house.'

In short, things were back again where they were before the talk with Robert. On the eve of Connie's arrival Martin writes with apprehension: 'When I tell you that Connie arrives tomorrow for luncheon with child, nurse and 20 thousand luggages you will imagine how things are. Nothing is really ready. We had not time. The nursery is papered but not painted, half the

bedroom things haven't come, Ann does not know her trade as
housemaid and has not mastered the 'nice tack' of parlouring, so
that is a lively state of affairs. Robert is amiablity itself, but his
idea of helping is to unpack bagsful of his own old clothes and
heap them all around him on the floor, call me to tell me the
history of them all, and then walks off and leaves the lot, and
starts on another in some other room. Mama as usual searches
for wholly useless things all day long, with a kind of anguish,
driving Biddy King before her as she goes. Selina is the only
one who is any use, and of course Nurse Barrett. I had a talk
with Robert this morning in which he said nothing was further
from his ideas than to disturb Mama. He was very nice about it
all, and I know he meant what he said.'

Then comes Martin's diary entry for the dreaded arrival:
'Maelstrom. Connie with Barbara and nurse arrived at 2 o'clock.
General convulsions and exhaustion of the most complete.' In
her letter to Edith, written the same evening, she is tired but
less pessimistic: 'Connie came today and is cheerful, practical
and so far all that could be wished. She does not seem daunted
by things here, praises what she can, and accepts the rest. But
it has been a nightmare day and I am about done.'

Edith had written to say she hoped Martin would come to
Drishane as they had to get on as quickly as possible with the
articles on the Connemara tour for the *Lady's Pictorial*. Referring to this Martin's letter has: 'Things cannot go on here
without me, and Mama will not stand the idea of my leaving
home. . . . Connie would never get on with Nurse Barrett, and
would probably be nasty to Selina. She has been that already.'
Edith must come to Ross. 'All will be well if Connie can only
learn politeness. God knows, I have as much talked since breakfast as would sicken an ass.' She is here quoting what Nurse
Barrett said about having continually to reprove Ann, the raw
parlour maid. It amused Martin so much that she 'carefully
entered it in the notebook,' the phrase book, already being
kept (and still extant), of things said by servants, country people
and the like. She ends the letter with another phrase: 'That the

world may wondher at your happiness,' a valediction in use
locally.

Martin's diary for the next month reflects improvement in
the situation. One gathers that Robert abandoned the idea of
setting up as resident Master of Ross. He and Connie, with
their little girl Barbara and her nurse, became boarders at £3
a week for the four of them. Mama was not displaced. Robert
soon found Ross dull and left for England where he toured and
made political speeches. Connie was amenable. The diary shows
them going for walks with her. Thus, 11 September, 'Went
with Mama and Connie to the weekly tennis party' at friends
in Oughterard. And she writes: 'Whatever may be Mama's
failings, she is seldom rude and it takes two to raise a ruction.'
On 18 September she urges Edith to come to Ross. 'I must make
money, so must you, and the Welsh Aunt (first name for the
novel *The Real Charlotte*) is an awful business.' She goes on to
say that they have had to get rid of Ann. 'She told Mama that "if
anyone 'd spake to her she'd bursht out sweatin'," This is not
what one wishes in a parlour maid.' As for herself, what with
her literary work, all unaided, and her labours in the house, 'you
couldn't pick me out of an ashpit and know me from one'.

Edith said she would come and Martin wrote: 'I am sure you
think you are coming to a cockatrice den, and it is awfully good
of you to come at all. But the sooner you can come without
seeming unkind to your family, the better.' (Ultimately Edith
found herself unable to come.) In the same letter she relates
what happened when she, Connie and Mama set out in the pony
trap to drive to a neighbour's house for tea. It is a good example
of the easy way she was able to throw off in a letter a brilliant
sketch of what was at once alarming and yet droll. 'We all got
into the pony trap, I with my back to the horse, Mama driving,
and were about three yards from the door when there came
terrific thumps on the splash board, I don't know how close to
my head, pretty close anyhow. The old mare kicking like a 3
year old. Connie was out like a shot and made for her head. I
was also out, and got hold of her. Mama sitting like an anvil,

with the reins. Judge of my horror to see the mare kick till she got her leg caught high up in the circle of the fore-carriage, in fact she did it just as I got to her, and immediately began to fall. Down she came like a fainting woman, with her head in my lap. Of course as soon as she was down I reversed the position and sat on her head. Mama was out by this time, and Robert had come tearing from the top of the house in answer to Connie's shouts. Then everyone came, Peter the stable hand, Mage the maid, and Nurse Barrett. Nurse was I may say more use than any of them, held the mare's other leg, and was generally admirable. I thought the leg must break from the horrid way it was caught, but by tilting up the trap they got it out with only a cut. The poor mare was in an awful fright and in great pain evidently when she was down, but by dint of two of us keeping her head down she didn't kick much and we got her to her feet without cutting the harness. Fancy Peter harnessing her without a breeching, and with the loops that the shafts run through put *behind* the little iron pegs on the shafts instead of before them. Of course the moment she started down the hill the forecarriage ran onto her hind legs. There was nothing on earth to stop it. Connie and Robert and I then walked to the Roberts and had the most delicious chocolate cake I have *ever* tasted.'

The few letters of Martin's which survive have never been published.* A fragment belonging to this date is too good to leave out. 'Yesterday I met Mary Mulloy on the avenue, bringing a present of eggs. "Tell me, oh tell me" she said (referring to Robert's little girl, Barbara) "is the child like yere family, or what is she like at all?" "Nurse Barrett says she has a look of *me*" I said. "God grant it." Mama came sailing down the avenue at this moment. "More power to ye then, ma'am, and long life to ye there, tis you's the lady," says Mary, beginning to cry and going on to the house. We met her sometime afterwards coming back with Ann Connor, both of them having

---

* In 1917 Edith included some extracts from them in her *Irish Memories*. The quotations I make are directly from the Martin MSS and sometimes differ slightly from Edith's, where they overlap them.

Edith (*left*) and Martin (*right*) composing in the Drishane dining
room (1888)

The Somerville brothers and sisters, with the exception of Jack
Back row, left to right: Hugh, Cameron, Aylmer
Front row, left to right: Boyle, Edith, Hildegarde

inspected Barbara. Mary took me aside. "Oh Miss Wylett" beginning to cry again "she has no look to any of yez. Oh but God protect the children of my own dear ladies—tis them is the ones, tis them belongs to yer own family." These things show the feeling. Tell them only to Hildegarde.'

Edith's sister, Hildegarde, was always the recipient of confidences both from Edith and Martin, because she could be depended on to keep her mouth shut. There was some blarney, no doubt, in Mary Mulloy's adoring protestations, but also something amusing and heartfelt which appealed to Martin. Though the old world of Ireland was passing away, she loved what remained of it and deeply valued the people's affection.

She knew that Edith liked best of all to hear the everyday news of Ross, particularly little anecdotes, like the one above, in which the people or the servants figured. (The letters do not contain any discussion of literary problems.) On 26 September 1890 she sends her another letter, written with her usual high spirits: 'I was sitting up here reading a letter when I heard a human tornado rushing towards my room—Ann and Mage— making such a dramatic burst into my room as they would get any money for on the stage. "The misthress' room is on fire." This with blanched faces and almost inarticulate utterance. I just put out for the water jug and went like the switchback railway. Arrived, I found Nurse Barrett, Murray, Allen and Robert sweeping and shovelling up a heap of red soot from the floor and hearthstone of Mama's room, and *cataracts* of it were coming down the chimney. The kitchen chimney on fire—that was all—and these little idiots frightened everyone's life out in succession, me last of all.'

The cat with three kittens was nearly smothered when next day one of the men about the place, Andy Welsh, started to clean the kitchen chimney. Soot, brick and jackdaws' nests fell on the cat which was in a disused oven whose flue connected with the main chimney. It and the kittens were 'disinterred quite unhurt but black and more entirely mortified than anything you can imagine.' Writing a few days later, Martin continues

F   [81]

on the subject of the chimney, her humour and choice of words making a trivial incident into something memorable. 'The tinkering at the kitchen chimney still goes on—still does Andy Welsh pound up and down the stairs with mortar on his boots, still do I hear his muffled jackdaw voice in the chimneys, still does the kitchen placidly puff smoke in his disgruntled face.'

Ross House remained infested with vermin despite efforts to clean it up. 'I caught a flea on my person with amusing brilliance and let it go by accident,' thus Martin complacently. But all the great houses of the gentry were in this state because the servants did not notice dirt. Drishane was noted for its rats, which flourished on the bits of food left lying about. If poison was put down they retired to die in some inaccessible spot. The stink of dead rats under the drawing room floor was sometimes strong. The air of the dining room was like a charnel house on occasion, and meals could not be eaten there. Martin's worst experience of rats was when staying with the Persses, one of the Galway families. 'Dined at the Persses' and slept there. Had a bad night surrounded by rats.' She enlarges on this diary entry in a letter to Edith: 'My bedroom was a very weird room on the ground floor with an earthy smell. The weirdness was the rats. Mrs Persse warned me about them and assured me they couldn't get into the room, but the row they made was intolerable. I wasn't frightened but just bored by the distracting courses of the rats on the ceiling and down the walls.' As she could not sleep she tried to read, but the only book in the room was Zola's *Nana*,* whose descriptions of the French slum dwellers *did* rather frighten her when read with the rats scurrying inside the walls. But finally she discovered a Bible and felt better.

So the summer at Ross passed into autumn. Nothing much happened. Nurse Barrett's mother died; she was over a hundred. Robert came and went; once he put up a fence. It had become quite clear that his fancy to take over Ross and retain his London establishment was beyond his means. Martin managed to keep the peace between Mama and Connie, superintend the household

---

* First published in 1880. A best seller of the time.

and get on with her literary work. It seemed a long time since
11 August when she had parted with Edith. At last on 21
October she felt able to rejoin her. At the moment Edith was
staying with friends in the County Waterford. Martin was
asked to join them there. 'Edith very fat and fit,' she notes on
arrival in her diary. At this time Edith weighed 9 stone 7 lb.
and Martin 8 stone 6 lb. They moved on to Drishane shortly
after and got to work on the last of the Connemara articles
'working double tides'. No news from Ross except that Nurse
Barrett's son has 'gone mad and tried to murder his mother,'
as Mama wrote. On 1 December she notes: 'Awful smells in the
billiard room.' More dead rats under the boards. She stayed till
22 December, when she had to get back to Ross for Christmas.
Going via Limerick, she found a strike there of porters, 'with
the result that all my boxes were left on the platform, and there
were neither lamps nor footwarmers'. There followed the long
cold drive in the mail car from Galway to Ross. She arrived long
after dark, quite exhausted and frozen.

7

Lady Zetland's visit to Ross

While Martin was finishing the Connemara tour articles at Ross in January 1891, a partial failure of the potato crop was reported throughout Ireland. Edith's father, Colonel Somerville, went to Skibbereen to organize relief. On 30 January she noted in her diary: 'Rode round the Toe Head country (two miles west of Castle Townshend on the sea coast). Sickened and stunned by the misery. Hordes of women and children in the filthiest rags. Gave as many bread and tea tickets as we could, but felt perfectly helpless and despairing in the face of such hopeless poverty.' Next day numbers of Toe Head women came for food to Drishane House. A difficulty was to be sure that all were genuine cases. Betty, the housemaid, however, was able to point out some old women she knew were in no need, wonderful actors and superb talkers. Egerton Coghill, the heir to the baronetcy, who had recently become engaged to Hildegarde, Edith's sister, was now appointed by the government to head relief measures in the southern areas. Early in February Edith joined Martin at Ross, where she stayed two months collaborating over *The Real Charlotte*, a stiff task as the novel was far longer than any previous one and contained far more characters.

At Ross relief measures were also in train. On 19 February Robert wired to say he would be coming that day. He was to go round Connemara distributing relief. Lord Zetland, the Lord Lieutenant of Ireland, had been instructed by the Cabinet to provide all able-bodied men with work on roads, bridges, buildings and the like, so that they could earn enough to buy food for their families. Free food was to be distributed to widows, old or disabled men and children. Arthur Balfour, Chief Secretary for Ireland, Robert's close friend, had the duty of setting these projects in motion. The government was anxious to avoid the odium it had incurred in the past, as in the great famine of 1847, when nothing was done by the authorities. The Home Rule party had grown to be very strong. It would certainly use any distress in Ireland to embarrass the government in the Commons and press its case for Home Rule, which the Cabinet continued to refuse. Robert wanted to show that his tenants at Ross appreciated the government's efforts to mitigate distress. On 11 April a letter was received from him to say that Lady Zetland, with Miss Balfour, Arthur's sister, who had been touring the distressed area in the west of Ireland, would be passing the gate of Ross in her carriage on the 13th evening. He would be in attendance, as A.D.C. for the occasion, and would like his sister to arrange a welcome by the people. The entry in Martin's diary for next day is: 'Spent the whole morning in painting Welcome in huge letters on 7 feet of white calico.'

Lady Zetland came by as expected. The occasion is vividly described by Martin in a letter to Edith (who was back in Drishane). It is an interesting document in the history of the times and indirectly reveals more than would pages of commentary on Irish politics. 'It was as bad a night as I ever saw, wind and real awful rain. However we got the arch and everything finished and the fire lighted by seven o'clock. Then dinner and then in buckets of rain Katie, Moolah* and I set forth in the van. K and I laughed feebly the whole way, in spite of the torrents, as we huddled in hay and rugs. There was something transcendantly typical of Ross about it. We had a longish wait. However we had the gate-house to sit in, where was Mrs Vereker, mountainous in her gray ulster, and a crowd of wet poor people,

---

* Kathleen Currey, Martin's eldest sister, and her little daughter, aged about five or six, whose name was Muriel, pronounced Moolah by the child.

amongst them a railway official with an accordion of 50 horse power, which he played many tunes on and nearly deafened us. Peter Connor sang *Ballyhooley* and *Mullingar* in a tight small tenor, and with a faint imitation of Robert oozing through shyness. I was in and out like a dog at a fair, and slowly getting soaked about the petticoats and feet, as Mr Vereker and I were organizing a set of men to hold in their hands long sticks with sods of turf, steeped in paraffin and set on fire, on them. These proved the most shining success, as they were posted along the road, and looked fine. The carriage came so quietly in the high wind that they had only just time to light up. It pulled up under the arch, Lady Z having stuck her head well out to see things. K and I were the wrong side of the bonfire and Robert lepped down off the box without seeing us, and began rushing to and fro among the people calling for us. "They're here" howled Nurse. Robert speechlessly seized me by the hand, dragged me through the thickest of the smoke and sparks, with Katie and Moolah flying behind, and precipitated me at the carriage door, where I had to try and say what politenesses I could. Katie then came along, and Moolah handed up a huge and lovely bouquet of daffodils, while the man with the accordion played "God save the Queen" at the full blast of his infernal machine. Lady Z could not get at Moolah to kiss her face but kissed her hand over the edge of the window. She was very civil, praised the arch, said we had done too much ("Ah go on" says I) but she seemed a person of not many ideas. She is fair and pretty and kind and quiet. R introduced me to Miss Balfour, but I couldn't see her well. She seemed dark, and she smiled very pleasantly; that was about all there was to her. These things occupied only about a minute, and the people were all the time forming up each side of the carriage, the 12 men with the torches high up by the walls, and the effect was intensely brilliant and picturesque. The turf blazed beautifully, the bonfire glowed in the background, and all the faces shone in the light with the rain streaming down on them. They began to cheer then, for her Ex, at R's bidding, then they themselves cheered for Balfour, for the Lord Leftnent

Lady Zetland's visit to Ross

and his lady, (Nurse screamed this above the row), for Mr
Martin and his family and for the Queen. Such a row you never
heard. I was astonished, both at the numbers and the noise.
Some of the men had walked up from the lake side in the deluge,
and they were determined to have some shouting for their
money. Robert then got a silence, and standing by the carriage
with his hat off, said about 3 sentences in excellent taste, nipped
onto the box again and off they went, to catch the night train in
Galway for which they had little enough time. Lady Z stretched
a slender paw over the door as she started and shook my hand
effusively. We wished them a pleasant journey and so farewell.
The men with the torches ran for a bit alongside and the railway
huts* were lighted up to show their beauties. Poor Selina, who
was afraid to come to the bonfire, stayed at home and had a light
in every window for them to see as they went along Coolaghy.
The fireworks did not come, and anyhow the rain would have
done for them. There was a man in the carriage with his back
to the horses, whether Lord Scarborough or the A.D.C. I do not
know. He looked young and grinned the whole time. After they
were gone we and the Verekers retired into the gate-house,
where I had ordained tea, and in the twinkling of an eye Nurse
and her two young ladies had got a cloth on a table and a comfortable tea and bread and butter, which we had with closed
doors, while the people yelled outside. I am glad to say that
they cheered Mr Vereker as he went home, no one ever deserved
it more. He was invaluable, hustling and cajoling, and keeping
a few who were negative in order. Mrs V also gave much moral
support, though not able to do anything beyond that, poor
creature. We huddled into the van again, being individually
cheered as we tumbled headlong onto the floor of it, and so full
gallop back here, and to bed. I could scarcely speak by that
time, but put my feet in hot water and went to bed and today
am nearly all right. We had a letter from Robert before he
started for England, congratulating us on the success of everything, and saying that Lady Z had desired him to convey her

* A railway line from Galway to Oughterard was being constructed.

thanks to us and to all concerned, and that she thought it a splendid wind-up to her tour. Robert's face of delight was quite repayment enough for all the trouble.'

A fortnight later Martin left for Castle Townshend to continue work on *The Real Charlotte* with Edith

8

The Somerville family at Castle Townshend

From this time onwards Martin stayed less at Ross and more at Castle Townshend, either at the Somervilles' house, Drishane, or at the Coghills', Glen Barrahane, or occasionally at one of the Townshends' houses, the Cottage; in the summer months the houses were full of visiting relations, and she had to go where a room was vacant. Edith was the eldest of the Somerville family, in 1891 being thirty-three. She had five brothers and one sister, Hildegarde. Cameron, the eldest of the brothers and heir to the estate of Drishane, was thirty-one and was a captain in the army, stationed sometimes in Asia and sometimes at the Curragh, a military headquarters in Ireland. When he got leave, he always spent it at Drishane. Edith was devoted to all her brothers, but loved him the best. Many of her letters to him are preserved. They always begin 'Dearest Chimp', his nickname from childhood, and she signed herself 'Peg', his pet name for her; no one else called her that. The letters, often very long, contained the sort of family news which she knew he would like to hear, when stationed far away. Read now they are rather flat. He had considerable musical talents and had probably read more widely than she. After him in age came Boyle, in 1891 a lieutenant in the Navy and stationed often in the Far East or Pacific. Of her brothers he had the strongest character and had a literary bent. On 30 March 1891, Edith's diary has the following entry: 'Received a play written by

Boyle and called "Captain Cook, an extravaganza in 2 Acts".'
Nothing more is told of this play but he wrote two biographies
later on, and was the only member of the family except Edith
who published anything. He was less often at Drishane than the
others at this time though he was to settle there after retirement. The third brother was Aylmer, aged 26 in 1891. He had
married in 1888 a Miss Emmeline Sykes of York, who had an
income of £500 a year and so was comfortably off. Edith and
he, sharing as they did a passion for horses and the hunting
field, combined to found in 1891 a local hunt, called the West
Carbery. This was an important event in Edith's life, for the
practical knowledge she gained of hounds, foxes and hunting
people fitted her, helped by Martin, also a keen horsewoman,
to write the hunting stories which made them famous. Her
other two brothers, Jack and Hugh, were still in their teens in
1891, the first studying for Sandhurst, the second for the navy.
They were both clever, able and pleasant boys and got on well
in life afterwards. Her sister, Hildegarde, now twenty-four,
was deeply in love with her first cousin, Egerton, the heir to
the Coghill baronetcy, who was now thirty-eight. He was an
accomplished painter, who for some years had been associated
in Paris with the Barbizon group of artists. Though he reached
a high standard of attainment he did not think of painting as
a profession but as a happiness for himself. He neither sold
nor exhibited his paintings in London. How good a painter he
was is shown by the fact that in 1965, forty-four years after his
death, when his heirs arranged an exhibition in the West End
of London, he was held by the critics to have been a considerable
artist.

The parents of these five young men and two daughters,
Colonel and Mrs Somerville, were in their late sixties. Much in
evidence were Mrs Somerville's two brothers, Sir Joscelyn
Coghill, Bart, whose seat was Glen Barrahane, and Colonel
Kendal Coghill, who lived close by at a house called Cosheen or
The Point. Colonel Coghill, always referred to by Edith as
Uncle Kendal, has been mentioned further back. He was an

Indian Mutiny veteran and a great character, devoted to his nephews and nieces, who returned his affection. Edith has a chapter on him in her book *Wheeltracks*. He had become intensely interested in spiritualism, as will appear.

Of what her parents were like Edith has left memorable portraits in her *Irish Memories* (1917). Of her father, the Colonel, she says in an Irish phrase: 'He was the gentlest crayture ever came into a house.' That he was a natural gentleman, she declared, was demonstrated by the fact that he fed 'his dogs from the dinner-table.' 'In him dogs recognized their slave. I can see him surreptitiously passing forbidden delicacies from his plate to the silent watchers beneath the surface, his eyes disingenuously fixed upon the window to divert my mother's suspicions.' He was in the now forgotten Kaffir wars of 1843 and 1846 and served throughout the Crimean campaign, winning the Campaign medal with four clasps for fighting in four major battles, including Balaclava and Inkermann. At the Alma he carried out on his back out of danger a wounded private. In recent days, after retirement, he had occupied the highest office in the County Cork, that of High Sheriff. Yet he was the gentlest crayture that ever came into a house.

Of her mother, *née* Coghill, she discourses in the same book. She first observes: 'My mother was a person entirely original in her candour, and with a point of view quite untrammelled by convention.' By this she meant that her mother had her own personal views on everything and expressed them without hesitation. She was a downright woman. What she said came gushing out; she did not think first. We have already seen how she regarded her daughter's writing—a girlish folly, her books so shockingly bad that the family name would suffer were it inscribed on the title page. Edith says: 'The character of Lady Dysart in *The Real Charlotte* was largely inspired by my mother,' one of whose dicta was 'I *hate* poetry, at least *good* poetry,' a sentiment she would blurt out and give a misleading impression of illiteracy. In short, she was a woman of very marked character, as was her brother Kendal, and as also was

[91]

her daughter, Edith, who after her mother's death dominated Drishane, none of her five manly brothers being able to stand up to her. It would be an error, however, to think of Mrs Somerville as overbearing. 'Handsome, impetuous, generous, high spirited, she had the softest most easily entreated heart.' Her *joie de vivre* made her the life and soul of any gathering. Practical and matter-of-fact though she was, she delighted in the occult, listened to palmists with close attention and joined her brother Kendal in his attempts to communicate with the dead. An unexpected side was her nervousness. She refused, for instance, to go in any vehicle driven by her sailor son, Boyle. 'He's no more use on the box than a bluebottle' was a characteristic sally of hers.

There is a letter of Edith's to her brother Cameron, which belongs to the date now reached in this book, and which gives a more homely and intimate glimpse of her parents in their old age. 'Mother has got another cold, I am sorry to say. So far it is only in her head, and if she can be induced to take care of it, I don't think it will be anything, but as a rule she is exasperating in neglecting all the precautions that she enforces on others. It is only sufficient for Hildegarde and me to beg her to take a tonic or port wine, or not to go out, for her to do just the opposite. Papa is nearly as bad and aids and abets her follies, besides not eating half as much as he ought himself. They really are very trying, and though they don't feel the result of their foolishness now, I am sure they will if they get influenza again or anything serious of that kind. Papa takes a sort of chastened pride in coming into lunch when everyone else has finished, and then eating one morsel of pudding with his left hand, to show how casual and unimportant he feels it to be, and drinking one drop of water. His circulation must be wrong, as he has chilblains on his hands and nose, but he won't believe that food and drink are the cures for it. I believe he thinks now that he is hard up, and is in consequence practising economy. He always believes he is going into the Poor House, and Mother has intervals of the same delusion. For your life don't give me away in your return letters, as they both get furious if I so much as hint these things to them. Mother for three or four nights drank port and began to look better and stronger, but then she suddenly refused to take any more, and neither entreaty nor abuse from Aylmer and me had the very least effect on her. She is headstrong as a child and often much more foolish.' Edith goes on to say that she realizes this is all very irreverent. 'But it is only a safety valve for my irritation.' She admits amusement, however, because her mother always mispronounces on purpose the great African hunter's name, Selous, as sea-louse. The letter concludes 'Much love from all, including Martin', whose position in the house was that of daughter and sister.

Edith and Martin's chief concern now was to cash in quickly on the success of their book on the Connemara tour. Their publishers urged them to write another travelogue. A tour in Lapland was mooted, but abandoned for a tour in the vineyards near Bordeaux, for which the *Lady's Pictorial* offered to pay expenses and three pounds for each article. On 24 September 1891 is the diary entry: 'Took out of the bank all the money I have bar 3 pence—viz £10.' She and Martin crossed the Channel on 30 September and stayed in France a fortnight, every day visiting different vineyards and being entertained by the owners. They enjoyed themselves very much. The articles were published in the *Lady's Pictorial* and soon afterwards in book form under the title *In the Vine Country*. The book is still readable. Its staple joke is that Edith and Martin spoke French abominably, which did not amuse the French at all. One has the impression that the text was mostly written by Edith and polished by Martin, whose task seems to have been to tighten the style and eliminate facetiousness. It is good journalism with an Irish flavour, illustrated with Edith's wash drawings. The commission enabled the authors to see something of the world free of charge, and led to two more commissions—one for a tour in Denmark, an account of which appears as a chapter in *Stray-aways*, and a tour in Wales, published later as *Beggars on Horseback*. These brought in enough money to keep them going and enabled them to struggle on with *The Real Charlotte*, which they hoped would firmly establish them as novelists. The travel books contained nothing to offend their hosts or upset the susceptibilities of the lady readers of the *Pictorial*, but the diaries are more blunt. The quotation from Martin's diary here given is closer to reality: '5 October. Went to the farm house of Jeanne, a vendageuse cook, and in pursuit of copy dined and slept there. Dinner good. Fleas awful. Was badly bitten by a mosquito. We scarcely slept at all or washed.'

There occurs a curious little note in Martin's diary after the return, when she was staying a few days with a married sister at Kew. 'Walked to Richmond in the afternoon, passing in the gardens someone who, it seemed to me afterwards, might have been the wreck of Willie Wills,' the elderly Bohemian friend of her brother Robert, for whom some years before she had had a mild affection. This entry is followed shortly afterwards by another: 'Heard that Willie Wills is dying of jaundice at Guy's Hospital.' Such is the end of that tiny romance in Martin's life.

While she and Edith were on the vineyard tour, Aylmer was getting together his pack of hounds at Castle Townshend in preparation for the hunting season. When back in Ireland Martin notes '7 December. Arrived at Drishane. Hunting in full swing.' Edith has details. 'Had a long stern chase of the hounds along the mountain tops . . . and saw them run into and kill the fox. Great glory.' Sometimes there were not enough foxes to be sure of a good run and so one had to be trapped and kept for the next meet, when it was let out and given a bit of a start. '4 December. Jack (Edith's brother) put his fox trap in the wood with a cock in it. 5 Dec. Walked with Jack and the little dogs to feed the old cock in the trap. 8 Dec. Found a fox at once and ran again to the wood where they dug him out and chopped him.' The local people also caught foxes as Aylmer was always ready to pay ten shillings for one. Sometimes they trapped them and sometimes they caught them with their bare hands. '26 December. They swam after him to an island and hunted him naked round and round until he lay down and was caught.' The creature was then loosed in a field. 'A nice chase ensued and after two checks he was run into after about twenty-five minutes and eaten.'

Thus Edith in her diary, despite the fact that her compassion for animals was intense. But it is impossible to chart the vagaries of the human heart.

Besides hunting, Castle Townshend society had another distraction. Led by Uncle Kendal, frequent attempts were made to communicate with spirits. In this it was following the fashion elsewhere. Seances were the vogue in London. Neither Edith nor Martin was as yet a convinced spiritualist. But nearly everyone they met at home or in England thought there was something in the cult. Robert Martin's friend, Arthur Balfour, the future P.M., after receiving a communication, as he supposed, from a dead girl he had loved in his youth, Mary Lyttelton, engaged a professional medium and for many years considered himself in communication with his lost love. The Society for Psychical Research, founded in 1882, became interested and in its Journal his seances are referred to as the Palm Sunday case. Uncle Kendal had no romantic reason for his probing into the occult, but he pursued his researches with the energy which he displayed in everything he undertook. There are stray references in Edith's diary to doings at his house, The Point. '26 October 1891. My grandmother was said to be the communicating force and made many strange statements.' '9 November. Sent a list of questions to Violet Coghill's gub.' The word 'gub' is employed by Edith at this date to mean 'familiar spirit'. She uses it, however, as a term of derision. Thus '14 November, Martin gubbing with the widow Currey.' '16 October 1893. Uncle Kendal full of his gubbing. He is in almost incessant communication with some spirit.' '6 January 1894. Hildegarde and Egerton went down to the first meeting of the Cosheen Psychical Society. Ordained by Uncle K and his head gub.'

At first the seances at the Psychic Circle were dull. 'Hildegarde had to go a-gubbing but no result.' A few knocks only were got out of the table. But at the gub meeting of 29 January 1894 'things began to go a bit holier', writes Edith. Two days later, at Glen Barrahane, Sir Joscelyn Coghill's house, 'strange lights were seen and gubs walking about'. Egerton, who had recently married Hildegarde, developed mesmeric powers and gave a demonstration at the same address. The wedding had been quite conventional, the church of St Barrahane decorated, Edith playing the organ, triumphal arches in the village, the rain pouring down in a typical Irish way. Two glimpses of it survive in the MSS., the one amusing, the other profoundly revealing. They are both contained in a letter written by Edith a day or so after the wedding to Hildegarde on her honeymoon. She asks her did she notice as she left the house with Egerton Mrs Leary, a dwarfish washerwoman. 'As you drove off, her feelings suddenly got too many for her and with a Central African yell she dashed from the ranks and hurled the most noisome old boot at the carriage. She ran right across all of us down to the dining-room window, and then the excitement died in her and she fled back almost on all fours, evidently realizing how greatly she had dared, and regretting her daring. Everybody went away then and I went up to your room and found the little dogs lying in moody coils with their backs to the world and I thereon put my face down on their backs and wept, and the Tothams licked up my tears with avidity.'

In her diary Edith lets one see a little deeper into her state of mind. 'The dogs' she says 'did not try to conceal their feelings and were exceedingly moody and disgusted.' The fact was that Edith had tried during the wedding to look as cheerful as custom required, but she had a deep-seated dislike of weddings, a dislike amounting to disgust. In declaring the dogs to be disgusted she was revealing her own feelings. Why she felt disgusted at her sister marrying Egerton, whom she knew well, liked, and who was an excellent match in every way, could only be fully explained by a psychiatrist, though perhaps enough has been said earlier in the book to hint at what his explanation would be. To say that her tears and disgust were

Hildegarde Somerville and Egerton Coghill (1893)

Robert Martin (about 1900)

caused simply by the departure of a sister whose congenial companionship she had enjoyed for so many years at Drishane, and without which she would feel lonely, is only a partial explanation, particularly as Hildegarde would be away on her honeymoon only a fortnight and afterwards would live at Castle Townshend in a house not five minutes' walk from Drishane House. In fact the marriage made no practical difference. The two sisters remained firm friends for more than half a century. When Egerton died in 1921, Hildegarde returned to live in Drishane. Nevertheless, the marriage when it happened was a profound shock to something fundamental in Edith's character.

For Hildegarde the marriage and the honeymoon were a great happiness, though one night at their hotel in France she had an alarming experience. While wide awake she saw a ghost walk from the window to her bed and vanish. It was said of Egerton at this time that he looked very different from what he did as an art student. Then he used to go about Paris, says Martin, in corduroy knickerbockers, a Tam O'Shanter and earrings. Now he looked like a very smart Major in a neat dark grey suit, close cut hair and a trim moustache. It was on the return from the honeymoon that he took up mesmerism seriously, and was in demand when people were ill and medicine did them no good. Even so, Hildegarde found Uncle Kendal's seances very tedious. Edith's diary has: '21 February 1894. H went cursing to her gub party. Emily Herbert (a spirit) says it is her crown of sorrow that she cannot materialize.' Uncle Kendal also took up painting. 'Went to The Point to see Uncle K's terrific paintings.' They were apparitional landscapes.

While these matters were going forward, hunting, seances, a wedding, Edith and Martin were hard at work, sometimes at Drishane, sometimes at Ross, or travelling abroad on commissions, a Danish tour,* a Welsh tour, a tour of the Aran islands, on which last, surprisingly, they were accompanied by Mama. They found the islanders rapacious and not at all as romantic as Synge was to dramatize them in *Riders to the*

* See *Stray-aways*, Chapter XIV.

Sea. The main endeavour, however, was to finish *The Real Charlotte*; money and reputation lay that way. The travel articles were badly paid and only journalism. '7 June 1892. We hurriedly wrote most agitating scenes.' '8 June 1892. We wrote feverishly in the train all the way to Mallow and succeeded in finishing off Francie', the heroine of *The Real Charlotte*. Then the triumphant entry: '4 February 1893. Actually and entirely finished *The Real Charlotte*.' And 'London, 16 May 1893. We went to Ward & Downey and sold *The Real Charlotte* for £250 and ½ American rights.' Edith's mother was less scathing than before; she thought the writing good though the characters detestable. The book was altogether too original for her conservative taste. Part of the time, as mentioned, Martin had to rent the house called The Cottage at Castle Townshend, where she engaged as servant a Mrs Whoolley, 'a genial savage, accoucheuse and layer-out to the village.' This woman is the subject of a letter written by Martin when Edith was temporarily absent in London, and is a splendid description of what an Irish servant at a place like Castle Townshend was like in the nineties. 'Whoolley came in to put on coal. She then easily fell into the prevailing conversation as she squatted on the floor, and proceeded to tell stories of confinements, birth marks and other appropriate matters. The talk turned on the topic of combinations. Whoolley, whose eyes were blinking in a most suspicious and owl-like way, suddenly whipped her petticoats up round her waist, declaring that she wouldn't wear combinations, and had a good pair of legs of her own. It was perfectly clear that she did not wear combinations or anything else.'

Edith and Martin were not so inseparable that they went everywhere together. The former still had her painting ambitions and in 1894 paid two visits to Paris to round off her studies. By this time she painted quite professionally though never reached as high a standard as Egerton, her brother-in-law. On her way to Paris in the winter of 1894 she went to stay with relatives in Leicestershire and hunted once or twice with the

Quorn, the smartest and richest hunt in England. A letter to Martin contains a description of the occasion; a fuller account is given later in her *Happy Days*. The comparison between the Quorn's solemn pageant and her own little happy-go-lucky West Carbery pack is entertaining. She could not help admiring and being impressed by the splendid thoroughbred hunters, the number of riders (three hundred compared with her usual turn out of twenty), the sartorial parade of well-tailored red coats, gleaming top hats, immaculate stocks, boots to dazzle. The respect she accorded Tom Firr, the Huntsman, would have satisfied a demi-god. At the meet 'the renowned Tom Firr, mounted on a splendid chesnut thoro-bred, took up his position on the cleared central space prepared for him; eighteen and a half couples of the beautiful Quorn Hounds surrounded him.' The moment was as solemnly correct as at a parade of Guards and 'profoundly impressed the Visitor from Ireland.' During the hunt she had a close view of Tom Firr in action. 'He came cantering majestically, certain that no one would dare get in his way.' She admits to a frenzy of excitement, her 'nerves as tense as a terrier's at a rat hole'; but her sense of the ridiculous came to her rescue. There was an element of comedy in the pageant. All of the three hundred splendidly dressed men, riding horses worth a fortune, did not ride to the hounds. At the cry 'Gone Away' two hundred and fifty of them jostled along the lanes and followed over the fields only where there were reliable gates and so no necessity to jump hedges.

In this letter Edith is at her most horsey, the side of her character one must not forget.

When she and Martin returned to Ireland after the Danish tour (end of 1893), they separated to their respective homes. Whenever Martin returns to Ross she is plunged in a stranger Ireland than when in the comparatively anglicized Castle Townshend. As she always wrote regularly to Edith when away, her letters (such as survive) give glimpses of mysteries. What she wrote in January 1894 about a suicide in the Wood of Annagh, at the edge of which stood Ross House, is as arresting

as anything she ever wrote. 'They have been two days probing
that awful pond that is on your left after you get into the Wood
of Annagh, Pooleen-a-fairla,' she begins, having in a previous
letter reported how a certain Shanneen Holloran had been
missing for some days. 'His scapular and Agnus Dei were
found on the brink, and his purse. The police came today, but
I don't think they got any tidings. They say there is thirty feet
of water, and unknown depths of mud. He is either there or
wants people to think he is. Mat told me "he took off the
scafflin and the Agnus Di the ways he'd be dhrowned. No one
could be dhrowned that had thim on him." The extraordinary
thing is that last Sunday a young man in Coolaghy rushed to
the lake and tried to drown himself. People saw him make the
spring and got there in time to save him. "He was lying on his
back" says Mat "and the Agnus Di without the sign of wet on
it." Much more did Mat say, and it is all written down, and
you shall hear it I hope soon. It is the makings of a story
almost.'

This letter also contains thanks from Nurse Davin, one of
the old wet nurses, for a message sent her by Edith, which is
too good to omit. 'Nurse Davin when I gave her your Christmas
messages, was overwhelmed with gratitude. "And would you
please to wish her every sort of good luck and happiness, and
the blessing of God on her. The crayture, indeed she was good
and clane and quiet and sensible, and her little dog, so nice and
so clever. She cried for him, the crayture. She couldn't do
more." ' To my taste this is more authentic than anything
Synge was to contrive, though I immensely admire his poetical
adaptations of the speech he heard in the Aran islands.

In a letter two days later Martin carries further her account
of the suicide. By that time the body of Holloran had been
fished up from the depths of the boghole and carried to burial.
She comments on the strange tragedy in her vivid style. 'One
could wish for that passion for death that that young fellow
had who disappeared. . . . I avoided the place throughout, and
did not look at the dismal procession. Need I say that Selina

went out and even permitted the face to be uncovered for her edification. I was at the pool yesterday and could realize very well what happened. It turns out that what chiefly played on his mind was that they had one day called him from his work to come and shorten up the chain of the chapel bell in order that when the new priest came to hold Mass the next Sunday, the bell could not be rung. When he found what he had done he was miserable, and ever since they watched him more or less. He tried to get away, as they think, to this pool a few days before, but he felt them following him and went back. On St Stephen's Day he went out with his brother to cut a rope of ferns, and took an opportunity of escape when his brother's back was turned. They found the rope of ferns flung down, and next the scapular on the bank and finally himself. Never was a more bitter comment on a parish feud, and never was there a more innocent and godly life turned to active insanity by bad treatment. It fills my mind in its dramatic aspect and perhaps after a talk with you it may take shape.'

Edith was greatly taken with this letter and requested Martin to supply further details, which she included years afterwards in her *Irish Memories*.

The household at Ross was much alarmed some months later because Mama, who had gone walking in the Wood of Annagh, did not return and could not be found for eight hours. It was feared that she had fallen into that very boghole, because a little time before she had suddenly fainted and fallen to the floor. 'She was in a dream for the rest of the day,' says Martin. 'Next morning her nose swelled. When Dr Gorham arrived it was 11 p.m. and he was drunk.'

If Martin at Ross was at the heart of the old occult, the denizens of Castle Townshend, absorbed in a modern rendering of it, were having their excitements. From a letter Martin wrote to Cameron, then at Capetown with his regiment, we learn more of what was going on there. 'You may think in your ignorance that your elders at Castle T are drowsing along in the lines of the Church of Ireland or in indifference to them, either way without excitement, but you are mistaken. A gentleman, called Stainton-Moses, has arisen, with a resident Djin for his prophet, called Imperator, and I solemnly assure you that on the creed of Imperator, Egerton, his father the Bart, Uncle Kendal and, in a kind of way, your mother are ordering their theories and lives. Egerton takes it with a sort of very logical, intelligent credulity. You know the kind of way the Coghills take new things, the Bart ditto, but without the desire to act on it, Uncle K very darkly and mysteriously, your mother by bursts of the most delightful kind. This time next year all will be forgotten, except by Uncle K, who has for a long time been going steadily on with his spirits and spirit writing. It has certainly improved his character and temper, and he says that it has made him believe in a hereafter, which strange to say he did not at one time. Nothing would ever surprise me about him, his reading the lessons in church or dancing in front of the Salvation Army or opening a faith-healing establishment at The Point. He has such strength of character that he would carry off anything he thought to be right. One respects him.'

9

The death of Edith's Mother

The Real Charlotte was published on 8 May 1894. It was well received by the press. 'Got excellent reviews from *Athenaeum*, *Pall Mall*, *National Observer* and a furious tearing from the *Westminster Gazette*,' Martin notes. There can be no doubt it was the most considerable of their novels, though it is not read so much now as their Irish R.M. stories, which were to take London by storm five years later. Edith and Martin were satisfied and certain of its quality. Its originality lies in it being a study of a girl belonging to the Dublin middle class, not the sort of heroine selected by any Irish writer hitherto. The plot is skilfully unwound, the girl is taken up by the class socially above her, her sensitive character and real worth are subtly suggested. The suspense is cleverly maintained until suddenly she meets with a fatal accident. The earlier chapters are in Dublin, which Martin knew well, having spent there sixteen years of her youth. The collaboration, however, is so close that it is impossible to distinguish for certain the two hands. The miracle of a joint style is achieved. One can, however, point to certain parts, such as the chapters with Dublin background, and feel that Martin had most to do with them. The conclusion, also, has the feel of Martin, when the mare which Francie, the heroine, is riding, startled by meeting a cart with a coffin and mourners, throws its rider, who breaks her neck. 'One of the women began suddenly to groan and thump the coffin lid with her fists, in preparation for a burst of the Irish Cry, and at the signal Norry fell upon her knees and flung out her arms inside her cloak, with a gesture that made her look like a great vulture opening its wings for flight. The cloak flapped right across the mare's face and she swerved from the cart. . . . Francie was shot into the air and fell headfirst onto the road.'

In January 1895, eight months after the publication, Martin went to Scotland to visit relations at St Andrew's university where Andrew Lang was staying. He asked her to dinner. In a letter to Edith she gives an account of her conversation with him. 'To me then with a kind of off hand fling he said "I suppose you are the one who did the writing." I explained with some care that it was not so. He said he didn't know how any two people could equally evolve characters etc, that he had tried, and it was always he or the other who did it all. I said I didn't know how we managed, but anyhow I knew little of book making as a science. He said I must know a great deal. On which I had nothing to say—and talked of other things. I hadn't the face to discuss Charlotte. I knew that he admired the book very much and that was enough. He talked of R. L. Stevenson, Mrs Humphry Ward and others, as personal friends, and exhibited at intervals a curious silent laugh up under his nose. He will be very nut-crackery as an old man, though his nose is straight. He was so interesting that I hardly noticed how ripping was the dinner.'

Back in Ross Martin writes two remarkable letters to Edith, moved to exert her full powers by the spectacle of death. The first letter has: 'William Mac's wife died suddenly two days ago, after producing a dead child, and was buried yesterday up at the chapel on the hill, where a graveyard has lately been opened. I went up to the back gate and walked with it from there and saw the whole thing. It was *extraordinary*. The people who had relations buried there roared and howled on the graves, and round Mrs Mac's grave there was a perpetual whining and moaning, awfully like the tuning of fiddles in an orchestra the whole time. The drunken men staggered about,

one or two smart relations from Galway flaunted to and fro in
their best clothes, occasionally crossing themselves, and three
keeners knelt together inside the inmost ring by the grave, with
their hands locked, rocking and crying into each other's hoods,
three awful witches, telling each other the full horrors that the
other people were not competent to understand. There was no
priest, but Mrs Mac's brother read a kind of Litany, very like
ours, at top speed, and all the people answered. Every saint in
the calendar was called on to save her, and to protect her, and
there poor William stood with his head down and his hat over
his eyes. It was impressive—very. The thump of the clods and
stones on the coffin was a sound that made one shudder—and
all the people keened and cried at it. Cremation for *me*—and
not this hiding away in the ground.' Nevertheless, Martin's
body lies in the ground of St Barrahane's churchyard.*

The second letter is concerned with the death of Thady, an
old retainer of the Martin family. It runs: 'Poor Thady died on
Thursday night, a very gallant quiet end, conscious and calm.
Anne Kinearey did not mean to say anything remarkable when
she told me that he died "as quiet, now as quiet as a little fish",
but those were her words. I went up there on Thursday to see
old Anne, and coming into the house, black with silent people,
was suddenly confronted with Thady's body laid out in the
kitchen. . . . It was very awful. And Connor three parts drunk
advanced and delivered a loud horrible harangue on Thady
and the Martin family. The people sat like owls listening, and
we retired into a room where were whiskey bottles galore, and
the cream of the company, men from Galway, respectably
drinking and magnificent in speech. It was *quite* disgusting and
the funeral yesterday only a shade better. At all events the pale
tranced face was hidden, and the living people looked less
brutal without that terrific purified creature.'† It is in such
passages that the great Martin appears. The desolation, terror,

* Edith valued this letter so much that she printed it in *Irish Memories*, though
she altered the text here and there and made some excisions.

† Part of this letter with alterations and suppressions was printed by Edith in
Irish Memories.

beauty of death fascinated her. Its spectacle she could not avoid, though it frightened her.

The year 1895 was to be a year of deaths. In November came the news that Mrs Somerville was dying. The letters Edith wrote to Martin in December give a full account of an event which resulted in her becoming mistress of Drishane, a position she was to occupy for over half a century. They are very moving and reveal the tenderness of her feelings both for her mother and for the whole family. It was a devoted family, though Edith and her mother were inclined to irritate each other. Mrs Somerville, for one thing, did not care for or understand her daughter's books and did not disguise the fact. Intellectually she was on a lower plane and failed to recognize that Edith's talents as writer and artist put her above her brothers and sister, though none of them were stupid and some were gifted, with enough force of character to rise high in their professions. In a letter of Martin's, which refers to an occasion when she was staying at Drishane while Edith was in Paris, she observes how curious it was that she got on better with Mrs Somerville when Edith was not there. In any altercation between mother and daughter, her heart obliged her to take Edith's part. 'It is not that I don't get on with your mother; I get on so well when I have her to myself that it is quite frightening,' she says. She kept Mrs Somerville in such good humour 'that a child might have played with her'. The truth was that Mrs Somerville was an overwhelming character. She was gay, lively, quick, but so accustomed to having things her own way, her husband being a very mild man, that she could not be opposed, even in a small matter, without risk. As Edith was a woman of equal assurance and force, altercations were inevitable. Yet Mrs Somerville was such a personality and had such immense warmth that she was adored by her children, and her death, which came suddenly, was a grievous blow. She fell ill on 25 November 1895 and on 4 December Edith wrote to tell Martin the sequel. It is a most touching letter and can still bring tears to the eyes. 'At about 6 a.m. the nurse woke me again. Mother was very wild,

feverish, and in great pain. We tried various remedies in vain.
At dawn I sent a man riding post haste for morphia. I can't tell
you the agony of waiting for him; she tried to bear the pain and
it would beat her. Then I sent for Uncle Kendal and Egerton,
and with mesmerism they soothed her a little. In the midst of
the worst she made me laugh by whispering that the nurse was
"a little old bit of red tape" because she refused to try some
unofficial remedy. At last came Hadden with the morphia. He
saw at once that she could not bear the pain and injected $\frac{1}{4}$ grain
morphia. In 5 minutes the blessed relief came, but soon the
mucous from the lung began, in the inertia of the morphia sleep,
to rise and rise in her chest. The breathing grew more and more
oppressed. They got a great quantity of nourishment down, and
we still hoped that she would wake relieved. . . . At midday she
seemed to rally and many symptoms were good, and we believed
in the Coghill constitution. At 10 they sent us to bed. At 11.15
Egerton called us. Her breathing then was almost peaceful. We
did not stay long. Egerton and Aylmer took us away. Then
Papa went in. You know he also has been ill. He tottered in
between the two boys. Dear Martin, I think that was almost the
worst moment; one could believe in that sorrow; the rest was
inconceivable, still is. He also was taken away soon. A few
minutes afterwards her life went out on a light gentle breath.
She had been unconscious throughout, and never, even in her
worst pain, thought she was in any danger. I am so thankful now
that we did not frighten her for nothing. She had too child-like
a soul to face death; it frightened her. . . . Poor Papa is quite
wonderful, so gentle and good and so utterly and entirely heart-
broken. It would wring your heart to see him. It was all so
sudden, we had about eight hours in which to face it, and till the
last we hoped.'

Martin replied at once and Edith writes: 'Your letter came
this morning, and the flowers came just in time [for the funeral].
Cameron opened them and put them in the carriage that was
full of flowers, then he came up to my room, where I was sitting
with Hildegarde, and Papa, and told me that they had come

[107]

and gave me the note. I made him bring them up to me. They were most beautiful and as fresh as if they had only just been gathered. . . . It all feels like one continuous dream of pain that began on Tuesday morning. I don't know when it is going to end. I know you will tell me it is morbid and foolish but most of the things that come back to me are of words and actions that I was sorry for even at the time and now—— And then I feel as if I had never been a bit demonstrative to her, or ever let her know what I felt, except indeed when I was angry or provoked. I know she took pleasure out of us all, but I feel now as if I might so easily have done so much more. Then there were so many times when I was snubbing or beastly. I don't say all this for you to contradict me, but because I must get it out of my heart. . . . Hildegarde's pluck was quite splendid but yesterday afternoon she broke down, in health I mean, and Egerton and I drove her into bed in my room. Hadden was here; we had sent for him to *order* Papa not to go to the funeral. He said she was all right but must keep quite quiet in bed, and be spared strong emotion. She is much better this evening, and has been in bed all day, a good thing as we managed to keep Papa down here with her, and he was spared all the sights or rather sounds. He never knew when they took the coffin up last night or brought it down this morning. I went in on Wednesday to see her. She looked most beautiful, but so terribly, utterly remote. I could not feel that it was she, it was a beautiful mask that her soul had worn, and now that it had been cast aside it had taken on a cold sort of serenity, a character of its own, quite apart from hers. In a curious way, seeing what had been her, reconciled me to leaving her alone in the cold, half dark, silent room; I felt that she was not there. . . . Aylmer and Emmie (his wife) went with me. It is no use to try and tell you what they and Egerton and Hildegarde have been. Whenever Aylmer gave himself time to think you could see how shattered he was by grief, but his pluck was beyond what I could possibly have believed. Boyle could not have been stronger or more reliable. As for Egerton I need not tell you of him. He has been everything, so helpful and tender and absolutely unselfish. And his and Aylmer's care for Papa was quite beautiful. On the night she died they sat up with him and sank all their own grief in trying to calm and comfort him. I could not cry that night. My heart felt like a hot stone and my mind was beating against the incredible truth like the sea against those awful Aran cliffs. Emmie and Hildegarde and I all huddled together in Emmie's room, and the house was all alight and people going to and fro in the passages. . . . When we were taken in to see her for the last time, the two nurses were standing with the tears running down their faces. . . . I can't believe it now. I can see her stumping up from Glen B to lunch, with her eyes on the ground. . . . Poor Cameron only arrived by the early mail this morning. He was quite broken down. Even Egerton's pluck gave way and he sobbed with us like a baby. What else could we do? Would you have had me sneak down to the cottage and cry there by myself? Martin, I know you wouldn't. Hildegarde and I had had a hard battle with Papa to keep him from going to see her. He is so broken down by his illness and misery that even his old obstinacy ("He's the *most* obstinate man I know!" as Mother used to say with a rolling eye) has left him and he does what we ask. Only when the coffin was shut and the violet cross, that was almost as long as it was, was fastened to it, we went in and knelt down by it and said goodbye to her in our hearts. Cameron saw her last in all her smart clothes going radiantly off to Christine Morragh's wedding; that is a better memory than the pale serene severe presence that had nothing of her own gay self about it. . . . From all round the country, from all classes, there is but one voice of grief. Aylmer said that every man and woman in Skib came up to him. Jack Buckley, who had written daily to enquire for her, was crying like a baby. "Your most affectionate and beloved Mother, that with her own hands made a wreath to place upon my dear daughter"—that was what he said in his letter of condolence. In the village they said every door and window was shut and not a sound in the street—"it was like there was death in each house". Papa had insisted on her being buried in Castle Haven,* and we can never be grateful enough to Mr Warren. He and his men went yesterday, opened the vault, cleaned and set everything in order, and then both lined and covered it all with moss and white chrysanthemums. Even Aylmer, who had had an unspeakable horror of taking her there, said it was beautiful and all the dreadfulness gone out of it. They carried her, in relays of six men, our tenants for the most part, and some of the coastguards and Jack Buckley and other farmers, who don't belong to us but wished to do honour to her memory. The tenants had gone out early this morning and had swept the road as clean of mud and stones as if it were an avenue. I think it was most touching of them. There were seventy carriages and cars, and hundreds of foot people. . . . Oh, dear Martin, it is a comfort to write to you but how Hildegarde and I wish you were here. After the two of us, no one knew her in and out as you do. I am so thankful to think that you stayed with her this time last year and she was so fond of you. She was always asking me when you were coming. . . . The Canon came down to read the service. He broke down two or three times. The poor boys also broke down quite uncontrollably, I believe. They were so far far nicer to her than I was, but it is no use saying so now. After it was all over the Canon came over and read some prayers to Papa and Emmie and the two boys and me, and gave us communion. It was Aylmer's suggestion and wish. I think it was very nice of him. My candle is burned out, but I feel better and as if I should go to sleep now.'

Two days later Edith wrote again: 'We are all better. Papa is sitting in the study. He is wonderful and tries to be cheerful and is so grateful for everything and so utterly uncomplaining. . . . I have got beyond the stage of tears now, only now and

* Instead of in the graveyard at St Barrahane, the church in the village of Castle Townshend. The Castlehaven graveyard near the mouth of the haven, opening on the Atlantic, is a wild and lonely place. The church had originally been there and the gentry of Castle Townshend had their burial vaults in its yard. When St Barrahane was built in the nineteenth century, the old church was disused and fell to ruin, but the vaults remained, tenanted by the dead. Colonel Somerville was the last of his family to be buried there.

then when some little foolish thing turns up unexpectedly, or I find myself quoting one of her absurd sayings from sheer force of habit, then it is hard. . . . Don't think of me as moping, or the like of that. I have more to do than I ever had in my life and am glad to go to sleep when I get into my bed.'

10

Edith becomes mistress of Drishane

The death of Edith's mother was followed two and a half years later (16 March 1898) by the death of her father, Colonel Thomas Somerville, aged seventy-three. Before describing that event, which was of capital importance in Edith's life, as it resulted in the whole management of Drishane devolving upon her, mention will be made of some happenings in the period 1895–98, which though of less weight, have their place in the story.

Three months after the death of Mrs Somerville a son was born to Hildegarde.* His aunt Edith took great interest in him from the first, despite the shrinking she had experienced at the time of his parents' marriage. Constant references to him appear in her diary. Thus on 22 May 1896 when he was two months old, she has 'Marmaduke immensely improved. He is a dear little chap.' (He began life with this name.) At the christening the entry is: 'I was a real godmother. Marmaduke was very good and only cried as much as was orthodox.' Martin, who was at Ross, had to be told all about it. To her Edith confides that the names selected for the infant were Marmaduke Nevill Patrick and that when, as godmother, she was asked by the presiding clergyman to say what they were, she couldn't

---

* This son succeeded in 1921 to the baronetcy, on the death of his father Egerton, who had succeeded his father Sir Joscelyn in 1905, and is now the Sir Patrick Coghill who owns the MSS on which this book is founded.

remember. However, they had been written down on a bit of
paper which was in the hand of an assistant. He rattled them
off and all was saved. There was the sad side: 'Hildegarde and
I had but one thought all the time,' their mother's recent
death, her absence on an occasion she would have delighted in
so much. 'However it is no good going on saying these things,
you know.' They had a splendid tea afterwards at The Cottage,
where Egerton and Hildegarde were living, 'at which all the
quality were present'. There was only one embarrassment
during the christening, or what in England would be so termed.
A Mrs Norris, one of the retainers, who was drunk, 'roared out
in the church "the Lord spare him to ye Mrs Coghill".' The
words were accepted as a blessing from the heart; that she was
drunk in church was overlooked. It is, I feel, otiose to continue
about Marmaduke, but I am unable to refrain from quoting a
few more dicta of his doting aunt. '29 November 1896. Marmaduke now bristles with teeth.' His early teeth were much
admired. Edith, quite carried away, compares them to shark's
teeth. When Hildegarde's second son Nevill* was born a little
later, we have: 'Paddy dislikes the baby excessively,' for by
now the name Marmaduke had been abandoned for Patrick.
But Edith remarks somewhere that she thinks having a brother
'will stop him from growing up an old-fashioned imp'. She
raves about Paddy. Seeing him after an interval she writes: 'I
never saw a child as improved in looks and health as Paddy. He
is most fascinating and good as gold. His hair is lovely. And
best praise of all, the puppy likes him'. But he could be naughty.
On 30 October 1898 'he had a day of badness, consequent upon
a double back tooth'. When he saw that his nurse's helping of
pudding was larger than his, he tried to snatch it and had to be
put out of the room. However, on his return he kissed everybody and promised to be good, but he wasn't.

When Edith wrote to Martin saying she had never been so
busy in her life, she was referring in particular to housekeeping. On top of her writing, her painting, the stables,

---

* To become Merton Professor of English Literature, Oxford.

maintenance of the house, taking her dogs for walks, sup-
pression of rats and the huge correspondence she carried on, she
now had to order the stores, arrange the meals, manage the
servants, many of them like those already described in these
pages, dirty, idle, violent—and devoted. The cook, Mrs Evans,
was said to be especially fierce. Of her five brothers, Cameron,
Boyle, Aylmer, Jack and Hugh, only Aylmer was in Castle
Townshend at this time, the rest being with their regiments or
on their ships. Aylmer and his wife Emmie lived in one of the
houses in the village. He managed the Drishane home farm for
a bit and saw to the horses, the hounds and their feed. Though
Edith did not care much for Emmie at first, she got fond of her
and found her a quiet, self-sacrificing, loyal and sweet person.
She was also a good housekeeper and whenever Edith was
away, moved into Drishane and took charge. Hildegarde helped
all she could, but at the moment with her two infant sons,
Paddy and Nevill, had to leave Drishane to Edith. Moreover,
she was rather pulled down by a pain in the spine. The papers
hitherto tell us little about her, except that she was a woman of
sterling character, Edith's constant companion, and confidante,
and Egerton's happiness. In January 1897, however, she comes
prominently forward for a moment. A letter of Edith's to
Martin tells the story. 'Let me tell you of the surpassing heroism
of Hildegarde. At about noon yesterday (11 January) she heard
a most awful bellowing in the street which stopped at her door.
Mary the Monkey,* roaring at full pitch of lungs and, literally,
tearing her hair. Hildegarde made out with some trouble that
a mad dog had run down from Skib, got down to the quay,
run quietly into the Monkey's house, sniffed round, and then
suddenly it had badly bitten one of the children, aged three, on
the leg. Hildegarde tore down to the quay; the wound in the
filthy little bare leg was bleeding hard. She sucked it. I say no
more, she deserves a V.C. One can't speak to her of it as she
has to go away and be sick whenever she thinks of it. It was a

* Wife of Donovan, a retainer, so called because it was her job to feed and look
after the Drishane monkey.

gallant act. She got sick and faint afterwards and no wonder. The dog tore Donovan's trousers but did no more harm before the police shot him. He is being sent to Cork for analysis today. Hildegarde said when she got there the house was crammed with people, roaring at the tops of their voices, and there was not a drip of water, and none of them had even thought of washing the wound.'

The child, however, died of rabies six weeks later. Edith's diary 2 March 1897: 'Mary the Monkey came up to say that her child was ill with pleurisy. Got it up to the big bath at Glen Barrahane and did all we could for it in vain. Stayed there all night. It went up to the Skibbereen hospital this morning and died there.' It was rabies, not pleurisy. Hildegarde was not told this. 'Her nerves are too shaky for the shock of hearing the truth.' She was left to believe it was pleurisy.

This mad dog caused an outbreak of rabies in that part of the County Cork. It bit several village dogs. By August the kennels at Drishane were infected. The first of the hounds to go mad, Countess, was shot on 22 August. By the 25th the whole pack had to be destroyed. Tim Crowley, their kennel man, had a risky job. A full account of what he had to do was printed twenty-six years later by Edith in her book *Wheeltracks*. She there relates how, when inspecting the kennels soon after Countess was shot, she saw four hounds 'sitting on the bench with their backs to the wall, silent and motionless, with feverish bright eyes, staring at us unrecognizingly—the dear hounds which had never before failed to greet us with extravagant affection.' They were in the first stage of hydrophobia. It was hopeless to expect that any of the pack could now escape. She and Aylmer hurried to Skibbereen to get poison. But before they returned, two of the staring dazed hounds had passed into raging madness. A couple of policemen with guns had been called to prevent any possibility of a hound escaping and were stationed outside the kennel yard. From where they were they could not see to shoot into the kennel and were afraid to enter the yard and get close. With two hounds mad and the rest going mad, a terrible fight inside the kennel seemed imminent. Tim Crowley realized that the only thing to be done was for him to enter the kennel. This he did, alone, caught one of the hounds by the neck and stern and dragged him out for the police to shoot. A policeman fired but missed, he was so agitated. Crowley then snatched his rifle, shot the animal 'and one by one dragged out hound after hound and shot every one of them with his own hand'. When Edith and Aylmer got back with the poison the corpses of the whole pack scattered over the yard were, she wrote, 'a sight of unbelievable horror'.

This catastrophe seemed like the end of the West Carbery Hunt, but Aylmer managed to replace the lost pack and when the season opened in October Castle Townshend was hunting again.

In March of the following year was to occur the death of Edith's father, Colonel Thomas Henry Somerville of Drishane, the head of the family. At the time of his death, to be described below, Cameron, his heir, was in Japan, Boyle was in Canada and Hugh in Australia. Of his other two sons, Aylmer was in Castle Townshend and Jack with his regiment in England. Martin was in Ross, where she had been putting the last touches to the little novel, *The Silver Fox*, in which some episodes recounted in her letters to Edith, such particularly as the account of the boghole in the Wood of Annagh and the suicide, were woven into the plot. She and Edith were now approached by London editors to write a series of short hunting stories. The success of Martin's brother, Robert, had created a taste for that sort of story. A few hunting stories of theirs had already appeared in magazines and readers wanted more. They had not yet thought of the form which in a couple of years they were to perfect in their *Some Experiences of an Irish R.M.*, but were close to it. As before, Martin found time to write long and amusing letters to Edith when they were separated. Those which survive continue to record whatever she found droll and arresting. Mama remained a continual source of wonder, amusement and delight. A fragment contains the following jewel: 'At Christmas I gave Bridget material for a blue serge dress. This, Bridget, in delirium of some sort, placed under Mama's table. Mama, coming on it there, joyfully and silently accepted it as a forgotten possession, and locked it up to make a dressing gown of. Bridget immediately recognized and sympathized with the theft, and said nothing until steps for the making up of the serge seemed imminent. Then with deepest reluctance she broke to Mama that she had seen the serge in Mama's press, and it was yielded, with I may say bitter disgruntlement on Mama's part. This transpired this morning. It is very typical of all things here.'

In the affair of the sweep Mama presides with dignity in an extravagant comedy. The sweep arrived at 2 a.m. by mail car from Galway and woke the household, but by breakfast nothing had been accomplished. Bridget declared that 'God forgive her, she never seen anyone she'd hate as much as the same sweep'. Every fire in the house had to be put out. 'Mama in high frump and chill retired to the garden house and had a fire there, loudly declaring that she much preferred smoke and chimneys on fire to a sweep. Things went apace till luncheon, the sweep on the roof bawling down the chimneys, bricks and stones avalanching down through the walls, the cook raging, the house black with filth, everyone perished with cold. However, all is now well but the memory of the sweep is accursed through all grades of the household.' Mama had sat out the whole hullabaloo grandly in the garden house.

After Christmas 1897 Martin went to Drishane for a short stay. A letter of hers to Cameron, in Japan, contains a passage about Colonel Somerville. Two years had elapsed since the death of his wife. 'Your father is much more silent, but he is really in better spirits. One sees that he never forgets, but is much better able to bear it. He potters round the fields with Yummy just as usual. Yummy is a wonderful pleasure to him, and sits on his lap all the evening and is really a paragon of goodness.' Cameron, when home on leave in 1895, brought Yummy with him. Edith's first impression was unfavourable:

'A degraded little long-haired lapdog named Yumyum.' But she was interested enough to record six months later: 'The foul Yummy, cased in mud, selected my bed as a couching place.' When Cameron's leave was up and he left for the Far East, he gave Yummy to his father. Yummy devoted himself to his new master, who returned his love.

Colonel Somerville liked to walk down alone with Yummy to the Castlehaven graveyard where his wife was buried in the Somerville vault, a distance of two miles on the lonely windswept road along the shore of the haven. He would linger by her tomb, as his little dog sniffed in the bushes. On Sunday 7 March 1898 he stood a long time in the graveyard in sad reverie, the wind blowing coldly. 'He got a chill there,' wrote Edith to Cameron, 'but said nothing and came to tea at Hildegarde's and then went to Church with me.' On Tuesday he had a cough, and on Wednesday stayed in bed. Dr O'Meara came on Friday from Skibbereen. It had not seemed more than an ordinary cold but on Friday was definitely bronchitis. On Saturday he was worse and O'Meara came again. On Monday he seemed better, but during Monday night there was a change. Early on Tuesday O'Meara came. He considered the bronchitis had taken a dangerous turn and took extreme measures, including cupping. 'Nothing was any good. The dreadful choking got worse. He did not suffer at all and was only semi-conscious, though he knew us when we spoke directly and loudly to him. He never once complained nor seemed to realize that he was very ill. He did everything we asked but I don't think he had any real wish to live, nor ever has had since Mother died. The parson came over and read some prayers. As he read the Benediction we saw the lines fade from Papa's face and he was gone.* It was the most peaceful thing you can imagine. We were all with him— Hildegarde, Aylmer, Emmie, Egerton and I.' He was seventy-four.

Jack, who had been wired for, arrived the next evening. Edith goes on to tell Cameron how much she feels for him, so

---

* These words are from the diary.

far from home, as she does too for the other two brothers, Boyle and Hugh. 'It is a crushing blow. It feels as though the tent pole had been broken, and our home and all its old happiness was gone for ever. He was so gentle and quiet and humble that one hardly knew how much one relied on him and his unfailing love and devotion to us all. I feel now as if I had never even half appreciated it. He was so strong and hale-looking and tramped about as well as ever, and had an excellent appetite, but the wish to live was not in him. His heart was with Mother on the other side and one cannot wish him back. His look of calm, and nobility and happiness was quite wonderful. We have put a cross of Mother's violets on his breast. There is but one feeling through all the country, high and low. I don't think there ever has been a man so loved and respected, not even Grandpapa. Dearest boy, how I wish you were home and with us. If he could only have lived two or three years more, just to let you see him again. . . . I felt that Mother was waiting for him. She seemed very near, and there was no faintest struggle as he crossed the bar. Yummy was the greatest pleasure and comfort to him. He lay on the bed all the time he was ill, and was so gentle and quiet, and when the doctor began to cup him and he groaned, unconsciously, from weakness, the poor little thing stood up on the sofa and kept watching Papa over the end of the bed with the most anxious little face. The last conscious word Papa said was a shout of "Yum" when Yummy barked at Egerton. He was a great and real amusement to him ever since you gave him to him and he has been a most faithful little adherent.' Yummy did not long survive his master. A month later Martin, writing to Cameron from Drishane to which she had hurried, says: 'Yummy has attached himself to Edith and they all take him for walks.' Two days later, however, Edith writing to Boyle in Canada, reports that Yummy was so badly bitten in a dog-fight that he died. 'Let us be thankful that Papa was spared the misery, as he was wholly devoted to Yummy. He always seemed like a part of Papa; when Papa was dying I lifted him on to the bed beside him.'

The funeral took place at 12.30 p.m. on 18 March. The coffin was carried from Drishane the two miles to the old graveyard at Castlehaven. Edith's diary entry is: 'By Uncle Kendal's suggestion we covered the coffin with a Union Jack. His sword, Crimean shako, spurs and medals were laid on it, and a branch of laurel. The weather was fine. Desmond* walked with Aylmer, and Jack and Egerton a part of the way. All the men in the country helped by turn to carry him.' His youngest son, Hugh, writing from Australia where his ship was stationed, to Edith on hearing the news, said: 'It is so hard that all the countryside could be at the funeral and we three, Cameron, Boyle and I, thousands of miles away. It was very touching to think how well all the people loved him.' He also refers to the fact, evidently reported to him, that the countrywomen in the procession raised the Irish Cry.

It had now to be settled with Cameron, who had become head of the family and owner of Drishane, how the place was to be managed till he retired from the army, which might not be for some years as he was only thirty-eight. There were Aylmer and Emmie, Egerton and Hildegarde, and Edith on the spot. As Edith was the eldest, had been presiding at Drishane since her mother's death and handling the accounts, it was suggested that she should continue to do so until Cameron's wishes were known. She sent Cameron a statement of the money position. Colonel Somerville's income was partly pension and partly rents. As the pension died with him, could Drishane be kept up on the rents? Edith had no money except what she made from her books, half of which went to Martin. Aylmer's income from his farm was small. Egerton had not yet succeeded his father, the baronet. As they all felt it would be dreadful to have to let or sell Drishane, they decided that each should contribute under Edith's general management. Writing to Cameron on 5 April 1898, three weeks after her father's death, she offers to carry on till he returns on leave. She warns him that Aylmer is not much

* Aylmer's son and present owner of Drishane, Brigadier Desmond Somerville, C.B.E., M.C.

use at business, though affectionate and good-natured. But he might act as bailiff and collect the rents of the estate, which amounted to £400 a year, and take a commission of 5 per cent. After a further exchange of views, it was settled that Edith should take over as Cameron's representative. She would live rent and board free at Drishane. Aylmer was to manage the estate farm in consultation with her, and with Emmie live at Drishane without being charged rent for his quarters. Edith should sit at the head of the table, Aylmer at the foot, and Emmie manage the housekeeping and, as their contribution, pay for the food up to £220 yearly. In this way it ought to be possible to keep Drishane as the headquarters of the Somerville family.

Cameron never interfered with these arrangements. When years later he retired and lived at Drishane, he did not take over from Edith. The management remained with her by general consent, as there was no one as competent as herself. It was not until forty-four years later when Cameron died in 1942 and the ownership of Drishane passed to Aylmer's son, the present Brigadier Desmond Somerville, that she, by that time aged eighty-four, gave up her charge. In 1903 she undertook further responsibilities when she succeeded Aylmer as Master of the West Carbery Hunt. Indeed, she was an indefatigable woman, her energies so various and interests so wide that everyone turned to her with confidence that her common-sense would solve their problems. She was careful, however, to take no steps of importance without consulting Martin and Hildegarde, and deferred to her brothers' opinions or appeared to do so. Thus Drishane passed under the rule of a woman; it became a matriarchy, though it had long been so, for her mother had ruled it before her. Her personality was the most marked in the family. At the time of her father's death when she took charge she was exactly forty years of age.

She was not a spiritualist as yet. Though she believed that the spirit of her mother was present when her father was dying, she made no attempt to communicate with either of them in seances. Whether Uncle Kendal did so is not on record in the papers. It was not until several years later that she became convinced of the validity of automatic writing as a means of communication with the dead. To what an extraordinary degree she indulged in the practice will be disclosed at length in due place.

11

Edith and Martin begin to write the R.M.
Stories

Added to her griefs, Edith's struggle to keep writing while she
supervised Drishane had been rather too much for her. She
became run down and began to suffer from gout, a rheumatic
disorder which in one form or another afflicted her for the rest
of her life. The waters at Aix-les-Bains were recommended by
the Coghills, who were also rheumatic, and she went there in
the middle of May 1898. Martin accompanied her only as far
as London. There she consulted J. B. Pinker, their literary agent.
He was one of the first men to set up as a literary agent in
London. Among his clients were such figures as Henry James,
Conrad and Lawrence. He had already advised Martin and
Edith of the demand for Irish hunting stories. He could place
them advantageously with the *Badminton Magazine* and later
find a publisher to bring them out in book form, the most
lucrative way of doing business. He strongly recommended
Martin to get to work on such stories at once.

After taking the cure at Aix for a month Edith went for a
holiday to Étaples, an artists' resort near Boulogne. Martin
joined her there on 15 June. Hildegarde and Egerton arrived a
week later. It was at Étaples that on 19 July they began writing
the first story of *Some Experiences of an Irish R.M.* (The date is
underlined in red in Edith's diary as if she knew it was an

important one in her life.) The story took them ten days. On
6 August Pinker wrote that Watson, the editor of the *Badminton Magazine*, was delighted with it and wanted another
for the next month on the same lines. By 20 September Edith
was back in Castle Townshend where shortly afterwards she
was joined by Martin. By that time the second story was done
and they were started on the third. The magazine paid them
£15.4.6. for the first story. They were to get a similar sum
for each of the twelve stories. That put them in funds for the
time being.

On 1 November Martin had a very serious fall while out
hunting. Edith's diary entry is: 'Martin rode Dervish and I the
King. About 16 riders out. Went to Kilnavoodhee and found
there. Ran very fast through Lakelands to Hollybrook. Martin
rode Dervish at a fixed pole into the 7-acre field. He took it
with his knees and fell right over it, pitching Martin in mud
and apparently falling on her. Mr Purdon and I picked her up
stunned. Thought her dead.' When examined she was found
not to have broken any bones and only to have been cut about
the face. She was, however, more seriously hurt than appeared.
Her back sustained an injury from which she never entirely
recovered. She was always very short-sighted and ought not to
have hunted because she could not see clearly what she was
riding at. A fortnight later she was well enough to be carried
downstairs to a sofa. Sometimes she got up for lunch, sometimes for dinner. By the end of the year she was still an invalid.
It was three months before she was down to breakfast. Her
diary has: '5 March 1899. Went to church for the first time for
four months. 8 March. Went to see Hildegarde. I slipped and
fell while playing the fool there for Paddy and got rather a
shake.' On 20 April she visited Hildegarde to see her second
son, Nevill, and records how Paddy had taken a strong dislike to
the infant and 'says his place is in the kitchen'. At last on
12 June she was well enough to go to England with Edith. They
saw Pinker and Longmans, the publishers. Despite her state of
ill health all these months she had pressed on with the stories

for the *Badminton*. They had by now written ten and had only two more to do. These were finished in August. Longmans contracted to publish the stories in book form by November and paid an advance of £50.

Some Experiences of an Irish R.M. is the central literary event in the lives of Edith and Martin. With its two companion volumes, *Further Experiences of an Irish R.M.* and *In Mr Knox's Country*, where the same characters reappear, it was the best liked of all their books and is read today, nearly seventy years after its first publication, by numbers of people all over the world. It has been called a classic in sporting literature, but more properly is a literary classic because the reader does not have to like hunting to enjoy it. It appeals equally to young and old and to both sexes. Like *Alice in Wonderland* it does not date; like André Maurois' *Les Silences du Colonel Bramble* and *Les Discours du Docteur O'Grady*, published about 1918, it is as fresh as when it appeared. The Ireland it depicts has passed away. Yet in a sense it has not passed away, for it lives in the stories.*

An R.M., or Resident Magistrate, a post which survives only in Northern Ireland, was a salaried judicial officer whose duty it was to visit the honorary benches, sit with the J.P.s, the unpaid justices of the peace, stiffen them by his support, advise them on legal points that might arise, and generally see that their administration of justice was dispassionate and free from local prejudice. He attended Petty Sessions in the various small towns, travelling from courthouse to courthouse in his dogcart or on horseback, and putting up at what hotels existed or with the gentry living nearby. In some convenient situation he had a house of his own. One has a glimpse of such a magistrate earlier in this book where Martin describes the intrusion of the Oughterard R.M. into the Martin family pew in church. The R.M. of the *Experiences* is not an underbred man of that sort. He is partially of Irish abstraction, but the Irish scene is quite new to him. Of an easy-going nature, with a good sense of

---

* All the thirty-four stories of the three original volumes are now collected in a single volume *The Irish R.M. Complete* (Faber & Faber).

humour, he has the gift of getting on pleasant terms with people of all classes. His wife is the stronger character of the two, a marriage relationship which Edith approved of. By employing the literary device of making the R.M. the narrator round whom all the stories revolved, the authors were able to give coherence to their picture of Irish country life. The result is more vivid than would be a series of unconnected short hunting stories. In point of fact, the *Experiences* do not all relate to hunting, though hunting is not very far away. In the first, for instance, we see the R.M. move into his house, which sounds rather like Ross. His cook, Mrs Cadogan, has the same downright and voluble personality as the domestics described in the diaries. In the second story we have not yet entered the hunting field proper. The form employed permits the authors to bring in all they knew of the rural Ireland of Connemara and Cork. And there were no writers then living who knew more. One observes at once how they made use of their own experiences. Thus, in the first story, the accursed sweep appears, almost word for word as in Martin's letter quoted further back. In the notebook already mentioned as containing examples of popular speech, are numerous picturesque sayings, now introduced with brilliant effect into the *Experiences*, which are thus solidly based on years of recorded observations. The result is a more authentic account of the lighter side of rural Ireland in the nineties than that produced by their Dublin contemporaries, the poets, dramatists and prose writers, whose intention was to present Ireland in a poetical rather than an objective light.

After serialization in the *Badminton*, the R.M. stories were published as a book by Longmans in October 1899. It was immediately acclaimed in the press as the most amusing book seen for many a year. By 12 December the first edition of three thousand copies sold out and a second edition was called for.

Since the publication of Edith and Martin's first book, *An Irish Cousin*, in 1889, ten years had elapsed during which they had produced *Naboth's Vineyard*, *The Real Charlotte* and *The Silver Fox*, together with three travel books and miscellaneous

hunting stories. Now with the R.M. they had made a big hit
and become widely known. They had worked independently of
the Dublin writers who, with Yeats as their most admired
figure, were beginning their literary careers. Bernard Shaw had
also been writing independently of Dublin. It so happened that
he was the first writer of importance they came in contact with.
Having little knowledge of what was happening in the literary
world or flair for the significant in contemporary writing, Edith's
first impressions of Shaw were very inaccurate. He came under
her notice, however, not in a literary but a social light. She
heard with surprise that he had married her cousin, Charlotte
Payne-Townshend, who belonged to a branch of that family
which lived, not at the Castle in Castle Townshend, but at a
house called Derry, some twelve miles distant. This branch of
the Townshends was much the better off. Charlotte and her
sister, always referred to as Sissy in the papers, were both
accounted heiresses, as their father had made money on the
London Stock Exchange. In reporting the marriage to Cameron
in a letter of 1898, Edith writes of it as a mésalliance and
repeats what gossip she has heard. 'Charlotte is now Mrs
Bernard Shaw and I hope she likes it. He is an advanced socialist
(all the same he has kept his weather eye open). They were
married at a registrar's office. I have, with much difficulty and
anxiety, written to poor Sissy. Of course he is an awfully clever
man. He began as office boy in Townshend French's agency
office in Dublin, and now he is distinctly somebody in a literary
way, but he can't be a gentleman and he is too clever to be
really in love with Lottie, who is nearly clever, but not quite.
However it may be better than it seems.' Of Charlotte she says
elsewhere, 'when she tells a story my mind begins to wander as
if it were the Litany.' In a subsequent letter to Cameron she has:
Sissy, who was married to a General Cholmondeley, 'can't make
it up with Charlotte and G.B.S. Clever as he is his personal
habits are so revulsive that she can't face asking them to stay
with her.' He was, as we know, a vegetarian, teetotaller and
non-smoker. The letter goes on: 'However Charlotte seems

perfectly happy and delighted with her cad, for cad he is in spite of his talent.' That her estimate of G.B.S. was ridiculous she soon perceived. In January 1899 she is writing to Cameron that she has just read Shaw's two volumes *Plays Pleasant and Unpleasant*, published that year, and finds they are 'very smart and unexpected from him'.

With the passage of time she found that she was quite wrong in thinking that G.B.S. was a dreadful man. Her diary has: 'Charlotte, Sissy and G.B.S. drove over from Derry to lunch. He was very agreeable and quite affable.' Sissy by now had got fond of G.B.S. who, of course, was one of the most amusing men alive. Edith records in January 1899: 'Heard from Sissy wanting me to do a drawing of her and G.B.S. on a tandem tricycle.' This was done, G.B.S. in his knickerbockers and Sissy in the volumin- ous skirt of the time, as amusing a period piece as one could desire. Somewhat later when Edith hoped to make money by getting a dramatized version of the R.M. stories put on the stage, she turned to G.B.S. for his opinion and humbly took his advice, though it was far from flattering.

At this same period Martin met Yeats for the first time. Augusta, Lady Gregory, as one of the Persses of Roxborough, was her cousin, whose wedding she attended twenty years before when she married Sir William Gregory, who had since died. Augusta, now a widow of fifty-one and mistress of Coole, her late husband's seat in County Galway, had become Yeats' patron in his project to found the Abbey Theatre in Dublin as a centre for the literary and intellectual life of the Irish capital. Since Martin had made a name for herself as an Irish writer, Lady Gregory felt she ought to meet Yeats and invited her to stay a night at Coole when he was there. She came on 8 August 1901 with Mama, and entered in her diary for that day: 'Had much literary conversation with the poet.' And the next day: 'More literary conversation and garden wanderings.' A letter to Edith written on the same day gives a full picture of the occasion. Yeats at this date was thirty-six and Martin thirty- nine. He had published two years before his third book of lyrics,

Hildegarde in the garden of Glen Barrahane, after her marriage to
Egerton Coghill

Edith on Bridget (1903)

The Wind Among the Reeds, the best poetry he had written so
far, a great technical advance in the opinion of critics on his
previous volume, *The Rose.* He was beginning to be held in the
highest esteem. Martin's letter about him is not adulatory. She
puts down frankly how he seemed to her eyes. 'The afternoon
and night at Coole were very interesting. Augusta Gregory,
her son Robert (at Oxford) and W. B. Yeats were the party. I
may mention that it is 20 years, or nearly, since I was there and
I was in the same room and the furniture was the same. Yeats
looks just what I expected, a cross between a Dominie Sampson*
and a starved R.C. curate—in seedy black clothes—with a large
black bow at the root of his long naked throat. He is egregiously
the poet, murmurs ends of verse to himself with a wild eye, bows
over your hand in dark silence, but poet he is, and very interesting indeed, and somehow sympathetic to talk to. I liked him,
in spite of various things, and I got on well with him, so far. He
gave an opinion of me to Augusta of which I feel inclined to
repeat only the remarkable adjective "simple". I didn't know
that I was that, nor perhaps did you.† It is strange to talk of
"deep subjects of life and death" without any selfconsciousness,
and I must say he induces that, and does it himself. He is not
at all without a sense of humour, which surprised me. He thinks
The Real Charlotte very big, in the only parts he has read, which
are merely quotations in reviews. He doesn't approve of humour
for humour's sake. . . . Today Augusta made me add my
initials to a tree already decorated by Douglas Hyde, AE and
more of the literary crowd. It was most touching. W.B.Y. did
the carving for me, I smoked, and high literary conversation
raged and the cigarette went out. I couldn't make the matches
light, and he held the little dingy lapels of his coat out and I
lighted the match in his bosom.'

Of a visit to Dublin in October of the same year Martin

---

* The schoolmaster in Scott's *Guy Mannering.*

† Twenty-two years later in *Wheeltracks* Edith replies to this question: 'No, I
did not; but I believe that the profounder insight of a Poet discerned the clarity and
purity of heart that was behind the subtle, meditative, inventing, ever-appraising
brain, and knew that in greatness there is ever simplicity.'

writes: 'Yeats's father and Nathaniel Hone have an exhibition of pictures on now, but on hearing that W. B. Yeats was incessantly there with Maud Gonne I thought I would stay away, as likely as not I should have found myself mixed up in a conversation with her, and that would have involved my doing something rude. I saw her at the Irish play on Friday night, and thought her looks terrific. The features still handsome, the nose salient and short, but the badness of the expression was startling. A huge mop of curly yellow hair crowned her big fat body. One look at her would be enough for anyone to form an opinion. Yeats was with her in a box all the time. I never looked his way and I daresay the Irish Literary Review was quite disastrously unaware of my presence in the shades at the back.'

Yeats had proposed to Maud Gonne several times but she would not have him. Bernard Shaw once described her (in conversation) as 'outrageously beautiful'. She was a little older than Yeats. Martin regarded her as a traitor because, though the daughter of an English Colonel, she was a Home Ruler of an extremist sort and had been mixed up in demonstrations against the Crown. She remained Yeats's close friend till his death thirty-eight years later. In one of his last poems he wrote: 'I thought her supernatural.' But she aroused no admiration in Martin's breast. She was altogether too flamboyant for that quiet intellectual. Even Yeats admitted that, beautiful though she was, she had rather a stupid look. Martin's objection to Maud Gonne made meeting Yeats awkward, but she did see him from time to time. She was invited later on to tea on the stage of the Abbey Theatre. 'I then talked to the leading comedian, Fay, a first rate little actor and as common as a little Dublin cabman, but most agreeable,' she tells Edith. After tea she was escorted from the stage door to her cab by Yeats. He and Lady Gregory pressed her to write a play for them. Augusta said: 'A week at Coole would do it. We could give you all the hints necessary for stage effects, etc, and even write a scenario for you, the characters and plot picked from your books. I will look through them at once.' But Martin did not fancy it. Perhaps she felt that she could not collaborate except with Edith. Besides, there was no money in it. An Abbey performance earned little for the dramatist. It was not worth it. Pinker would be against it. Edith and she had developed an original line of their own, where humour played the principal part. She knew Yeats wanted humour to be subordinate to his poetico-nationalist themes. She and Edith had better stick to their independence. There was the further reason that her brother Robert, the friend and associate of Arthur Balfour, the Chief Secretary, whose life as journalist and lecturer, and as the head of the great Martin family, had been spent in support of the Unionist cause, as opposed to the Home Rulers' ambition to end the Union and establish an Irish government of their own, would be much embarrassed and chagrined if his sister, his distinguished sister, should join a literary group identified with Irish nationalism. In the letter to Edith where she relates how, after tea on the Abbey Theatre stage, she was conducted to her cab by the leader of that group, Yeats himself, she adds: 'Robert would have had a bad relapse if he could have viewed me emerging from the stage door.' So she and Edith, though they admired Yeats' poetry and were fond of Augusta Gregory, remained disinclined to join up with them.

12

The end of the Ross period

A quick glance through Martin's diary for the period between the publication of the *Experiences* and her meetings with Yeats and Lady Gregory will reveal how things in general were going with her and Edith.

Martin's hunting accident had left her with a delicate back, a tendency to get bad headaches and lose weight. Her nerves, too, were not as robust as before. In March 1900 she went to Buxton for baths and massage. She was there for a month and a half, after which she paid visits to friends and relations in England. In October she was in London and drove one day to see Pinker in a fourwheeler accompanied by her sister, Edith Dawson, to whose husband, it will be recalled, Ross was let at this time. 'At the corner of Arundel Street our cab was turned over. Horse and cabman in a heap outside and we in a heap inside, but no one hurt. We were dragged forth and went to Pinker, who coped with the situation and gave us lunch.' This accident threw back Martin's convalescence, and when staying with her sister Katherine Currey at Gravesend she had to be wheeled about in a bath chair. She and Edith had got to like Pinker very much. When it was reported to them that Watson, the editor of the *Badminton* who had published so many of their stories, had been 'drunkenly impudent to Pinker, we ceased to write for him'. On 28 December 1900 there is a characteristic entry: 'Raging storm all day in London. A man outside a pub said: "Why you're blown all to bits. Better come in and 'ave a drink." I wished I could accept.'

It had been found convenient to close Drishane for a while, in spite of the arrangements made after Colonel Somerville's death. In April 1900 the great house was opened again by Edith, whose naval brother Boyle, back on leave from his ship, moved in with his recently married wife, but he immediately 'tumbled downstairs with 2 jugs, cut himself, twisted his foot and broke jugs. I had to send him to see O'Meara,' the family doctor who lived five miles away at Skibbereen. This was the month when Queen Victoria visited Dublin, arriving in the Royal Yacht and escorted by a line of battleships, the new Dreadnoughts. Edith sent her a copy of the *Experiences* and received a pleasant letter of thanks from the Private Secretary, Arthur Bigge. Maud Gonne took a different line. She paraded the streets in heavy mourning with crape and jet beads. 'She dressed in black, to welcome me back,' as the Queen is made to say in a ballad by Percy French, Dublin's amusing artist and singer. The closing of Drishane had given the rats their chance. Edith, while tidying her other naval brother, Hugh's, dressing room, in expectation of his arrival on leave, 'found a mangy rat crouching in a torn pillow case covered with feathers.' But that was nothing to the dining room. 'Moved the old grand piano into the dining room which is now a howling wilderness, given over to rats and filth.' This was the room in which for so many years her father and mother had entertained the landed gentry of Cork.

Aylmer, who had founded the West Carbery Hunt, now gave it up. The subscriptions did not cover expenses. But the indefatigable Edith has: 'A dozen women to tea to talk over means of raising the wind and managed to buy four new hounds.' Other news there was little that year, 1900, except that Paddy fell into the sea again and had to be rescued, and that Uncle Kendal was giving lectures on spiritualism, a subject in which Edith was beginning to take more serious interest than heretofore. The expense of keeping up Drishane, she found, was more than she could afford, even with the help of her brothers.

To make money she took up horse dealing. When lucky she could pick up a likely looking colt for £20 and sell it for £70.

To turn back to Martin's diary, she begins the year 1901 by recounting how a man arrived at Castle Townshend with a fox to sell. It was in a barrel in a mule cart. There was a row over the price. One of Edith's guests 'was knocked down and walked on by the mule that drew the cart, that held the barrel, that held the fox, which in the *mêlée* escaped'. Good news arrived about the popularity of the R.M.'s *Experiences*. Mr John Dillon, an M.P., 'tried the R.M. for seasickness with perfect success'. But though it was doing so well, Martin only got £150, her share for sales to date. She was so short of cash that she was glad to get £1 from Hildegarde to pay for massage. At Ross at the end of the year, she was nearly prosecuted by the police. On the way back from the Oughterard workhouse, where she had gone to arrange for a tea which her sister, Edith Dawson, was giving the inmates on Boxing Day, her coachman 'drove against a drunken man and sent him headlong. He lay senseless until a policeman came by when he got up and walked off shouting "Where's the man that knocked me down?" The policeman was warlike till he found I had been at a concert in Spiddal where he had sung a song. He then assured me that the man was quite unhurt.' When the tea came off two days later, the Matron and the workhouse teacher danced a jig and a reel to a concertina, and Martin, in spite of her poor state of health, felt strong enough afterwards to dance waltzes and barn dances, presumably with the workhouse people; as a real grande dame she knew how to do so in a natural way, as Mama did. Her health remained uncertain for some months. Later at Castle Townshend she had a relapse, with pain in the back and weakness in the legs. 'O'Meara came and applied "Corrigan's Button" red hot to my back in 14 places. Very startling but brief.' O'Meara with his cupping and his blistering was a country doctor old style. But as he was the only doctor within reach, they had to put up with him. Four days later she was well enough to drive with Edith to Skibbereen 'and was nearly run over by a carload of people drunk in honour of Ascension Day'. She had a relapse again in the autumn of 1902 and had to go into a nursing home in London, where she remained till the close of the year. Pinker had been to stay at Drishane in June 1902 and pressed them to do a second volume of R.M. stories, for which he said he could get them £2,000. On a further visit in December Edith persuaded him to go out hunting on New Year's Eve. She mounted him on her horse, the King. He started away all right, but presently fell off and then got lost in the Carbery hills, quite a dreadful misadventure, as Martin noted, for a London literary agent. A search was made, they found him at last and he got home in time for tea. During this visit he again urged Edith to repeat the success of the first R.M. volume. 'The poor authors yearn towards the bait, but doubt their ability, physical or otherwise,' notes Martin. A compromise, however, was achieved. As a stop-gap they would collect odd hunting stories, already published in magazines and, adding a few more, make up a book. Longmans published this on 30 March 1903, a 'new book of old things, nice looking but not up to the R.M.' says Martin modestly. It sold well, however, because of the popularity of the other. It was called *All on the Irish Shore*, contained eleven stories, all but one connected with hunting in the County Cork, and had ten drawings of Edith's as illustrations. It includes the remarkable story, 'A Nineteenth Century Miracle', and 'The Dane's Breechin', a country farce with a horse, not a hunter, for theme. Though the book hardly sustained the authors' reputation, it served its purpose for the moment. Pinker understood its quality well enough and continued to press them for further experiences of the R.M. for which editors were clamouring.

During this year, 1903, Edith became M.F.H. of the West Carbery Hunt. Since Aylmer had given up the Mastership and left Castle Townshend for England, she had been trying to put its finances in order. Master of Fox Hounds is normally a man's job, but it seemed to the subscribers that the hunt was more likely to prosper under her management than under any available man's. She herself, though now a successful author, a professional painter and the mistress of Drishane, the centre of Somerville family life, did not regard the Mastership as a burden. Hunting was her great distraction; moreover, she was proud to be doing a man's work as well or better than a man, for among much else she was a staunch supporter of the feminist movement of the day.* She remained M.F.H. for five years, though the subscriptions were never enough to cover expenses. Later she was to take on the job again. What she learnt as M.F.H. was invaluable when she and Martin were writing the *Further Experiences*. Martin was not sufficiently recovered from her fall to hunt, though she rode to meets or the like. In March 1904 she describes herself in her diary as looking like a white rat. But she continued doggedly to write, her powers unimpaired.

Events now began to close in at Ross. In April 1905 Martin received the news that her brother Robert was seriously ill in London. He had contracted a disease of the kidneys. Hoping that rest and his native air might restore him, he decided to give up his London career and retire to Ireland. He was nearing sixty. To make Ross available for him, his sister, Edith Dawson, who had rented Ross from him, now moved to a house called Waterfield at Oughterard. Robert and his family left London in May 1905 and after a short stay in Dublin came on to Ross. He seemed better for the moment. On 2 September, however, Martin, who was at Drishane, received 'a very bad account of him' from her sister Edith and left Drishane at once. On arrival at Oughterard she found Robert on the sofa of his room in Waterfield, the Dawsons' house. 'He was much wasted since last I saw him and weaker.' Connie, his wife, was in the Oughterard railway hotel; there was no room for her in Waterfield, as Robert had two nurses. Martin went on to Ross that evening and found Mama there. Next day she took the 7.20 a.m. train back to Oughterard.† Her diary for 7 to 9 September has: 'All

---

* She was Chairman of the Munster Women's Franchise League.
† By this time a railway had been built from Galway to Oughterard.

through this week Robert became weaker. I slept at Waterfield and went over to Ross every day to see Mama. Robert not suffering but the nights terribly restless.' On 10 September she notes: 'I went over to Ross in the morning and came back with Mama, who saw Robert for the last time.' On the morning of 12 September he seemed 'wonderfully better, but began to sink in the afternoon and passed into a deep sleep about nine o'clock. He slept more and more quietly till 3.30 a.m. when he passed out of life with perfect peacefulness.'

The funeral was on 16 September 1905. For a reason not disclosed Robert had expressed the wish that his body be buried in the graveyard of Oughterard church and not at Kilannin in the vault where his ancestors for many generations were laid. It was a quiet funeral attended by a few of the landed gentry, such as Hugh McCalmont, Edward Hewson, the husband of his sister Geraldine, and Bob Martin, a cousin. 'Many of the outside people came for it.' His tenants at Ross were extremely put out that he was not buried at the family graveyard of Kilannin. Though generally absent in London he was popular with them. One recalls how at the tenants ball a few years back he had sung his famous song, *Ballyhooley*, and danced jigs with all. They wanted to carry his body to the grave, for though times had greatly changed, he was still a great lord of the old stock in their estimation. It had been the custom for centuries to hold a splendid drunken wake when there died a Martin of Ross. Oughterard churchyard has none of the wild beauty of Kilannin. It has no enchanted Wood of Annagh beside it, nothing of the air of Connemara. Though but a mile or two from the bogs, the heather, the little lakes among the hills, it might be a hundred miles away.

Over his grave there was erected a tall cross of granite, on the base of which he is described as 'Master Robert of Ross.' the name Martin being omitted. I have seen no explanation of this departure from the practice at Kilannin, where on the ancestral vault are the full names of the dead within. His sister Edith only survived him till 1908. Her grave is beside his. His wife, Connie, was buried on the other side when she died in 1914.

It had now to be decided where Mama was to live, at Ross with Connie or at Oughterard in Waterfield with her daughter Edith. She had been a widow now for thirty-three years since her husband, James Martin of Ross, died in 1872. She had given birth to and brought up three sons and five daughters. Edith Somerville had an immense respect for her and in *Irish Memories* writes of her imposing presence, her stately walk, her sound critical taste in literature, her agreeable manner with the lower orders, to whom she knew exactly how to speak, her intolerance of bores, her great sense of the ridiculous, her fits of wild laughter and her fearlessness; she remained calm in all emergencies, on land or on water. As Martin had written after seeing her dancing with Paddy Griffy in 1886, she was a wonderful woman. She decided a fortnight after Robert's death to leave Ross and live with her daughter at Oughterard. Martin's diary gives: '4 October. After arduous day of packing Mama and I left Ross in the afternoon and drove with bag and baggage to Oughterard. Breathed a freer air.' They had never cared much for Connie. After leaving Mama with Edith Dawson, Martin returned to Drishane to continue writing the new R.M. book. It was while she was at Drishane that old Sir Joscelyn Coghill, the head of the Coghill family, father of Egerton, Hildegarde's husband, died on 20 November 1905. He was just eighty, a man of gentle character. It was said of him: 'Ah, Sir Joscelyn, he was no more use in the house than a feather.' His brother, Uncle Kendal, had a much more assertive character. Sir Joscelyn's place as head of the Coghill family was thus taken by Egerton, whose eldest son was Paddy, aged nine. Edith had given him on his birthday a fancy waistcoat with the Hunt buttons, she notes in her diary. He was coming on. A groom said he had a better seat on a horse than his cousin, Desmond, who was seven years his senior. And Edith wrote to his mother: 'The tea parties rage antiphonally. Paddy summons his guests on the telephone with almost dwarfish precocity and skill. I cut his hair today—it really wanted it awfully.'

A few days after Sir Joscelyn's death Martin had a letter from Oughterard to say that 'Mama was sinking into feebleness of mind and body'. She was not ill, but merely very tired. Three weeks later Edith Dawson wired for Martin to come, as Mama was getting very weak. She left at once and 'found Mama much changed, in bed always and living on liquids'. This state continued into the New Year (1906). Edith now joined Martin, wishing to be of some help in the emergency. Soon after her arrival, on 8 February 1906, Mama quietly expired. Martin's entry in her diary is as follows: 'At 6 a.m. the nurse called me, Mama having taken a bad turn. Found her breathing very fast and laboriously, one valve of the heart having stopped working. Looked on helplessly until 9.45 when she ceased to breathe. Edith Somerville was present. Spent the day in a maze of telegrams, arrangements and distress. Edith was invaluable.' Edith Dawson, who was away that day, hurriedly came back. The vault at Kilannin was opened and lined with moss and ferns. On the 10th a big cross of violets arrived from Hildegarde. The 12th was the day of the funeral. At one o'clock the coffin was taken to the Oughterard church where the funeral service was held. After the service the hearse was driven the five miles down the Galway road to Kilannin. The turn to the graveyard is a quarter of a mile before reaching the gate of Ross. There at the little hamlet of Rosscahill tenants met the hearse and thence carried the coffin some three or four hundred yards to the vault in the graveyard. 'All that friendship and good feeling could do was done. All the men of the neighbourhood were there.' Connie, however, did not attend, though the burial was so close, nor did Barbara, her daughter, by now a girl of about eighteen, though she had called on Martin to enquire about Mama and on the day before the funeral called again. Martin had called once at Ross on Connie but 'was perished with cold. There were no fires worth mentioning. The drawing room not used at all.' Since Robert's death and Mama's departure to Oughterard, the huge house was empty save for Connie and Barbara who evidently were only living in a corner of it. Connie continued to reside at Ross till her death in 1914, after which Barbara, who had married in October 1912 a Mr Mascie-Taylor, sold the house to its present owner, Mr Chavasse. Martin was hardly ever at Ross again though she attended Barbara's wedding there. Drishane became her home. The Ross period of her life was ended. Occasionally she went to see her sister at Oughterard, and looked in on Connie once.

13

Edith and Martin's humour

Martin was back in Drishane a week after her mother's funeral.
It was now February 1906. Longmans, their publishers, had
written to say they wanted something at once; it was three
years since the publication of *All on the Irish Shore,* which had
sold remarkably well, considering that it was no more than a
collection of old magazine stories. Edith and Martin had not
done enough of the new R.M. stories to promise that book in
the near future. Longmans accordingly asked for a collection of
their published articles and occasional pieces. This was feasible;
indeed, it was the only thing to be done, as money had run out.
They set to work at once. In Martin's diary for 20–21 April
1906 we find: 'Worked all the morning on the old stuff. Finished
up all the tidying of the articles and sent twelve of them with
22 pictures to Pinker. Thankful to be rid of them.'

Longmans were pleased and on 20 April offered '£150 and
excellent royalties for the rubbish volume', as Martin puts it.
It appeared in October as *Some Irish Yesterdays* and had fourteen
articles in it. The money enabled them to spend a fortnight of
June in London. Among other things they went to the National
Gallery to have a look at the Rokeby Venus, the famous nude
by Velasquez, which had just been purchased from two old
ladies in Yorkshire for £45,000. 'Very lovely,' noted Martin.

Another day they went to a function at the Lyceum Club, a
so-called Irish Evening. Standish O'Grady, the grand old man

of Gaelic letters, was the guest of honour. Edith wrote a description of the occasion to Hildegarde, which is lively and revealing. Among those present was a Mrs Esler, 'a frightful little woman, exactly like a shaved griffin'. O'Grady came off little better. 'He was like a little sad old country man, and his wife is a massive female in weird blue draperies held on by Tara brooches, supposed to be the Garb of Old Gael. His speech was very long and wandering and dreary. I thought it a pity that he should—as they told us—have left a rest cure in order to make it.' At this date Standish O'Grady had published twenty-three books. In 1872, when Edith was fourteen, he had, as a student at Trinity College, Dublin, come upon the Irish epics and in 1878, after an intensive study of Gaelic, published his *History of Ireland: Heroic Period*, which critics have regarded as the start of the Irish literary movement. Meeting him now in London, in the rather stupid setting of an Irish Evening, he seemed a tedious old man, though he was not actually more than about fifty-five to her forty-eight. Misled by the company in which she saw him, she underrated him as a literary personality, as she had underrated G.B.S. on first acquaintance, for she was prone to hasty judgments. Another speaker seemed to her 'a horrid youth who spoke as if his mouth was full of fish bones' and she was dreadfully fatigued by a certain Miss Hull who lectured them on her achievements in the Gaelic field 'in a thin mouselike squeak'. The letter goes on: 'I longed for poor Robert Martin to have been there or G.B.S.' How salutary would have been their abounding humour. 'Percy French sang very moderate songs afterwards and told a few good stories.' Percy French, though an amusing little song-writer, was nothing like as robust as Robert Martin, she felt. However, she was introduced to 'a most capital woman, a Mrs Uniacke, maddish and handsome like Mrs Noel Guinness, who was as furiously bored by all the spouting cads as I was'. It was of course silly of her to have gone to such a gathering. Yeats would have been just as bored as she was. Such functions almost always drag; distinguished people, if any are present, tend to talk down, deadened by the audience, while the common run try to talk up with ludicrous results. There was this, too, that the people at the Irish Evening were not quite Edith's class.

Martin's comment in her diary is not nearly as caustic. 'Standish O'Grady,' she writes, 'spoke interestingly and pessimistically. Several mediocrities followed, and a mad parson from Australia. Afterwards Miss Coleman Smith chanted Yeats's poetry. A moderate show all round.' Her view was much the same as Edith's but was more forbearing. She had spent most of her youth in Dublin and was used to people who were not members of the Irish landed gentry. Edith had not so high a degree of sang-froid. There are instances in the papers of her taking offence and standing over much on her dignity, as when it was reported to her that a certain Dublin woman spoke of her by her Christian name at a party. The woman received a very stiff message of rebuke. Martin would not have cared. Nevertheless she could be more freezing than Edith. She could alarm more, could even frighten Edith, who admired her more than she admired Edith. Martin presided without assertion. As will be shown, she presided both in life and in death.

When in the autumn of 1906 they were back together at Drishane, their book of articles, *Some Irish Yesterdays*, came out and had very good reviews. Edith records in a note that seven of the fourteen articles were the work of Martin alone, and specifies two, 'An Outpost of Ireland', about the Aran Islands, and 'In Sickness and in Health', citing them as 'instances of Martin's command of prose that is rhythmic, poetic and subtly harmonious, a combination of qualities that is as rare as it is delightful'. Edith had a wonderfully generous character. There is never a trace of envy in her devotion for Martin.

To pick out the other five articles which Martin wrote by herself is no easy exercise in criticism, but one may hazard a few guesses. One of hers is 'Boon Companions' where the scene is Ross and the Wood of Annagh, and the characters are dogs and other animals of Martin's childhood. 'Faith thim was the dogs!' as Rickeen, the Martin retainer, said. 'The grandest dog

ever was in this counthry was Mullowny's. You couldn't know
what kind of a breed was in him, but you'd *have* to like him, he
was that spotted.' With such a sudden slap of fun does Martin
summon up the shade of the cur dog, a jest infinitely to Edith's
taste, but with a distinctive flavour of Martin about it. While
Rickeen spoke, his own dog waited in a brake nearby 'where
the young bracken stems curled like bishops' croziers round her
crafty snout'. Such a phrase was a bit beyond Edith's power.
That is why she wrote so admiringly of Martin's subtle combination of poetry and humour. It is in this article, 'Boon
Companions', that Mary the Monkey appears, who in real life
was the mother of the child bitten by the mad dog as recounted
further back. Here in *Irish Yesterdays* she is a tender-hearted
kitchen maid who nurses a sick monkey in front of the kitchen
fire and gets bitten for her pains.

To continue the investigation, the article called 'The Biography of a Pump' is clearly the work of Martin smiling in her
chamber apart. It contains an adorable peep at the servants'
ball in Ross on New Year's night, when Pete-een bawn, the
albino fiddler, played his jigs. Any doubt of the ascription to
Martin is banished by the lovely sentences: 'Outside, a light
snow was on the ground, the north wind blew dark in that
bitter midnight, and the ice on the lake uttered strange sounds
—hollow, musical shocks with the voice of the imprisoned
water in them. Every tree in the woods stood separate in white
silhouette, the rime sifting through the branches in a dry
whisper.' This is Martin, the poet Martin.

'Alsatia' is another article of Martin's for sure, an exquisite
reminiscence of childhood at Ross. 'I look back and see a procession advancing from the most ancient places of memory.'
Edith's style has not this solemnity. But with the anecdote of
the bitch, May-fly, humour takes first place. May-fly, a name
which 'held for us the glamour of a hundred springs', was a
white creature with sore eyes, which had some bull-terrier
blood, but very little.* The children were proud of her and led

* See drawing of May-fly in *Maria and Some Other Dogs*.

[144]

Edith (*left*) and Martin (*right*) with dogs, Candy and Sheila (1907)

Uncle Kendal dancing with Hildegarde in the garden of Cosheen
(1910)

her out to do battle with Boiled Rice, a bitch they held to be the meanest among the mean cur bitches of the village, small, old, toothless and to all appearances broken spirited. But she bustled to meet May-fly when the two were confronted in the village street, 'and rising upon the shortest pair of hind legs ever put under any four legged creature save a lizard laid her paws upon May-fly's shoulders and yapped harshly in her face'. May-fly, despite her reputed bull-terrier blood, 'gave a squeak of resentful alarm and fled', as if Boiled Rice was an apparition.

So much for five out of the seven articles ascribed to Martin by Edith. Of the remaining two, 'Out of Hand' must surely be Martin's. But the seventh remains in doubt.

In 1920, five years after Martin's death, Edith brought out a book called *Stray-aways*, a collection of twenty-four articles, fourteen of which she certifies as the work of Martin writing alone and ten by the two of them in collaboration. The fourteen articles by Martin have the same distinctive flavour as those selected above from *Some Irish Yesterdays*.

The stories for *The Further Experiences of an Irish R.M.* on which they were now engaged were so much the result of a close collaboration that the style is perfectly even; at no point does Martin's style obtrude. The two authors achieve such a coordination that even with the knowledge we have of Martin's manner it is impossible to point to individual contributions. This was already clear in the *Some Experiences* of 1899. *Further Experiences* of 1908 dovetails into the other. Some later attempts to throw light on the absorption, not by one writer of the other, but of the two into one, will necessarily recur after the death of Martin in 1915, towards which tragic date this narrative is now approaching. As if Martin had some intimation of an early death, she made her will on 29 March 1906. The document, which was signed at Castle Townshend and witnessed by Egerton and Edith's brother, Hugh, then a Commander in the Navy, runs as follows:

'This is the last will and testament of Violet Florence Martin. On this twenty-ninth day of March, nineteen hundred and six,

I, Violet Florence Martin, give and bequeath to Edith Œnone Somerville, all my worldly possessions, of which I am possessed at the time of my death, or may be entitled to afterwards, to be disposed of by her, as absolute owner, according to instructions which I shall give her.'

This bequest had the effect of giving Edith the copyright of all Martin's letters and writings, which copyright passed on Edith's death to her sister Hildegarde, and on the latter's death to her son, Sir Patrick Coghill, the present owner.

By dipping into the diaries between 29 March 1906, the date when *Some Irish Yesterdays* came out, and September 1908, when *Further Experiences* appeared, a rough narrative of events, none of them of capital biographical importance, but all lending colour to the story, may be extracted. On 18 June 1906 at Drishane Martin notes: 'Fell to work again with Edith in the morning at the R.M. story.' In July a certain M.P., by name Henniker Heaton, asked Martin to London, as he wanted her to write a memoir of her brother Robert. 'Dined at the House of Commons with Mr Henniker Heaton and afterwards sat out on the terrace and discussed the memoir. H.H. very unattractive, superior and patronizing, though obviously very fond of Robert.' Nothing came of this, though Martin did write part of such a memoir, which was published in 1917 by Edith as the first chapter of her book *Irish Memories*. In August, when on holiday with Edith in Sligo, she records: 'Pulled a mile against a stiff wind to the island of Innisfree, a mound of boggy heather and rocks and bracken,' the spot immortalized by Yeats in his early poem, 'The Lake Isle of Innisfree'. Thence she went alone to her sister Edith at Oughterard and dropped in on Connie at Ross. Back in Castle Townshend in September, she found Bernard Shaw and Charlotte staying at the Rectory which they had rented for a month. Of him she wrote: 'Very sane and affable.' In November she went on her own to London and stayed with Pinker and his wife at their luxurious house in the suburbs. One perceives that she and Edith were taking it easy over the R.M. stories.

There is nothing in Edith's 1906/07 diary of moment, though here and there are amusing touches, as always with her. For instance, a Lady Parker, who was taking Drishane for two months in summer wrote that 'she hoped I'd arrange that her servants should not hear any rats during their stay' or they would leave. Drishane, though overrun with rats, was not as frightening a place as Glen Barrahane where Hildegarde was much perturbed on more than one occasion by the apparition of two long dead relatives at her bedroom window. Rats were everywhere in these old houses and so were ghosts. News came in from Meath that when Lord Gormanston, the 16th Viscount, lay dying nine spectral foxes circumambulated the house.* Uncle Kendal, too, was continually dropping in with news from the spirit world. His other favourite topic was the Indian Mutiny. It is expressly stated that on a certain day he 'talked Mutiny' to his nephew, Hugh Somerville, home on leave from his ship. The dogs have their share of space, as when Edith's pet, Candy,† after having six pups, got pneumonia and had to be fed every twenty minutes, night and day, for a week. What with that and other trivia, they did little work on the R.M. stories.

The diaries give many quick peeps at the daily scene which help to sustain an unbroken narrative of people and events, so that even the lesser actors do not disappear. Thus, Edith and Martin were asked to be the guests of honour at the Lyceum Club, this time at the St Patrick's Day dinner of 1907, but remembering the last function there which was so painfully boring, they refused to go. Or again, a passage from their first novel, *An Irish Cousin*, was quoted by Lord Lansdowne in the House of Lords in support of a proposal for a Channel Tunnel, which remains to this day no more than a proposal. On 8 April 1907 Paddy's brother, Nevill, aged eight, 'got a heavy smack

---

* Sir Patrick Coghill states that when his body lay in the Gormanston private chapel the night before burial, a succession of ghost foxes were seen to enter and go up to the coffin.

† A section in Edith's last book, *Maria and Some Other Dogs*, published when she was ninety, is devoted to Candy and has a drawing of her.

in the face from his French governess's golf club and is a good deal swelled.' When Martin was given for her forty-fifth birthday a copy of Synge's *Aran Islands*, illustrated by Jack Yeats, the poet's brother, she liked the book but not the illustrations. In June 1907 she was in London and had tea with friends in the House of Lords. Pinker asked her to go to the Derby, but she didn't. The visit over, she was on her way to Paddington station when, 'as usual, the cab horse fell'. In July she was at Oughterard with her sister, whose house, Waterfield, had now become the centre of the Martin family. One Sunday she attended evening service at the Oughterard church when 'a terrible being with a heavy moustache held forth intolerably'. In August she left for Devonshire where Edith, having let Drishane, rats and all, to Lady Parker, had rented a house. Edith painted and no writing was done. At the end of the month we find them in Dublin at the Horse Show. By November they were back in Drishane at work. Pinker, now a close friend and concerned at the pause in completing the *Further Experiences*, came on a visit. '24 November, talked business with Pinker.' On the 26th, 'Pinker taken hunting'. On the 29th, 'Pinker got the brush'. A triumph for Pinker. But he failed to keep his two clients working. Martin admits their perverseness. They are likely to lose money, 'all owing to our slowness, sickness, slackness and the Dublin Horse Show'. The publication of the *Further Experiences* was deferred till the autumn of 1908, though some of the final stories were serialized in the summer by the *Graphic*. All the others had appeared previously in some magazine or periodical.

In February 1908 Edith Dawson died at Waterfield and was buried in the Oughterard churchyard next her brother, Robert. An Irish cross similar to his marks her grave. This event finally severed Martin's connection with the Ross country.

In spite of interruptions of all sorts, the completed book was sent off to the publishers, and advance copies were received on 29 August 1908. As a big sale was expected, 10,000 copies were printed for the first edition.

Martin's health was by this time quite restored. She had at last thrown off the effects of her bad fall out hunting in 1898. She began hunting again regularly. The hunt was still managed by Edith. A letter of hers to her brother Cameron, dated 20 August 1908, gives an analysis of her financial position. The hunt was clearly a luxury which she could not afford unless the subscriptions covered expenses. In the Cameron letter, written before the royalties for the *Further Experiences* began to dribble in, she informs him: 'At this moment I owe £80 to the bank, and have only just enough to get along by renewing my bill—Egerton backs it for me. But till it is cleared off I could not raise any more. Though I now have no other debts it is big enough for me not to feel happy till it is finally wiped off. I have not yet come level with the expenses of the Hounds, and the new stables aren't paid for yet.' (£40 was owing there.) She hoped, however, that her horse dealing would bring in the £40, but unfortunately her most likely horse had sprained a big muscle and was unsaleable at the moment. But if 10,000 copies of the *Further Experiences* were sold, all would be well. 'I will send you a copy directly it appears,' she tells Cameron. 'It will be interesting to see how many of the papers regret its inferiority to No. 1. I don't think there is much intrinsic difference, but of course the first had the great advantage of being the first.' There was no fear of a decline, however. The book was not a weak follow-on, but the continuation of a theme, as solidly founded on personal observation as the first. Helped by their industrious way of noting down at once whatever struck them as typical or amusing, the authors were well supplied with tit-bits of all sorts. The notebook, marked 10, already referred to, was the chief repository of these notes, though some were made at the end of diaries, as when Martin jotted down in hers the following, overheard on the Cork steamer: 'Child: "Ma'ma, what's a hippopotamus?" "I don't know, child." "But *what* does it do? Do it run or do it lep?" "I don't know, child." ' There are many such delicious asides in Notebook 10, some used in the *Experiences* and some never used. As one reads them now,

hidden away in the notebook, Edith and Martin endear themselves to us, as if one saw their happy smiles as they related
to each other some fresh find of local drollery and set it down
with the relish of a connoisseur adding a new piece to his
collection.

They were partial to out-of-the-way fancies and were pleased
when a cottage woman told them of 'a rich man of great age
who had bribed the people on the other side of death to leave
him here'. And of an old and diseased woman of whom it was
said that 'she will get a fine throuncing in the next world for not
having come before', because it was wickedness for her to have
burdened her family for too long. Old curses, too, and the
way they were delivered to enhance their magical effect,
were copied out. Says a woman: 'I heard him cursing me and
coming on his knees and wishing everything might melt from
me like the froth of the sea.' The following praise of a boy was
just to their taste: 'He's a good boy, he is, and that willin', if
you sent him to bale the wather out of the sea, he'd do it, and
he'd live forever with donkeys.' A milkmaid's effort to explain
how love took her, they inscribed: 'Indeed, I don't know how
I got it, but the same you'd get a stitch over a churn.' They
were fond of fights. An old man complains how hardly he was
used by another: 'He was going on with a great flurry of capers
and he put his hand into my mouth and took out both of me
teeth, and they're very scarce.'

A mad old retainer's distaste for Edith's brother, Aylmer,
comes out this way: 'And he'd talk of everyone only Masther
Aylmore, and he never dhrew down Masther Aylmore between
his lips.'

Mat Kenealy, a Ross tenant, gave the following account of a
mare of his which Martin found touching: 'I sold her before I
wint to America. God knows afther she going from me,
whinever I'd look at her winkers hangin' on the wall I'd have
to cry. I never seen a sighth of her till 3 years afther that, and I
going to Galway. I was talking to a woman and we coming
down Dangan hill, and what was in it but herself coming up in

a cart; and I didn't look at her good nor bad, nor know her, but sorra bit but whin she knew me talking she turned in to me with the cart! "Ho-ho-ho," says she, and she stuck her nose into me like she'd be kissing me. Be damn but I had to cry, and the world wouldn't stir her out o' that till I'd lead her on myself. As for cow or dog or any other thing, there's nothing would rise your heart like a horse.'

A man's simple remark about a dog that went ranging at night was felt to call up a picture, as a line of verse can do: 'There wasn't a yard of wather in Ross but he had it barked over.' And Martin was moved by hearing it said of a dying man: 'There was the blaze of darkness in his face,' a wonderful vision. Edith admired the phrase so much that years later, in 1920, she used it in her book *Stray-Aways*.* The reassuring promise about a dog entrusted to his care made by the guard of the Irish Mail when it stopped at Crewe was good enough to go in: 'I'll put a curtain unther him, and he'll be as safe with me as if he was in God's pocket.'

There are many other jewels in this repository that have never seen the light. Edith asks Macarthy, the ferryman at Castle Townshend, what he has been doing to his eye. He replies: 'Tis true for ye, Ma'am, I have the countenance of a blackguard on me this morning and I'm not fit to face the ginthry.' He goes on that to steady his nerves the night before he took a drop of whisky. 'Upon my soul and honour 'twasn't dhrunk I was.' His eye was swollen because the ground seemed to come up and hit him. Martin delighted in sayings about drunkards. 'She's very clever. She'd never turn her mouth to you when she's like that,' (because of the poteen on her breath). And the answer to the question: 'Is it drink?' was 'he'd dhrink the eye out of a cat.' She also recorded many splendid blessings given her by countrywomen such as, 'that every hair of your head may be a candle to light ye to glory'. And they collected curses, in which the countryside was rich. 'Where is she? says he to me—Well, God forgive me the fearful curse I let loose

* It also appears in the story 'Oweneen the Sprat', in the *Further Experiences*.

[151]

from me—Where is she? I says, but lying up in her bed like any old dog.'

But one must stop and consider the *Further Experiences*. After browsing for so long among their private papers, one has got to know Edith and Martin so well, that on turning now to read their principal work, the thirty-four stories of the Irish R.M., the very sound of their voices seems to reach us. The illusion of their presence is complete. They are in good spirits. The stories are among the happiest ever written.

Edith declared in the preface to the 1928 collected edition of the stories that all the characters were fictitious except the disreputable hanger-on, Slipper, and the incorrigible dog, Maria. It is a common practice, however, for writers of fiction to make such a declaration. In fact, anyone acquainted with the life at Ross and Drishane through a study of the diaries and letters, will find a real name often coming to mind. Mrs Knox, the mistress of Aussolas, who dominates the scene again and again, is not exactly Mama, yet is so like her both in word and action as to be her free portrait. Take the following from the opening passage of *The Finger of Mrs Knox*. It is twilight at Aussolas Castle. The hall door is open and Mrs Knox sits at the far end of the hall. 'A being who had arrived noiselessly on bare feet now revealed its presence by hard breathing. "Come in, Mary," commanded old Mrs Knox without turning her head; "make up the fire." "I will, Ma'am," murmured the being, advancing with an undulating gait suggestive of a sequence of incipient curtsies. She was carrying an armful of logs.' After making up the fire she 'retired by way of the open hall door with the same deferential stealth with which she had entered.' She was the henmaid, one of whose duties was to bring in logs from outside, because she was the only member of the staff who knew the difference between a dry log and a wet one. The scene is built up from memories of Ross and Mama, as is the following. Mrs Knox's woolly dog was on the steps and barked. 'A slow footfall ascended the steps and the twilight in the hall deepened as a man's figure appeared in the doorway.

"Who are you?" called out Mrs Knox from her big chair. "I'm Casey, your ladyship," replied the visitor in a deplorable voice.' Casey, a former tenant of hers, but now a man whom the recent Land Act had made a peasant proprietor, was in debt to a money lender who had a writ from the court to seize all his stock, wanted Mrs Knox to come to his aid. 'Great trouble I got, Mrs Knox, your Honour ma'am. The few little bastes I has and me donkey and all, he's to drive them tomorrow.' Mrs Knox let him run on about his wrongs, which he did at great length in a lamentable voice, the tears running down his cheeks, while she fed the woolly dog, which had thrust its nose under her hand, with hot buttered scones. Casey ended by saying that he knew Mrs Knox would not let one of her own tenants be wronged. 'I have no tenants,' she replied, 'the Government is your land-lord now.' 'Then I wish to God it was yourself we had in it again,' cried Mr Casey. 'It was better for us when the gentry was managing.' 'Well, that will do now,' said Mrs Knox. 'Go round to the servants' hall and have your tea. I'll see what I can do.' Next morning she was up early and drove a distance to see the money lender. He was unable to stand up to her overwhelming personality and Casey was saved from ruin.

At Ross and Drishane there were still a few tenants, but the bulk of them had taken advantage of the Land Acts and been able to buy the land they held as tenants. A tenant who became the owner of his land had to stand on his own feet. And some-times he was too improvident, too stupid, to maintain himself. As a tenant, if he did not pay his rent, his landlord had the right to eject him; as a proprietor who failed to pay his debts, he was at the mercy of the money lenders. Mr Casey felt that the old gentry had had more patience with defaulting tenants than had money lenders with defaulting debtors. But the day of the landed gentry was past. They now belonged to history. Ross and Drishane and all the other great houses might make a show of maintaining their ancient standing, but their time of power was over. Edith was intelligent enough to realize that nothing could stop the advance of Catholic home rule, though naturally the prospect was rather alarming for her. In the R.M. stories she and Martin are not describing the Ireland of 1900 to 1915, where a new epoch was brewing; their theme is what was left, as at Ross and Drishane, of the old order. There is no lament, however, for what was passing away. In the stories all is laughter, drink and sport. Even the foxes are represented as sportsmen, slipping over stone walls like cats, going to ground like rabbits, fooling the hounds, and glorying in the chase. No wonder the Dublin literary group, who had aligned themselves with the national movement in politics, thought the R.M. stories not serious enough at a time when the Irish were preparing to spread their wings. They could not help laughing a bit at the fun and the drink and the dogs, but were half ashamed of admiring what they held was too funny to be called literature.

The thirty-four stories are all comedies. Nothing is to be taken over seriously, not even hunting. The R.M., Major Yeates, appears in each, as he is the narrator. By his own admission he is continually being taken in, cheated, made a fool of, but he manages to laugh off such mishaps. He is a figure of fun, yet a good fellow. His wife, Philippa, though very feminine and good hearted, is sharper; she is devoted to him but has a poor opinion of his wits. She would like to admire him, but can't. Not that she is really a clever woman; it is just that she is a woman of sense. She is given one of Martin's traits, being subject to convulsions of laughter, but otherwise has no resemblance to that eminent woman. Her prototype, one feels, is among Edith's sisters-in-law, while the R.M. himself is an amalgam of her brothers, Cameron and Aylmer, both mild decent men. High comedy is reserved for Mrs Knox, much cleverer than any man, her personality more pronounced, who has her finger in everything and never loses face. Her resemblance to Mama has been noted. What she stands for is Edith's feminine ideal, a matriarch. When she is present the story leaves farce and becomes high comedy, in which she has the laugh of everyone else. Mrs Cadogan, the cook, is the same type in the world below stairs, her prototypes being the many powerful females who lorded it in the kitchens of Ross and Drishane.

Some critics have found that the best of the thirty-four stories is 'The House of Fahy', whose technical perfection puts it on a level with Maupassant at his most skilful. Mrs Knox does not appear in it. The leading protagonist is the dog, Maria, introduced thus by Mrs Cadogan, whose vocabulary is gorgeously displayed: 'I can't put a thing out o' me hand, but he's watching me to whip it away. 'Twas only last night I was back in the scullery when I heard Bridget let a screech, and there was me brave dog up on the table eating the roast beef that was left after coming out from the dinner! And I had planned that bit of beef for the luncheon, the way we wouldn't have to inthrude on the cold turkey!* Sure he has it that dhragged, that all we can do with it now is run it through the mincing machine for the Major's sandwiches.'

Major Yeates, Philippa and friends were starting on a yachting cruise along the Atlantic coast of Cork. Yeates refused as flatly as his character permitted, to bring Maria, but as usual his arrangements were disregarded. Maria followed and went aboard the yacht with them and provided a climax as neat as the best masters of the short story could achieve. From first to last everything in the comedy has, one feels sure, happened in reality. And that is true of all the thirty-four R.M. stories. More than any other part of the two authors' fiction, they are autobiographical, a picture of their life at Castle Townshend and at Ross.

When reading the tenth story, 'The Policy of the Closed Door', a hunting comedy with a love interest, it is curious how the narrator, the R.M., seems to lose his identity and merge in Edith Somerville. The metamorphosis becomes marked when the excitement of the chase is most intense. The R.M. ceases to speak. His rather jaunty way of expressing himself is drowned by the urgent tone of Edith's voice. 'The brown mare came out

---

*This phrase, evidently heard at Ross or Drishane, was jotted down in Notebook 10 for further use.

through the trees and the undergrowth like a woodcock down the wind, and jumped across a stream. . . . The hounds splashed and struggled after and as they landed the first ecstatic whimpers broke forth. In a moment it was full cry, discordant, beautiful and soul-stirring, as the pack spread and sped and settled to the line.' This is totally out of character for the R.M.; it is the impassioned voice of Edith Somerville, M.F.H. The fiction has become autobiography. But in the last page of the story where the hunt is over and the love interest comes into the foreground, Edith's voice begins to die away and Martin's to take its place, as when the girl speaks 'with a sudden stagger of a sob in her voice, as she escaped into the house'. When dealing with love, Edith does not achieve so emotional and wild a note. Major Yeates' manner is something quite other.

14

From 1908 to the outbreak of War

The R.M. stories, which bring the reader so close to Edith and Martin, contain no reference to spiritualism or the occult except in jocular form. Nevertheless, Edith's interest in the subject, which at first was tepid, had been growing since the death of her parents. In her diary of 9 January 1908 she notes: 'Uncle Kendal came back from London having had a very remarkable seance, at which something purporting to be the Bart talked to him.' The Bart, Sir Joscelyn Coghill, who was Uncle Kendal's brother, and Egerton's father, had died three years before in 1905. Since the foundation of the Psychical Research Society in 1882, London had shown increasing interest in supernormal phenomena of all kinds. Many persons eminent in the sciences were engaged in investigating them. Mention has already been made of Arthur Balfour, who for a time was President of the S.P.R. In 1908 the President was Annie Besant, the disciple of Madame Blavatsky, the most sensational of all the spiritualists of the period. Numbers of professional mediums and countless amateurs existed in London. Communications in the form of automatic writing purporting to come from the dead filled hundreds of pages in the publications of the various societies devoted to the cult. This was the milieu which Uncle Kendal was in touch with on his visits to London, when he stayed at the Cavalry Club. Back in his house, The Point, he never tired of relating the strange things he had seen and heard. Little was

known at first in so remote a spot as Castle Townshend of the
serious attention paid in London to occult matters by persons of
standing. Uncle Kendal was regarded as a credulous old man
(in 1908 he was seventy-six), but as London opinion became
better known, his reputation went up, and his nephews and
nieces (Cameron, Edith, Boyle, Aylmer, Hildegarde), began
to listen to his accounts of London seances with more attention.
There were no professional mediums in the County Cork so far.
The old women of the mountains, certainly occultists, were
illiterate and useless for any sort of modern psychical research.
Edith had not yet met the London medium, Geraldine Cummins,
who was afterwards to become her close friend. The entries in
her diary, however, which relate to supernatural appearances,
become more frequent. Thus on 16 July 1908 we find: 'An ugly
ghost was seen on the stairs of Tally Ho,' a house off the main
street of Castle Townshend owned by the Coghills.

Making up her bankbook on 8 October 1908 Edith noted:
'Have £2 2s. 6d. with which to face a frowning world. Haven't
enough money to buy stockings but keep hounds. How very
Irish!' Here we have the reason why Edith had had to resign
from the M.F.H.ship of the West Carbery pack. Now in an
effort to make some money she and Hildegarde started a dairy
farm on the demesne for which Cameron bought twenty-five
Friesian cows, and so founded the first herd of that breed in
Ireland.

Edition after edition, however, of the *Further Experiences*
was called for in 1910 and the author's financial situation
improved, as did their literary standing. In March 1910 a
Dublin body known as The Corinthian Dinner Committee gave
a banquet for Irish women writers. It was a big function,
presided over by the Lord Lieutenant, Lord Aberdeen. Twelve
Irish women writers came, along with some two hundred guests.
Edith and Martin were seated at the high table, Martin being
some places closer to His Excellency than Edith, an indication,
perhaps, that in the Committee's opinion she was the more
distinguished of the two. She was asked to make one of the

speeches but declined. The only Irish women writers at that
date whose names are now remembered besides those of Edith
and Martin are Lady Gregory, Eva Gore-Booth, Miss Purser,
Emily Lawless, Susan Mitchell and Katherine Tynan. Martin's
diary gives her account of the occasion. 'Began to dress after
tea, Edith in black sequins over white, I in pink with gold. Got
to the Gresham Hotel at 6.40. Found throngs already there of
all sorts. Edith and I and the other authoresses were then drafted
into another room and there awaited Their Excellencies and
were introduced and curtseyed.' At dinner Martin sat between a
head of the Land Commission and a judge of the High Court.
'Finished at 12.15. Home much spent.' Next morning they found
their photographs in the *Irish Times*. A private luncheon was
given for them that day, at which George Moore sat next to
Martin. She describes him as 'very entertaining, and discom-
posing and alarming'.

The Corinthian dinner was the first public recognition of
Edith and Martin by Dublin literary society.

The seven years that followed the publication of the *Further
Experiences* in 1908 were years of less literary activity. It should
be kept in mind that the third part of the R.M. group of stories,
In Mr Knox's Country, did not appear until 1915, though Pinker
and Longmans continued to urge Edith and Martin to complete
it. For some reason not fully explained they brought out in 1911
a book called *Dan Russel The Fox*, a single hunting story of
novel length in which the R.M. does not figure. Of this volume
Edith recorded a note: 'Martin Ross and I have written many
times of hunting in Ireland, but in this story, above all others,
we have told faithfully, and with the emotion of enthusiasts, of
the sport that we knew and loved, what time my brother Aylmer
and I successively Mastered the West Carbery Foxhounds.'*
The book is a light amusing little novel, and it does reflect in
places the frenzy for the chase which possessed Edith. Take this
emotional passage:

' "It was beyond under the rock he was lying!" shrieked one

* See *A Bibliography of E. Œ. Somerville and Martin Ross* by Elizabeth Hudson.

[159]

of the men. "The Villyan! Dhrive on your dogs into the smell!"

' "They have it! They have it!" shrieked the other. He struck his hands together, his face scarlet, his eyes blazing. Whatever the madness of the chase may be, he too was possessed by it.

'A clash as from a steeple-full of bells shook the air; the hounds snatched at the line, a big white and yellow dog-hound drove out to the front with his head up, vociferating.

' "Leu! Trumpeter boy! Trumpeter!" cried his huntsman, in a rapture of love, his voice piercing the din. "Get to Trumpeter there!" The hounds crushed in together, as if they were squeezing through a narrow gateway, they lengthened out into a stream, they fleeted, they sped, and the river of their music flowed back to Katharine and she galloped in it, and there was nothing else in Heaven or earth.'

The composition of *Dan Russel the Fox* and *Mr Knox's Country* was all the writing done between 1908 and 1915. But the diaries and letters of the period provide lively biographical facts, which, though often trivial, help to round off the picture.

As we know, Edith and Martin never stayed at Drishane all the year round, but now they seemed to be more constantly on the move. In the autumn of 1910 they went to stay with the Pinkers in Surrey where they had acquired 'an extremely nice house and place'. Pinker met them at the station with his carriage drawn by a handsome pair of greys. 'Saw the horses and the farm. The coach horses, 4, quite a nice lot. Ditto the cows. It is more blessed to be an agent than an author,' observes Edith. During the same visit to England they stayed with Cameron at Kneller Hall in Twickenham, where army bandsmen were trained. He took Edith to the British Museum, a place she had never entered before, to have a look at some Chinese and Japanese pictures, which were of special interest to him as he had been to Japan. The pictures were too exotic for Edith to appreciate and she bluntly records that she didn't like them. This was characteristic of her. When confronted with objects of art or books which were unfamiliar to her, she had

The dying Martin, drawing by Edith, 18 December, 1915

Landscape in oils by Edith: Roger's Island in the Harbour

insufficient instinctive taste to guide her to a just appreciation. But she could learn and was able in time to correct her first hasty judgments. She need not be blamed in this case of the Chinese and Japanese masterpieces, which even today are not generally appreciated at their real value, as the figures they fetch at auctions testify. Martin, too, made her mistakes; for instance the first time she saw at the Abbey Theatre in Dublin Synge's masterpiece, *The Playboy of the Western World*, she recorded in her diary an adverse opinion of it.

Later in 1910 Edith had to go over to London again to attend her brother, Jack's, wedding, a fashionable affair at St George's, Hanover Square. She records that there were 'about 400 guests, including the Japanese Ambassador. Great crush at the reception at 18 Grosvenor Street.' The bride, Vera Aston Key, came of a wealthy family. Jack, then aged thirty-eight and a Captain in the Army, had of course only his pay. But Uncle Kendal managed a dinner at the Cavalry Club for his relatives. Martin had intended to go over, but at the last moment Candy, Edith's favourite little fox terrier, got a bad cold and was snuffling so much that Martin gave up the idea and stayed behind to look after her. Edith was away for a week, during the whole of which Candy sneezed and wheezed. On 8 November when Edith got back she found Candy still 'sneezing and snorting but in excellent spirits'.*

Edith often took her dogs with her when she crossed to England. It was, and still is, against regulations, on the cross-channel steamer for passengers to have their dogs with them in the cabin. But Edith could not bear the idea of her dogs being locked up in the steamer's kennel on a night crossing and used to smuggle them into her cabin when the stewardess was not looking, though some stewardesses were complaisant. The diary has: 'Had dogs in our cabin. Abstracted meat from dinner for dogs.' And again, when some dog owner protested to the stewardess that Miss Somerville had her dog in the cabin, the stewardess, evidently an Irishwoman, replied: 'Is it Miss

* Candy died in 1915, aged sixteen, to both Edith and Martin's grief.

L   [161]

Somerville! Sure she has nests of them!' Of this occasion
Martin's diary has: 'Had perfect crossing with the three dogs
concealed in our cabin. All slept well. The stewardess very
favourable to the dogs.' One's affection for Edith and Martin is
increased by such escapades. On one occasion, it may be recalled, they took a very small dog to France and got it back
through the British customs by Martin concealing it in her
sleeve.

It was Edith's turn to stay behind at Drishane to look after
the dogs and the new dairy, which was not doing well, when
Martin went over to London to attend George V's coronation
in June 1911, along with Hildegarde, Egerton and others of the
family. There are one or two passages to quote from her
account of what she saw: 'Walked across in front of Buckingham
Palace where the new memorial to Queen Victoria was surrounded by India, Malay and all sorts of dark soldiers,' a
reference to the groups of statuary round the base of the huge
monument. She had been invited to join a select party on the
roof of the chapel in St James's Palace. From there they saw the
royal procession leave Buckingham Palace, and could hear the
chiming of the Abbey bells. The procession's return was via Pall
Mall. The two sovereigns passed at two-thirty wearing their
crowns. 'The Queen dead pale but very fine looking; the King's
crown rather overwhelming to him.' There was a royal progress
through London later that afternoon. In the procession Martin
caught sight of Winston Churchill who made this impression:
'Winston Churchill, flaunting in a Victoria as Home Secretary,
was hissed by the crowd and looked very angry.'

Some of the Dublin literary group, including Yeats, had come
over for the coronation. Lady Gregory was staying with Sir
Hugh Lane, her nephew, whose splendid collection of French
Impressionists was afterwards the cause of so much con-
troversy. Martin called at his house to see her. It is evident that
she was keeping on good terms with the Abbey Theatre crowd
in spite of her refusal to write a play for them. Indeed, in the
next spring we find her staying at Coole with Lady Gregory

and having, she says, 'much interesting talk'. Lady Gregory
had shortly before returned from an American tour with the
Irish Players. Though Yeats was not at Coole on this occasion,
she met him not long afterwards at Sir Horace Plunkett's house,
when he was 'very agreeable'. Before going to Coole she was
taken over to see Tyrone House, a visit that suggested to her
the plot of a novel, which Edith thirteen years later used in a
book called *The Big House of Inver*. Tyrone House had been
the seat of an old Galway family, the St Georges, but was
now 'a wonderful wreck of a place'. Writing to Edith shortly
after the visit she describes it as 'a bigger and much grander
edition of Ross, a great square cut stone house of three stories
with an area, perfectly empty, and such ceilings, architecture,
teak doors, and chimney pieces as one sees in old houses in
Dublin. It is on a long promontory by the sea'. In early days
the St Georges were very grand, but in the late eighteenth
century they abandoned their aristocratic tradition and let the
semi-barbarism of their remote situation engulf them. They
made alliances with the village girls, dispensed with legitimacy,
fought among themselves, drank heavily, neglected their estates
and lived in squalor, crowded into the big house. Martin and
the friends who had brought her over explored the house,
which was empty. 'As we were leaving an old Miss St George,
daughter of the last owner, was at the door in a little donkey
trap. Since her people died she will not go into Tyrone House
or into the enormous yard or the beautiful old garden. She was
a strange mixture of distinction and commonness, like her
breeding, and it was very sad to see her at the door of that great
house. If we dared to write up that subject!' The theme, Martin
felt, provided scope for a powerful drama. But, as will be disclosed, much was to happen before the attempt to write it was
made by Edith.

At Drishane the dairy farm turned out badly and early in
1911 Edith sold for £66 what had cost £240 to stock. Relieved
of the supervision of what did not much appeal to her, she
decided to take over again the Mastership of the West Carbery

Foxhounds. The Hunt had suffered from bad management under the man who succeeded her in 1909. She could not live without this winter amusement, the excitement of galloping over the little fields, jumping the banks and looking after the hounds in the kennels. But it was a luxury. The first year showed an expenditure of £505, a subscription of £249. However by 1914 she was only £100 out of pocket.

Spiritualism had now begun to fascinate her. This was partly due to the friendship she formed with a certain Jem Barlow, an amateur medium, who in September 1912 came to stay at Drishane and next year decided to rent a house in Castle Townshend. By the autumn she was holding seances with Uncle Kendal, in which they were soon joined by Egerton, whose keenness had been much enhanced by his experiences when in London staying with Cameron at Kneller Hall. Edith records on 14 February, 1915: 'Egerton and Cameron went to a seance with an American Miss Whist and heard strange things. Voices spoke to them and said things impossible for a stranger to know.' Edith herself began reading books on the occult; one by A. P. Sinnett on elementals is mentioned. In a letter to Cameron dated 30 December 1914 she describes at length what happened at the dining room table one night at Drishane when she was convinced she saw elementals mixed up with the dogs' dinner. She had three small female fox terriers, Candy, Sheilah and Dooley, and at the end of her dinner began to make up theirs in three soup plates which were on a tray on a stand near the door. As she was lifting down Candy's plate, in which was a mixture of bread, cabbage, soup and some bits of raw meat cut up into small squares by the cook, 'two conglomerated lumps of meat and slush rose out of the plate. One fell on the floor, the other flopped back on the tray and fell on the edge of Sheilah's plate, and as it lay there it *squeaked*, a very faint dry little squeak.' Martin, who was the only other person in the room, was sitting by the fire a little way off. Edith rushed over to her in a fright and told her what she had seen. Martin said she must have jerked the plate. Reassured, Edith went back to the tray.

Suddenly, when mixing Sheilah's dinner with a spoon, she saw 'a lump of stuff like two or three of the raw bits of meat, move of its own volition from the middle of the plate and creep up on to its edge, a shapeless mass trailing with vermicelli, altogether horrible and awful. I dropped the spoon with a yell and jumped back from the tray. The next instant the thing uttered a far louder squeak.' Martin came to her rescue and with a lamp they advanced together on the tray. But nothing was now to be seen. The first bit which had fallen on the floor had been eaten by Candy. What was the explanation? Could it have been a mouse or small rat which had got mixed up with the bread and cabbage? Drishane was so infested with rats and mice that this might have happened, but on reflection was seen to be very improbable. 'Martin's idea was that it was one of old Sinnett's elementals, who feed on raw meat and somehow tumbled out of the fourth dimension or wherever he lives, and was materialized for a minute or two.' Cameron is asked to find a better explanation if he can. Her account is absolutely true and unexaggerated, she insists. 'Martin did not see the thing, as it had vanished when she got over to the tray, but she heard it squeak, a low and reedy sound.'

Edith was fifty-four at this time. The tray was some distance from the lamp. The semi-darkness, perhaps a flicker from the fire, could explain what she saw. As for the squeaks, dogs when waiting for their food often give little squeaks of impatience while they watch their owner mixing it up. But Edith was in no frame of mind to entertain such natural explanations. Her head was full of stories of the occult.

It was a moment, too, of strain and worry. The first World War had just begun. She was anxious about her brothers in the services; her nephews, Desmond, Paddy and Nevill, also might later become involved. Rumours flew about; a German invasion of Cork was thought possible. On 23 August, 1914, nineteen days after the declaration of war, she recorded in her diary: 'Strange cryings over in Reen like a mad creature roving and calling. We all heard it here, but no one else had heard it.' In

Martin's diary reverberations of the storm without are heard. '4 May, 1915. Edith had a letter from Aylmer to say that Desmond (his son) has been wounded with the Dardanelles expedition. 5 May. A German submarine is sinking ships off the Kerry coast.' And Cameron wrote of the occult background. He went to see Sinnett and 'heard strange things of the conflict of white and black magic, and good and evil powers', noted Edith. The death of Candy two months after eating the elemental was very perturbing as well as sad. On 7 May Edith has: 'At 7 p.m. heard the ghastly news that the *Lusitania* had been torpedoed off Galley Head' fifteen miles east of Castle Townshend. Six bodies were washed ashore in the harbour not far from Drishane, where a dog was reputed to have swum ashore. An oar belonging to the liner was found and today is to be seen at the main door of the church of St Barrahane in Castle Townshend. Sir Hugh Lane was on board the *Lusitania*. In a letter dated 14 May 1915 from Lady Gregory to Martin she tells of the last sight of Lane. 'Lady Allen, one of the survivors, said Hugh had been near her on deck. He had no lifebelt, was very pale but quite calm. He said "I will try if I can do anything to help the Pearsons" and went towards the bow of the ship—and that was the end.'

On the literary side, however, the news was good. In Martin's diary we find: '1 August. A noble review of *Mr Knox* in yesterday's *Spectator*.' This, the last third of the R.M. stories, so pleased Rudyard Kipling that he 'sent us his respectful love, his obeisances and his salaams'. One would never have guessed that Kipling, whose sense of humour was boyish and whose creation, Mulvaney, the Irish soldier in India, was a ridiculous travesty of Irish character and speech, would be so carried away by *Mr Knox's Country*. *The Times* conceived that soldiers overseas would be cheered by the R.M. stories and printed broadsheets for distribution in the trenches containing extracts from the three volumes.

In July 1915 their doctor, O'Meara, advised them to take a quiet holiday, now that *Mr Knox's Country* was out. They spent

August at Waterville, a Kerry beauty spot, and did not return to Drishane till 18 September. They were both in normal health. There was not a hint of the irreparable disaster that was closely at hand. Martin was destined to die in three months.

15

The death of Martin

The first hint that all was not well with Martin is contained in Edith's diary entry for 24 September, 1915: 'Dr O'Meara came to see Martin who is having a lot of pain in her face.' This was diagnosed as due to two bad teeth. On the 28th she was in bed and very wretched. As she was reported no better on the 30th, Dr O'Meara brought a dentist and the two teeth were extracted. But she still remained in great pain and it was thought that perhaps her eyes were the cause of the trouble; they had never been very strong. So on 12 October Edith took her to Cork to see the oculist, Dr MacMahon. He did not think there was anything wrong with her eyes and put the pain down to a neuritis in the facial nerves, for which he prescribed remedies. These were ineffective at first, but by 17 October she was a little better and on 31 October was able to sit in the garden in the sun. They all thought she was mending. She had never had anything serious the matter with her except the headaches and weakness following her bad fall out hunting in 1898.

But on 23 November she took a turn for the worse. 'Martin's head gave her a very bad time during the afternoon and evening.' O'Meara was sent for and prescribed massage of the neck. The headache, however, did not cause Edith any great anxiety for she went hunting on the 25th. On returning from a poor run, she found Martin alarmingly worse. The pain in the head, aggravated by nausea, had increased. O'Meara advised her

going to the Glen Vera hospital in Cork, where her case, which
seemed a puzzling one, could better be studied.

So on 27 November Edith with Hildegarde took her to Cork,
a room having been reserved for her there at the Glen Vera by
Dr MacMahon.

Edith stayed with her that night in the hospital, and next day
moved to a friend's house in Cork university, as there was no
proper accommodation in Glen Vera for relatives of patients.
From this address she was able to visit Martin without difficulty,
and found her on the 29th morning cheerful and comfortable,
already looking better though with some pain in her neck. She
sat with her all the 29th till the evening train for Drishane.
There was a hunt the following day which as M.F.H. she wished
to attend.

On the morning of 2 December she received a note which
Martin had dictated to the nurse, saying that 'she was going on
nicely'. But at 9 p.m. a message came from the nurse asking
Edith to come to Cork at once; no reason was given, but an
emergency was implied. Late though it was, Edith managed to
get a car and motored the fifty miles to Cork through rain and
cold, arriving at the hospital at 1.45 a.m. on 3 December. She
was extremely alarmed as the message, conveyed to her by the
Castle Townshend coastguards, whose phone was the only
one working after a violent storm of two days earlier, made her
think Martin must be dying. At the hospital she was told that
Martin had suddenly become unconscious shortly before the
nurse sent the message, but had now regained consciousness
and was asleep.

When she woke up she knew Edith only vaguely. Edith saw
she must consult the doctors at once. Dr O'Meara, who was
staying at a hotel, was fetched. Dr MacMahon was then consulted. Their report was exceedingly grave. A tumour had
developed at the lower part of the brain, at the back, and they
regarded the case as hopeless, an operation being impossible.
'They told us to wire for Jim Martin,' her brother, who was in
Galway, back from his tea plantation in Ceylon. This was done.

'Martin was very sleepy and dozed almost all day.' Hildegarde and Edith were now putting up at a Cork club they belonged to.

Edith's diary continues: 'Saturday Dec. 4. Jim Martin arrived. . . . Martin was about the same in the morning, but was taking food, liquids only, better. She knew us, and Jim, quite well. She put her hand over her left eye, the one of which the lid is paralysed, when Jim spoke to her—such a familiar movement and one which showed she knew him. She explained to the day nurse who he was and said that his son, Richard, was with the army in Serbia. The doctors seemed inclined to let us have a shred of hope. On Dec. 5 she slept most of the day. She knows us, says my name, but she is very far away. It seems as if she were lost in mist, but she seems quite happy. Her voice is not quite natural and has a sort of formal tone, as if she were speaking to strangers—but is very cheerful. When we ask how she feels she says: "Oh, *very* well!" Dec. 6. About the same, but once in the morning she came nearer. I sat by her holding her hand and she said my name. Then Hildegarde held her hand and kissed her. She murmured "You and Edith are always faithful." After that we could not understand what she said, but her tone was contented.' Hildegarde was obliged to return to Castle Townshend that afternoon. On 7 December the Castle Townshend parson, Mr Madden, came to read the Communion Service. 'He was anxious that Martin should in some degree realize the service. I knelt by her holding her hand and told her what was proposed. She gave my hand a little pressure. Mr Madden read some of the prayers. She could not swallow, but after Jim and I had received I whispered to her, and her lips were touched with the Bread and Wine. She again gave my hand a faint pressure.' She was faintly conscious and able to utter the word Edith. 'After Mr Madden and Jim had gone she fell asleep, the quietest sleep imaginable.' On 8 December Martin was only very faintly conscious. On the 9th 'her breathing was awfully bad'. On that day Hildegarde was back and Egerton arrived.

By 10 December 'the nerves of her throat had now become

involved'. She could only take one spoonful of milk at wide intervals. 'Her breathing and temperature kept continually changing. Her face and hands got stone cold more than once. Hildegarde and I, kneeling by her side, believed she was dying.' But she rallied. About 2 a.m., however, 'her breathing became desperately laboured, very painful to hear. Each moment it seemed that it must cease, but it again improved. . . . We went away for a couple of hours.' When they left at 8 a.m. she was sleeping.

On 12 December they 'found her in the same tranquil sleep. Her brow, the purest and most noble in expression imaginable. Hilda and Jim went to church. I stayed with her and wrote letters. At three, Dr Hearn, the rector of this parish, a very kind and quiet man, came and read an intercessery service. The three of us knelt round her bed. I thought that she pressed my hand, and Jim said she opened her right eye while the service was going on.' On Monday 13 December there was no change. The doctors were astonished that she was still alive. 'Jim Martin went back to Galway today. I begged him to go. He could do nothing. I sat in her room all day.' It was believed that Martin was just sufficiently conscious to know when Edith entered the room. 'There was some faint difference of breathing hard to define, yet perceptible. Her colour varies in a curious way; sometimes her face gets flushed all over and the forehead becomes very hot, and then the reverse happens and her whole body gets cold. I held her hands in both mine.' This seemed to soothe her.

On 14 December there was no change. Edith stayed on till late before returning to her lodging. 'I walked back—the streets noisy and blazing, a big recruiting meeting raging in Patrick Street.'

As Martin was receiving by now no more nourishment than a spoonful once in three hours, she was starving to death. She was now completely unconscious and one side was without feeling. On 17 December she seemed weaker 'and is deeper in a trance of peace'. On Saturday 18 December Edith resolved to

draw the likeness of her dying friend, the person she loved best
in the world. 'Got some paper, a carbon pencil and some white
chalk to make a drawing of her in her beautiful tranquil repose.
Nothing could be more still; only the faintest and most gentle
breathing. It was hard to get the point of view, harder still to
concentrate' solely upon the effort of creating a work of art.

The original of this drawing, reproduced here, is in the
possession of Sir Patrick Coghill. Edith was satisfied with the
likeness. It is a very moving portrait. Martin is just alive, but
very remote, unconscious as in sleep, but a little more rapt and
more utterly relaxed.

During these days of agonized waiting for the end, Edith
wrote constantly to Cameron, the eldest of her five brothers, the
head of the family, the owner of Drishane, who was in England,
addressing him as 'dearest Chimp', his pet name since childhood. He was two years her junior. The letters follow the diary
and amplify it. 'There is no more to be said. She sinks a little
deeper into unconsciousness daily. There is no suffering. There
is nothing to be done. Every possible care is taken of her, and
she seems happy in a dim far place. I can write no more. It is
no use trying to say anything. No one but she and I can know
what we were to each other. Dearest boy, I know you sym-
pathize and grieve too. Your loving Edith.'

And again: 'She is farther away today, she can hardly be
made aware of us, yet I think she knew it when I kissed her;
she murmured something. But she spoke from this far-off place
that she has been in throughout. You can understand. Dear
boy, I can say no more.'

And this heartrending cry on 12 December when death was
still a week away: 'Nurse does not expect her to see another
morning. I am sitting in her room. Half—the best half—of my
life and soul is torn away. There are no words and no tears that
can cure my trouble. If it weren't for you all, I would be
thankful and joyful to follow her, that we might go together, as
ever. I will try and do what she would like and not break down.
I suppose it won't hurt so much as time goes on.'

The death of Martin

On the day she made the drawing she wrote to Cameron: 'One line to say that she is still lying in a most profound trance of peace, absolutely still with the most unclouded and serene brow. The doctor says that her brain could never clear and that I ought not to wish her to live. He is right, no doubt, yet it is something to feel that she is still here.' She was not yet gone from her, though her departure was close. She was still alive, her darling, there in the room. She could still be served, kept warm, kissed as a living being. The last terrible words—Martin is gone, is dead—had not been uttered.

So much till 18 December. Her old intimate friend Ethel Coghill, whose marriage had been such a shock to Edith, came now to Cork. 'Ethel came quite unexpectedly. She is staying with me.' After the end of their emotional attachment a gentle friendship had grown between them. Ethel accompanied her to the hospital. Together they gazed at the dying Martin. As Edith drew the portrait, Ethel stood by. 'The result is, Ethel and I think, fairly successful.'

'Sunday 19 December. Found Martin almost exactly the same in appearance but the nourishment—such as it was—is no longer possible. Did a little more to the drawing.' Afterwards she and Ethel went to church to pray for Martin. 'Spent the afternoon with Martin's hand in mine, as it was very cold. She sighed sometimes, but did not move. I thought she pressed my hand once as if with intention, but it is hard to say. The nurse thinks she is now too far away for any consciousness of us.'

On Monday 20 December Edith went to the hospital as before and sat with Martin most of the day. 'Mounted and made safe the picture of her. She sighed rather often and uttered several moans that might have been pain' but her face showed no trace even of discomfort. 'I thought that she seemed soothed and quieted by my nearness. Before I left she was entirely peaceful and deeper than ever in the trance.'

The rule was for the night nurse always to telephone to Edith at 10 p.m. and report Martin's condition. If no change,

Edith went to bed; otherwise she came over again. On this night the nurse telephoned not to come over again as Martin seemed likely to continue peacefully asleep. Edith, by now nearly worn out by the strain, did not wait up any longer. But at 5 a.m. Martin's breathing changed and began to fail and at 7.45 a.m. it ceased. When Edith appeared early at the hospital she was met by the news that Martin was dead. She had planned to be with her when she died, but as often is the case, the moment of death came suddenly. She had missed the moment, an intimate moment which she had ardently desired to share.

Her grief on the day of Martin's death, 21 December, did not permit her to make an entry in her diary, except the words: 'Only goodnight, Beloved, not farewell.' On the 22nd Martin's body was taken to Castle Townshend, and the coffin laid before the altar of St Barrahane's church. On the 23rd, the day of the funeral, Edith wrote: 'Got up early and made a big E with violets. Took it to the church and laid it above her heart. Afterwards it was put into the grave with her.' Her grief was so terrible that she felt unable to attend the service in the church and in the graveyard. Supported by Hildegarde, she 'went away to the Cromlech field where Martin and I have so often sat and stayed there while the incredible impossible happened'. It seemed to her unbelievable that the dead body of Martin was being put into the ground nearby.

Later the tall cross standing there today was raised over the grave and carries this inscription:

In dear Memory of
Violet Florence Martin
youngest daughter of
James Martin
of Ross, Co. Galway
Obiit December 21, 1915

Underneath was inscribed these words from the Apocrypha (Wisdom 3):

The death of Martin

The Souls of the Righteous are in the Hand of God.
In the sight of the Unwise they seem to die but they are in Peace.

The grave is near the eastern wall of the church, on high ground
which commands a view of the Haven below.

Next day Edith has: 'Notices of Martin in the papers, all alike
saying a light has gone out.' And on 24 December: 'Letters impossible to enumerate—over a hundred already. A wonderful
flood of grief and sympathy and kindness.' Martin had a wide
circle of friends and cousins with whom she was on the best of
terms. Moreover, her fame as a writer had given her a host of
acquaintances. All agreed, indeed, that a light had gone out. At
the moment Edith felt in total darkness. Her whole life was so
interwoven with Martin's that she saw no future for herself as
a writer. On the last day of 1915 she wrote: 'This black, black
year goes out in despair and tears.' She had written to Cameron:
'Dearest Chimp, you mustn't mind a brokenhearted companion.
It isn't that I don't love you all. It is only that she was a part
of myself, only unspeakably higher and nobler.'

On New Year's Day, 1916, she addressed a humble petition
to God:

'Suffer her to know, O gracious Lord, if it may be, how much
I love her and miss her, and long to see her again; and if there
are ways in which her influence may be felt by me, vouchsafe
her to me as a guide and guard, and grant me a sense of her
nearness in such degree as Thy laws permit.

'If in anything I can minister to her peace, be pleased of Thy
love to let this be; and mercifully keep me from every act which
may hinder me from union with her as soon as this earth-life is
over, or mar the fullness of our joy when the end of the days
has come.'

There are phases in this prayer which suggest that Edith in
her desolation was already thinking of how to communicate
with the spirit of Martin.

16

The Apotheosis of Martin

The Somerville family, and their close relations the Coghills, suffered frequently from various kinds of rheumatic ailments, due partly to the extreme dampness of Castle Townshend, exposed as it was to the storms and downpours sweeping in from the Atlantic. Moreover, the big houses were damp inside, as they were inadequately heated. Edith seems to have been the most susceptible of them all to rheumatism and did not take adequate care of herself. She hunted in all weathers and often got soaked. Riding side-saddle, as she did, was also harder on her right leg than riding astride would have been. She now went down with a bad attack of sciatica in that leg, the worst bout of rheumatism she had ever had, and aggravated by the strain of Martin's illness and death. The attack came on in February 1916 and her leg was so bad by the 20th of that month that she went over to England for treatment and stayed with Cameron. The pain, however, increased. For several weeks she was laid up in bed. Not till June* was she back in Drishane and able to go about her normal duties. But home again she missed Martin at every turn. On 6 June she writes of 'the deadly details that go to the making of each futureless, featureless day'. When away she had heard that one of the Sassoons had had messages

---

* Edith was therefore not in Ireland at the time of the Easter Rebellion, 24 April 1916, and records no opinion of it, though later she wrote to *The Times* pleading that mercy be extended to the rebel rank and file.

Tally Ho House, Castle Townshend

Edith autographing a copy of *Happy Days* at Tally Ho (1947–8)

The Apotheosis of Martin

from her son killed in the war. Now in Drishane she seems to
have thought seriously of trying to get into touch with Martin's
spirit. For years she had heard Uncle Kendal talking of his
seances, but it was only recently that she had put some faith in
spiritualism. On 16 June, 1916, she went to dine with Jem
Barlow.

Jem Barlow had been resident in Castle Townshend for some
four years. She was a woman in early middle age, unmarried,
very slight of build, and not as poor as she made out. The
Somervilles and Coghills had taken a fancy to her. When it was
known that she was a medium, their interest in her increased.
Her psychic powers were virtually that of a professional
medium. Professor Coghill writes: 'Her prominent blue eyes
had an expression of permanent wonder, with a hint of coyness
or slyness, one couldn't be sure which. How much she deceived
herself and how much she deceived others, I shall never
know.'

Edith wrote an account of what took place after dinner on
16 June. 'Jem wished to see if she could communicate with
Colonel Isherwood, who was killed in the war a short time ago.
Jem held the pencil in her right hand and I put my left hand very
lightly on hers. In a minute or two the pencil began to move
and, without our asking any questions, wrote. The writing
was very clear and legible, though sometimes it failed and
became difficult to read. I can truly say that neither of us had
any idea either before or during the writing of what was being
written or at first who the writer was.'

When it became clear that they were not in communication
with Colonel Isherwood's spirit, but with Martin's, their
surprise was great. The sense of the automatic script was at first
confused but became quite clear when the pencil wrote: 'You
and I have not finished our work. Dear, we shall. Be comforted.
V.M.' In her diary of this day Edith has: 'Received communications of which I hardly know what to think.'

Two days later a second seance was held. 'Jem came to dinner.
We again wrote for nearly an hour. If only one can dare to

M   [177]

believe that such happiness can be permitted.' The automatic
script ran as follows:
'June 18 Sunday evening 9.30 p.m. at Drishane.
Martin. Edith I am with you. Did you think of me when you
were playing this morning?
(The allusion here is to Edith playing the organ in the St
Barrahane church, where for many years she had been organist.)
Edith. Can I ever write alone? (The questions were put by word
of mouth, the answers came in the automatic script.)
Martin. Yes, some day. Jem can help you now.
Edith asks whether Martin was aware of the drawing she made
of her while it was being done.
Martin. Yes, very wonderful, but a melancholy remembrance.
My dear, did it comfort you at all? You have been so brave.
Edith said she would give anything to be convinced that she
was really speaking to Martin.
Martin. You will gain conviction.
Edith. Are you permitted to tell me how you are occupied?
Martin. Not yet.
Edith. Are you happy?
Martin. Yes. I am very often with you.
Edith. Are you ever lonely?
Martin. Sometimes.
The questions go on in this manner. Martin is asked whether
she has seen Edith's mother, but replies 'not yet'. She has
found the dog Candy, however, and is looking after her. And
writes: 'Edith, if only we were together.'
Edith. Do you know when I shall be with you?
Martin. No.
She says she travels to all sorts of places on earth. When
Edith was in London at Kneller Hall with Cameron, she was
there and adds 'Can you feel me near you now?'
Edith. When shall I try and write again?
Martin. When you feel impelled, my dear.
Edith. Shall I go on trying to write alone?
Martin. Not just yet.

Edith was now quite convinced that she was talking to Martin and was profoundly moved.

The next seance was two days later, 20 June. The transcription of what occurred is given thus:

Martin. My dear, I am feeling so happy today. You are nearer. I wonder why that is. (I said that possibly I was beginning to realize better that it was she.)

Martin. I know you must be convinced.

Edith. How did you know that you could communicate with us. We were trying to find out about Colonel Isherwood.

Martin. I had so often watched and I knew that sooner or later Jem would help. Of course, Edith, I wished to speak to you. In fact I have spoken, but you cannot hear my voice.

Edith. Shall I ever hear it?

Martin. I cannot say. I suppose you might develop what is called clair audience.

Edith asked again if she was happy and the automatic writing gave the answer: 'I am happy, but sometimes so sorry that I have no more material power of consolation. You must not think of giving up this one little means of communication between us.'

Edith, after questions on the best methods to adopt, asks: 'Must I speak my thoughts aloud?'

Martin. I both hear and feel, but I fancy the thoughts must be transmitted through Jem's mind.

Edith. Can I never transmit my thoughts unaided?

Martin. I do not know quite so definitely yet, but some day I shall.

Edith. When Jem is away, shall I be cut off from you?

Martin. Not entirely. Try Hildegarde.

Edith. Are you lonely?

Martin. Yes, I miss you inexpressibly.

Edith. I had hoped that the condition would be happier for you than for me.

Martin. It is. We are nearer to the realization of all our hopes.

Edith. Do you now feel that you are justified in the religious beliefs you held here.

Martin. I do indeed. I am very sure now.

After a few more questions to which the answers were dis-jointed and vaguer than before, Edith made Jem stop her ears and said aloud: 'Can you hear me speaking to you now?'

Martin. Yes—nearly over the boundary.

Edith now tried to get some definite information from Martin about her life in the place where she seemed to be, whether it resembled her life on earth, whether she wrote, read, slept, etc, whether those of her family who had died, such as her father and mother, were with her. But no clear information on these subjects was transmitted and the pencil in Jem's hand began to run backwards. Afraid that she had put inadmissible questions, Edith expressed regret, but was informed: 'It is not that, but the power is running out.'

Edith. Will it be best to stop?

Martin. Yes, I think it will be best. Goodnight. Sleep well.

On 21 June, 1916, Edith gives one more full transcription of an automatic writing session with Martin. She had been made happy by the news that Candy, the best loved of all her little fox terriers, was with Martin, and at the start of the present seance asked: 'Do you and Candy understand each other better than you did here?' This was a question to which Martin could give no better answer than: 'Yes, I think certainly.'

Edith. Have you met other of our dogs?

Martin. Several.

Edith. How did you find Candy?

Martin. It just happened.

Edith. Did she know you?

Martin. At once.

Edith then proceeds to ask questions about the other deceased dogs and is assured that Martin is looking after them all. Martin then volunteers the information that she has met Edith's mother, who is now a young woman again and very interested in the news Martin can tell her of her daughter. Her husband is with

her, the quiet old Colonel, Edith's papa. Martin refers vaguely
to the tasks which have been allotted to her, but when pressed
to state who is instructing her in her new duties, replies that she
is not permitted to be more specific.

There is, however, one point on which she is emphatic. Edith
must not give up her writing. She has not written a line for
over a year. No doubt she has hardly been in the mood for the
humourous vein for which their stories in the past have been
admired. But she should not give up. Edith replied that she
could not write without her.

Martin. I cannot help thinking that I may be allowed to help.
Edith. I shouldn't know which were my own thoughts and
which yours.
Martin. That would not matter.
Edith. I don't feel any desire to write.
Martin. Not now, but perhaps you may.
Edith. I don't feel like being amusing.
Martin. Yes, I know that, my dear, only too well.
Edith. Shall I try and collect your writings and add an account
of you?
Martin replied that she would like that, but warns her to tell
nobody at present that they are collaborating. Not even Ethel.
'I do not believe that they would understand.'
Edith. But I can't write without Jem.
Martin. I may be able to influence you later in another way. On
Edith pressing her to be more explicit, the pencil in Jem's hand
'paused and wandered vaguely for some time'. The seance ends.

Though this is the last full account of a seance with Martin,
the papers show that from this date Edith continued to consult,
as she now firmly believed, her former collaborator and considered that the fifteen books which she subsequently wrote
between 1915 and her death in 1949 were their joint work. As
no full account of such collaboratory seances is extant it is not
possible to be clear how such a collaboration could have
operated. It is true that at times Edith seems to have been able
to get the automatic pencil moving without the assistance of

Jem Barlow or any other medium, but how the question and answer went in so difficult and technical a matter as writing a book is hard to conceive. Nevertheless, Edith was satisfied that such a collaboration was taking place.

How the seances went on during the rest of 1916 may be gathered from short references to them in the diary. '23 July. Jem and I do writing with ever increasing and welcome conviction.' '29 July. Jem leaves. Much missed. I try every evening to write (with Martin) but so far have failed to write or even scribble.' On 24 September Jem Barlow returns. 'Jem had tea with me and we wrote a little but very interestingly.' By mid-October Jem has left again and alone Edith 'can do no good with writing' to Martin. 27 October 'My single-handed writing progresses.' 4 November 'I write a little bit to Martin every evening.'

Edith's note on 26 November tells us her reaction after reading Sir Oliver Lodge's *Raymond* which had just come out. She bought it at once and read it eagerly. Lodge, one of the well known scientists of the day, describes at length how his much loved son, Raymond, killed in France, spoke to him at length in a series of seances. Edith's comment is: 'The book probably marks the beginning of a new epoch in spiritualism.' She was enormously cheered and reassured by it. Lodge was doing precisely what she, with far less resources, far less knowledge, was striving to do. If he had contrived to speak so familiarly with his dead son, could she not hope to achieve as much with the dead Martin? On 31 December her diary has: 'Wrote alone (i.e. without Jem Barlow). On the last day of this miserable year, 1916, I can at least record my thankfulness for this wonderful privilege.'

Here one may pause. In plain language what had happened? However one grades Martin's or Edith's contribution to the literary fame which they enjoyed by 1915, the death of one of them was a potential disaster. Could the survivor carry on? There was only half as much talent available. As revealed by her diary Edith at first regarded Martin's death as fatal. In her view

Martin was the greater. What could she do without her? But the seances raised her hopes. Martin would help her. It would still be possible for the two to write together. So Edith comforted herself. She would be able to continue her literary career. And she would also be able to continue an emotional intimacy, the total loss of which had caused her such anguish. The fact of death could be circumvented. Things would not be quite as they were before, but nearly so. In some ways Martin would be a more puissant collaborator than when on earth.

As time went on Martin was to grow into a being resembling a guardian spirit. She would be consulted on all matters, not only on questions of composition, but on the problems of the day, on coming events, dangers, war, politics, on what to do in certain contingencies, on medicine and about the dogs. The whole family would be grouped round her, made to look to her in life and in death trust themselves to her care. For the next thirty-three years, until Edith's death in 1949, such was to be the pattern.

By the time 1916 had passed into 1917, Edith had begun to write her *Irish Memories*, the book which Martin in one of the seances had encouraged her to try and write. It was published in November 1917 and was favourably reviewed in *The Times* on the 23rd of that month. The frontispiece is a photograph of Martin and though some chapters are devoted to Edith's youth before they met in 1886 and to certain members of both families, the central theme is Martin. There are passages where Edith's admiration for her is given full rein. 'Intellectual refinement was hers, a mental fastidiousness; personal refinement in her dress, physical refinement in the silken softness of her hair, the slender fineness of her hands and feet, the flower-bloom of her skin; and over and above all she had the refinement of sentiment, which when it is joined with a profound sensitiveness and power of emotion, has a beauty and perfectness scarcely to be expressed in words.' Here the bereaved Edith already depicts her beloved friend as a virginal saint. In the chapter headed 'When First She Came' she describes the idyllic summer when Martin first came to stay at Drishane. There were calm evenings when she, Martin, and members of the family used to row up the haven towards its mouth on the Atlantic. 'Nothing more enchanting than resting on one's oars in the heart of that dark mirror, with no sound but the sleepy chuckle of the herons in the tall trees on the hillside . . . or at the mouth, the boats rocking a little in the golden fields of moonlight, golden as sunlight, almost, in those August nights, when, as Martin said "Land and sea lay in rapt accord, and the breast of the brimming tide was laid to the breast of the cliff, with a low and broken voice of joy".' In these words Martin gave utterance to the intensity of their dawning love.

Irish Memories contains no account of the death of Martin. What has been given here comes from the diary whose contents hitherto have never been made public. Nor does the book reveal how Edith, frantic with grief, strove to communicate with the spirit of her dead love, who came back from the grave to comfort her and promise to help her write. There is not a word in it about the seances. Yet on the last page, where she writes of the kindness shown her, she professes particular gratitude in a matter of which she will not now speak. Here she is guardedly referring to the seances and Martin's messages. It would seem she was unsure how the general public would take the story, though spiritualism was in vogue. The book ends in a mood of melancholy. 'I will try no more. Withered leaves, blowing in through the open window before a September gale, are falling on the page. Our summers are ended. Vanity of vanities.' And she quotes the words of an old woman who has lost her husband: 'Death makes people lonesome, my dear.' Her nature demanded a woman to love. She loved Martin but Martin had become a celestial personage. To love a spirit, even though one spoke to her, was not enough. One was still lonely. Only a mortal could fill the void.

17

The meeting with Ethel Smyth

Irish Memories did very well. By 18 January 1918 there had been four reprints. Encouraged by its success Edith decided to try a novel next, to be called *Mount Music*, but felt very nervous about how she would manage it alone. She tried to make a habit of writing every morning from eleven to half past one, but was often interrupted by urgent demands to settle this or that household problem. Then in the evening she read over to Martin what she had written, and received from her through Jem Barlow suggestions, emendations and encouragements.

Among a number of letters from admirers of *Irish Memories* she received in July 1918 a letter of congratulations from Dr Ethel Smyth, whom she had never met but knew to be a musician of wide celebrity. The letter was enclosed in one from the Countess of Kenmare, who was a friend of both women. Nothing came of this at the moment. Not until the September of the following year, 1919, did they meet at Killarney House, the Kenmares' seat, as will be described in its place. The episode will be found somewhat strange.

In July 1919 Uncle Kendal died aged eighty-seven. He had been an invalid for some time on account of his heart. Colonel Kendal Coghill of the XIXth Hussars, whose name has frequently cropped up in this narrative, particularly in reference to spiritualism, was unlike most of the Coghill and Somerville men, who could, I suppose, without offence be called mild, retiring and gentlemanly figures. He on the contrary was a character, with a quick temper, a daring dashing Irish soldier, like the famous Gough of the Chinese and Indian wars, who when things looked black in a battle invariably ordered a charge, which he led in person, and won the day. The older Uncle Kendal grew the more popular he became with his nephews and nieces. In some ways he was, as described by Edith, a ludicrous figure, but his simplicity, his faithfulness, his genuine goodness and high spirits won all hearts. His tempers were violent while they lasted, but they never lasted more than a minute. His warmth was such that even people he had insulted loved him. Edith devotes a whole essay to him in her *Wheeltracks*, published in 1923. She describes his last days and death thus in her diary: '22 June 1919, Uncle Kendal had a stroke. Dr O'Meara has little hope of his recovery. 13 July, Uncle K had a bad heart attack but was full of talk when I went to see him. 14 July, Uncle K very much oppressed but wonderfully alert and interested as ever. 15 July, Uncle K breathing very bad and he was very weak, but was talking and uncomplaining as ever. 16 July, Uncle K died at 3 a.m. this morning. Egerton and Hildegarde were with him. He had a fit of very violent sneezing, and then his breath gradually and quietly ceased. The standard bearer of his generation had fallen.' Edith, matriarch though she was becoming, thought no end of him. As he was eighty-seven and had long since retired, his funeral on 18 July might have passed unnoticed by the military authorities; his rank was not high and his exploits in the Indian Mutiny, when he was a subaltern, were hardly remembered outside his immediate circle. But so striking was his character that Lord French,* then Lord Lieutenant in Ireland, sent a staff officer to represent him, a Guard of Honour to fire the salute over the grave and a trumpeter to sound the Last Post. Edith adds: 'Uncle K had left directions that I was to play in the church (1) Wrap me up in

---

* Lord French had been Adjutant to Colonel Kendal Coghill at the battle of Tel el Kebir in 1882 on which occasion Colonel Coghill was in command of the XIXth Hussars. They remained warm friends ever afterwards.

my old stable jacket, (2) The XIXth Hussars March, Men of Harlech, (3) The Dead March in Saul. Everyone came in spite of torrents of rain.'

But this is not the last we hear of Uncle Kendal. Later as a spirit he terrified marauders in the Troubles of 1922.

Besides Uncle Kendal Edith lost in 1919 another of her little fox terriers. Candy was already in Martin's keeping and now Sheila goes to her. 'Martin wrote to me and met her and comforted me.' Martin remained in constant attendance. When Desmond Somerville, Edith's nephew, was reported killed in France, she declared he was only wounded, which was shortly shown to be the case. She advised against the purchase of farm land from the Townshends; and when in June 1919 Edith went to London to negotiate, with Pinker's help, an advance from Longmans for *Mount Music*, which she had by now finished with Martin's help, Martin accompanied her. '6 June. At 11.30 Jem picked me up and we went to Miss Key, where was Mrs de Crespigny (a professional medium). We wrote with the alphabetical table. Martin came.' Another medium said that Martin who was present, might materialize and Edith see her. But that did not happen.

After the death of Uncle Kendal in July 1919 Edith went to stay in Dublin with Sir Horace Plunkett, who took her to call on George Russell (A.E.) at his office where he edited his weekly, the *Irish Statesman*. Edith was not as well acquainted with the Dublin literary set as had been Martin, and had never met A.E., mystic, poet and journalist, who, after Yeats, was its most striking personality. Edith, however, was not a woman who kowtowed to eminent men, or any men, and particularly Dublin men, and she describes A.E. the way she sometimes used to describe Uncle Kendal, as a slightly ridiculous yet lovable creature. 'He is very much the hairy fairy cum Pantomime ogre, but delightful to be talked to by (one does not talk oneself).'

Next month, September 1919, she had an invitation from Lady Kenmare to stay and meet Dr Ethel Smyth who was coming over from England. This had been fixed some time before. A letter from Ethel Smyth to Edith dated 12 July refers to a possible meeting in September at Killarney House. 'I really do want to know you so,' she wrote, 'as I believe no one gives me more pleasure than you and Martin Ross.' She is referring in particular to *Irish Memories*, which as the record of the love of two women for each other had for her a special appeal.

The first meeting took place, not in the Kenmares' house, but at Mallow junction. Edith had to change trains there and wait for the Killarney train. It so happened that Ethel Smyth, accompanied by Maurice Baring, Lady Kenmare's brother,* a brilliant London man of letters, was in the Killarney train when it came in, also heading for the Kenmares. 'I was accosted by Dr Ethel Smyth,' noted Edith in her diary of 16 September 1919. They arrived at Killarney House in time for lunch, after which Lady Kenmare took them motoring to see the lakes. 'After dinner, Dr Smyth sang and played enchantingly.' She was exactly the same age as Edith, sixty-one, and had written several operas and a quantity of orchestral and chamber music. Her personality was ebullient, she was well known in London society, had an international reputation and was very much a woman of the world, which Edith was not, despite her celebrity in London as a writer. The two took to each other at once.

Edith's first recorded opinion of Ethel Smyth is in her diary of four days later: 'Dr Smyth is a very interesting and affable companion, absolutely devoid of the side and swagger she might very lawfully indulge in.' She invited her to come and stay at Drishane after the Kenmare visit.

Back at Drishane on 22 September Edith wired for her new friend to come immediately. She arrived next afternoon and stayed a few days. When she saw Edith's paintings, she was so taken with them that she offered to try and arrange a London

* In a letter to Hildegarde of this date Edith gives her first impression of Maurice Baring, a little caustic as was usual with her. 'A huge pleasant being, an ugly likeness of Robert Martin, who talks as if his tongue was too big for his mouth.' His pet name was Mumble.

exhibition. This was an important offer, for though Edith had had a Paris training, had exhibited a few paintings in Cork and Dublin, she had made no attempt to win the wider reputation which only a show in London could give. Ethel Smyth's opinion was also sought on *Mount Music*, the first proofs of which had just come in. It was favourable. The visit was a great success, the weather perfect, excursions every day, music in the evening when Ethel sang and played her own compositions. Cameron and Jack (one of Edith's two youngest brothers), were in the house. Both were musical and much enjoyed Ethel Smyth's virtuosity at the piano. She was a woman nearly as versatile as Edith, being an excellent writer as well as a musician. Her book *Streaks of Life*, chiefly about her close friendship with the Empress Eugénie, came out shortly afterwards and was a best seller. It is lively reading even today.

There was thus much in common between the two women. On the practical side Ethel Smyth could be of great use. Besides introducing Edith as a painter in the London art world, getting her money, which she badly needed, from the sale of her paintings, and reputation in a new sphere, she could also introduce her into a much wider section of London society than she had enjoyed as yet, enlarge the circle of her admirers, and bring her more fully into the public eye. But it was not such practical considerations that counted with Edith. She was fascinated by her new friend, this brilliant woman of the world. She fell wholeheartedly in love with her, as Ethel Smyth did with her.

Edith poured into Ethel's ears the story of her love for Martin, their long collaboration, Martin's death and how she was now in constant communication with her spirit. She assured her that Martin, when told of the new happiness which so unexpectedly was hers, would join in their happiness, for her happiness was Edith's happiness, and she would receive Ethel Smyth into her heart.

Ethel Smyth left Drishane early on 11 October to stay with her brother who commanded at Fermoy. In a seance held the night of her departure, Edith received a message from Martin declaring her joy at Ethel's coming. The message was sent at once to Ethel at Fermoy. In her reply she begs Edith to thank her for the message and writes: 'Tell her that it is one of my greatest sorrows not to have known her, one of my great joys that I may hope to know her elsewhere. Tell her that I have loved you ever since *Irish Memories*. You have changed the present and the future for me.'

The tone of this letter reflects the emotional pitch of the moment.

But the emotion experienced by the two women was not quite identical. Ethel Smyth had had in the past several affairs with women, in which mutual devotion included a conscious element of sex; that element was latent in her love for Edith. Edith's nature, however, was such that she was unconscious of any element of sex in her devotion. Ethel Smyth assumed that Edith's passion for her was not totally devoid of sexuality, while Edith assumed that Ethel Smyth knew that there was no trace of sexuality in it. This misunderstanding had its course and its resolution, as will be traced later on. The phenomenon of the utter devotion of one person for another is so mysterious and subtle, that, in fact, the intellect cannot exactly define its variations and decide what belongs to consciousness and what is hidden in the subconscious. It is not possible to be sure whether the rejection of what may be prompted by the subconscious is a rightful inhibition or a limitation. As will appear, Ethel Smyth felt that the inhibitions, which Edith held to be right, were in fact limitations.

To proceed, however, with the narrative. Ethel Smyth, who had been in and out of Drishane since 25 September, left for England on 27 October 1919. The diary for 28 October has: 'Nice letter from Ethel Smyth. Wrote to her, Martin helping.' From this on there are entries which show how very frequent was the exchange of letters. Edith's letters covering the first phase of the romance are not extant; they survive only from January 1921. But Ethel Smyth's survive and in one dated 29 October 1919, two days after her arrival in London, she describes to Edith the efforts she is making to arrange an exhibition for her. She first took the canvases which she had brought over to the Goupil Gallery, a leading art gallery of the period. As its director made no immediate offer, she carted them round to the Grosvenor and the Leicester Galleries, not an agreeable task, which only a very good-natured person would undertake for another, as dealers are hardly polite to such suppliants. In the end, the best offer she could get was from the Goupil. They said that as Miss Somerville had never exhibited in London and was totally unknown as a painter, they could not incur the risk of an exhibition without an advance of £100 to cover preliminary expenses, such as catalogues and advertising. As Ethel Smyth knew well that Edith did not possess £100, she offered to pay it for her on her undertaking to repay the sum out of profits. 'You will not make a fool of yourself by exhibiting,' she wrote. Everyone outside the dealers had frankly admired what paintings she had shown them. There might be a loss, of course; an exhibition was always a gamble. But there was a good chance she might make some money, and anyhow, if she wanted to win London recognition, it was the only way to start. So the exhibition was fixed at the Goupil for 7 January 1920.

This businesslike communication was followed two days later by a letter which is a reply to a loving letter from Edith. 'Your letter has made me very happy. To believe that anything I am or can be lessens in any degree your loneliness makes me wonder if it is a dream, but best of all that your cousin (Martin) is glad of me in your life. I will try to be the sort of friend she wanted for you and not lose myself merely in the unutterable joy of having found you. Edith, don't forget me. Leaving you was so hard to me. I am glad now to go to bed with my letter— with my letter.' This was followed by another letter containing this sentence: 'In 1918 I had long been as lonely in a way as you.' She may here be referring to the death of Henry Brewster, her lover. Though Edith replies daily to Ethel Smyth's letters, she only notes their receipt in her diary and makes no comment on their emotional contents. Her 4 own letters were equally warm, judging by Ethel's answers.

On 1 December Edith crossed over to London and confirmed the arrangements made at the Goupil Gallery. On 6 December she went to stay the weekend at Ethel Smyth's house, Coign, near Woking. They had already discussed the possibility of a trip together to Sicily at the close of the exhibition. Ethel Smyth says she wished she could take Jem Barlow's place in the conversations with Martin when abroad. But as she has no psychic powers, she fears that Edith will be cut off from her dead love during the whole of a trip due to last three months. Edith, however, does not think this ground for cancelling the tour. She hurried back to Drishane for Christmas, returning to London in time for the exhibition on 7 January 1920.

During her absence Ethel Smyth wrote to her nearly every day a long letter. In one she says: 'Edith, I think it would break my heart if you don't let me privately pay for your ticket to Sicily.' Her heart is 'passionately set' on the trip. 'Let me spend my money on the greatest and only true joy life has to offer me.' Edith is 'unutterably dear' to her.

The private view of the exhibition was a social event, thanks to Ethel Smyth's efforts to interest her large circle of friends. Edith was introduced as the famous Irish writer, whose new book, *Mount Music*, was just out. The occasion gave Edith her first experience of what it was like to be lionized. Dublin had never lionized her, London now did. During the fortnight her pictures were on view and many sold, she lunched and dined out every day with people in society. But though she certainly enjoyed the experience, which enlarged her outlook and got her away from the tribal atmosphere of Castle Townshend for a while, she kept her head and, despite flattery and promises, found no inclination to leave her retreat in the County Cork and move to London. There are, indeed, signs in her letters that she found the round of entertainments rather exhausting and, at times, vapid. After all it was her knowledge of the Irish background, her ability to express it and her native humour which had made her famous. London had nothing to give her but a tonic for the moment.

The departure for Sicily was fixed for 10 February 1920; Edith however had first to run over to Drishane for a week or so. While there she received and answered promptly long letters from Ethel Smyth, which reflect the increasing warmth of their relationship. Such phrases as: 'Your letter moved me so that I could hardly go on reading. You know what you gave me in saying certain things' and 'I am utterly in the hands of some-one I love, as I love you' hint at something more than Edith ever consciously contemplated.

Back in London a few days before 10 February, Edith writes to Hildegarde: 'Much as I enjoy the thought of Sicily, I should love to come straight home.' Was this a momentary revulsion at the thought of a tête-à-tête trip with Ethel Smyth, or was it that she found it tactful to cool the thing down, and avoid giving the impression of deserting her family and rushing off with a new-found friend? One cannot be certain. The letter, however, contains the suggestion that Hildegarde and Egerton might well join in the tour. When Ethel Smyth learned that Edith thought a party of four would be more enjoyable, she was very astonished. How could Edith want such an intrusion on their intimacy? However, it fell through; anyway the two Coghills had not the money.

The tour is described in Edith's diary, in her letters to Hildegarde, and more at length in her essay in *Happy Days*, a book published in 1946 when she was eighty-eight and enjoyed recalling a delightful time. The three essentials for happiness were present, she wrote, spring, lovely scenery 'and chief in importance a thoroughly complete and well-found Loved One, endowed with a heart for any fate' and an ability to swear in the Sicilian dialect. The letters give glimpses not to be found in the essay, particulary about their stay with the Duke of Bronté at Randazzo near Taormina, a beautiful spot within sight of Etna. The Duke was a descendant of Nelson's sister, who took on the Bronté title conferred on the Admiral by the King of Naples, when her other brother became Earl Nelson on Nelson's death. 'The little duke' Edith writes to Hildegarde on 29 February 1920 'is quite a pet, like a little band-box duke on the stage. He and his old sister in a gorgeous chestnut wig and pearls as big as eggs pay me a formal visit each morning.' He introduced her to all the local notabilities. She painted industriously in his garden. That was all very well, but she feels too cut off from Drishane and the animals. 'I am longing to see my puppy.' On 20 March she has another attack of homesickness, brought on by Hildegarde sending her shamrock for St Patrick's Day. She wants to come home, but Ethel Smyth won't hear of it.

On 1 April she records in her diary that she suddenly got bad lumbago, due to painting too long in the evening dew. This turned out to be the beginning of a long and serious rheumatic illness. Besides writing to Hildegarde, she kept up her usual practice of letters to her brothers, and wrote also to Jem Barlow, telling her of her longing to get home and reopen the seances. She has attempted to write with Martin, but finds it very ineffective, though she is assured of Martin's presence in Sicily.

Towards the third week of April she was free enough of the lumbago to stay again with the Duke of Bronté. Her letter to Hildegarde, written on his own notepaper, with a coronet over the address, 'Bronté, Sicily', tells how he sent a carriage to the station to meet her and Ethel, 'a wonderful little light victoria drawn by two mules'. Beside the coachman was a guard in uniform, armed to the teeth, for the locality was infested with bandits. The feudal atmosphere appealed to her.

Edith was back at Drishane by the middle of May, as was Ethel Smyth at Coign, who immediately wrote how dreadful it was to be without Edith, 'My whole mind harks back to what I have had and what I have not today nor will have tomorrow.' Every other day she posted a long letter, often with as many as 2,000 words. They contain such innuendos as; 'It is late and I seem to hear you, well, not snoring, but let us say breathing deep. And I shall be unable to read even—thinking——and saying a name—again and again.' She begs Edith to come over and stay at Coign and offers to pay her ticket.

On 26 June she wrote a letter which contains passages bearing on the intimacies of their relationship, and makes it clear beyond question that Edith remained governed by her inhibitions, no matter how much she loved, and was loved by, another woman, and that Ethel Smyth had to accept this. The letter is the only one of its kind in the correspondence. It amounts to a protest, almost a rebuke. Yet Ethel Smyth feels there is no remedy. She must accept Edith as she is, or in spite of what she is. The case was the more intricate in that Ethel Smyth was bisexual. Among other love affairs, she had spoken to Edith about Brewster, her dead lover, terming it her profoundest experience.

'Your instincts and education make you fastidious and . . . rather virginal. Your charm is to be thus. But don't you see that I am not all this—your law is not my law. That I can do and risk things that you could not—because in your case the inner sanction is lacking. I don't mind your feeling as you do —you and V.M. (Martin). It goes with your type. It is yourselves. I should *not* say certain things before you that I could take a shot before' and she cites friends, including Baring and Storrs and even Lady Ponsonby ('the greatest lady I have ever known'). 'Why make you uncomfortable? I have others I can talk this foreign language to. I have more experience of life stored in my little finger than you in your whole body, I mean of a certain kind of experience. I have a different stride to you. It does not follow that I run about Hook Heath with no clothes, no. To do that I should have to be very innocent or very thick skinned, and I am neither. I want you to understand all this, Edith, my dearest. You know I can put my shoulder to other wheels. Why, why should you imagine that I have *not* done so. I do feel—miserably sometimes—she *is* fond of me, but she does not really see me. What can I do to make you? I shall be agonizing lest I have hurt your feelings. If so trust me—my loved one—and don't be hurt.'

Edith's reply to this letter is not extant, but one can deduce it from a further letter of Ethel's. It appears that Edith excused herself and took the blame. Ethel Smyth promises not to offend against her delicacy again. She declares Edith was never worse than a bit 'governessy'. It is noteworthy that Edith's diary contains no reference to this letter of Ethel Smyth's nor her reply to it.

A further letter of Ethel Smyth's dated 10 July 1920 closes the subject. She declares she is very glad that Edith feels the way she does. 'Never would I have called you a prude or—good heavens—wished to pull you round to my point of view. It all came about because you were so often—or anyway sometimes— a little shocked at me.' Ethel Smyth, however, feels that she is in the right. Edith has not her wide experience of the world. If she had she 'would feel some of the things that I do or at least allow that they may be so'. And, she goes on, 'tell Martin she mustn't like me less because I think as I do. You know you don't, so she mustn't, as I couldn't at all bear that.'

Ethel Smyth had from the first accepted without question all that Edith told her of Martin. As she was in no doubt that Edith was in almost daily communication with Martin, and was guided by her advice, her desire to stand well with her was natural.

After this exchange of views, the two women held each other in no less affectionate regard than before. They were very fast friends and were good to each other. Both suffered misfortunes at this time. Ethel Smyth, who for some months had been worried about her ears, so vital an organ for a musician, found that she was going deaf and went over to Paris to consult a specialist. Writing from there she tells Edith she has little hope that he will restore her hearing. 'Pray for me. Not that the thing may not be . . . only that I may have courage. My greatest comfort and help is the thought of you.' Edith consults Martin, who, however, can promise nothing. For her part Edith seems in tolerable health. The alarming attack of lumbago had passed off. Her diary records the ordinary round of happenings at Drishane, the doings of those of her brothers

in residence and the state of the animals. She was rash enough
to do some riding. It was not the hunting season, but she could
not resist the temptation to try out the horses over jumps.
Suddenly she was struck down by sciatica and had to go to
bed.

As soon as Ethel Smyth had news of this, she left Paris and
hurried over to Drishane. There she stayed two months, nursing
Edith, in whose diary we find: 'Ethel Smyth is a great solace.'
As is often the case with rheumatism, the nights were the worst
time. 'The minutes pass and pass and I swallow bottle after
bottle of O'Meara's pain killer, and wake every two or three
hours during the long long night and make tea or boil milk and
try to read.' Ethel Smyth did all she could to amuse her. Her
reading was far wider than Edith's and she tried to introduce
her to books by the best English and foreign writers. During
the visit she finished the volume of her memoirs called *Streaks
of Life*, which contains a flattering essay on Edith's *Mount
Music*.

Though Edith highly valued Ethel Smyth's opinion in
literary matters she by no means always agreed with her. They
had quite a sharp difference of opinion over Anatole France.
Edith could not see anything in him. Ethel found it very curious
that a woman of Edith's mental equipment could be so limited.
She had small liking for what she didn't know. Novelties
repelled her. This idiosyncrasy irritated Ethel Smyth at first
but she got to like it because it was 'so Edith'.

Edith was well enough to continue the seances with Martin
through Jem Barlow. Martin informed her that Uncle Kendal,
who since his death had joined the family circle round her, had
announced his intention to see if he could cure Edith. 'Whatever
he did I had an awful night of torture from my brutal leg,'
wrote Edith to Hildegarde. 'I wrote with Jem next day and
Uncle Kendal himself wrote and said he was so sorry, but he
thought it was all his own fault. Then Martin said that Mother
refused to let him try again—for which I am thankful. Jem
said that while he was writing her arm had neuritis in it. He

is far too strong and does not know how to control his magnetism.'

As by the end of September Edith was no better, she was advised to try the baths at Dax, where she remained for the month of October 1920. Cameron went with her. Still suffering much pain, she returned to London, and stayed at Coign with Ethel Smyth, who pushed her about in a bath chair. She wrote Hildegarde an amusing account of how she attended a concert at the Grafton Galleries, arranged by the Music Club, where various compositions of Ethel Smyth's were played before a large and fashionable audience. On entering she saw Clara Butt standing in front of her. 'She is vast and white and soft as a snow mountain. Six feet tall and weighing over twenty stone, she looks as if she came from another planet.' Her face was childish. The honorary secretary of the club, who 'looked like a passée houri who had fed exclusively on Turkish delight' now led Edith to an armchair in the front row, to which she hobbled on her stick. The concert was opened by a speech delivered by the President of the society, a dwarf 'with a face like a squashed toad, someone having trodden on his head,' who called Ethel Smyth 'our greatest woman composer'. Ethel Smyth, dressed in her Doctor's robes and looking very handsome, replied in an amusing way and the concert began. Of a flute soloist who followed later in the programme Edith's description is: 'The little flautist stood looking down his long nose smiling, like a little cur greyhound waiting to be patted.' The letter ends with Edith declaring: 'I was dog lame by the time I got out to the taxi, but it was well worth it.' She believed that Martin went with her to the concert. A few days later a friend, called Miss Garstin, a medium, called: 'While she was talking to me she gave a start and said "I saw her again! The same whom I saw with you before. She was smiling, very brown hair and an oval face." I had asked Martin to come if she could.' On Armistice Day 1918 Miss Garstin 'had a very wonderful vision, while in St Mary Abbot's Church, of soldiers, Lord Roberts and Kitchener among them. The day I came up from Coign I made my taxi go up Whitehall and saw the cenotaph and the astonishing embankment of flowers all round it. The long train of mourners was still creeping past it, with the traffic roaring on both sides of them.' When she remembered that all her brothers served in the war and her four nephews, including Paddy and Nevill, her favourites, and came through it safely, she wept with emotion and thankfulness.

Edith got back home at the end of December 1920, after an absence of three months. She notes that she was now able to walk from Drishane to the Red House in the village, about a third of a mile, 'the longest effort since this decay started'.

In spite of her long and painful illness Edith had managed to produce another book. This was *Stray-aways*, published in the course of 1920 and consisting of twenty-four essays illustrated by thirty-four of her drawings. All the essays had been published before in various periodicals. Fourteen of them were written by Martin and ten by Edith, as specified in the table of contents. One of the objects of the book was to show Martin writing alone, and so making it possible to compare her style with that of the books written in collaboration, and also with Edith's own style in the ten accompanying essays. The characteristics of Martin's style have already been mentioned. The fourteen essays in *Stray-aways* confirm what has been said. Edith drew particular attention to Martin's essay 'At the River's Edge', and declares it a piece of prose worthy of any anthology.* Edith's admiration for Martin was unlimited. As more than half of *Stray-aways* was written by Martin, the attribution on the title page 'by E. Œ. Somerville and Martin Ross' was not questionable, but the attribution of the book which preceded it, *Mount Music*, written by Edith after Martin's death but attributed to both, raised comment in the press and made Longmans, the publishers, fear ridicule if this practice were continued. The Hudson Bibliography† contains Edith's protest in the form of a note: 'I cannot help feeling that I am the person

---

* See *A Bibliography* by Elizabeth Hudson (1942), page 39.
† Page 41.

best qualified to give an opinion whether or not it was a work of collaboration.' Longmans, however, remained dissatisfied and her next book, the novel *An Enthusiast* (1921), appeared under Edith's name alone. On her protesting to them, however, at the omission of Martin's name, they gave way, inserted it on reprinting, and in all subsequent books the double attribution was allowed.

18

The Troubles

The Edith-Martin papers, voluminous and detailed though they
are, contain few references to the political background. This is
the more noticeable since the revolution, which ended the
Union government and culminated in an Irish republic, was a
contemporary event of the greatest importance. The Home Rule
movement had made itself felt long before the death of Martin
in 1915, though it was after her death, with the Easter rising of
1916, that events began to move to their climax. Briefly put,
the progression was this way. The Easter rising of 1916 was
not seen as an aspect of the constitutional demand for home rule
which had been developing since the start of the eighteen-
seventies, when, as mentioned early in this book, it had dis-
illusioned Martin's father, James Martin of Ross. The law
classified it as rebellion against the Crown, and those who took
part in it were hanged as traitors, a piece of legal barbarity
which shocked many people. We have seen how Edith's tender
heart moved her to petition for clemency, though her upbring-
ing tended the other way.

Two years later, in 1918, an election to the Unionist
parliament at Westminster was held and all seats in Ireland
were won by candidates who supported the aim of the 1916
rising, the establishment of an Irish republic. The elected
members, however, refused to sit at Westminster and set
up a parliament of their own in Dublin, called the Dail,

and sought to take over the administration of the country.

This move was met by an attempt by the English government to suppress the Dail and all that it stood for. In 1920, the year when Edith was mostly away from Ireland, savage affrays began between the Crown's forces and those of the Republicans. A body of troops employed by the Crown became known as the Black and Tans, and the atrocities which have been attributed to them seem in retrospect the prelude to an era of atrocities throughout Europe which have revealed the human mind to be far less stable and far more sinister than was formerly supposed. When Edith landed at Cork in December 1920 after her absence abroad, she was appalled by the look of the town after the Black and Tans had done with it. To quote Frank Pakenham's* book *Peace by Ordeal*: 'It may have been the quality of the men chosen, it may have been the nature of the task set them; whatever the cause, the Black and Tans and auxiliaries had done enough long before they left Ireland to dishonour the British government, to defile by association the name of the British fighting services, and in the words used by *The Times* "to make Englishmen bend their heads with shame". Whatever their origin, whatever the provocation, history will record that after a few months in Ireland a large proportion of these, the most active British forces, had ceased for the time to deserve or count as responsible human beings. Or that was how it seemed to those who saw them strutting down the streets of Cork, crazy with drink and nerves, lashing passers-by across the face with riding whips stolen from the shops.'

For the first half of 1921 the struggle between the Crown and the Republicans continued, reprisal being matched with counter-reprisal. In July 1921 a truce was arranged and con-versations opened in London culminating by December in a treaty by which Ireland was granted dominion status and called a Free State. This treaty, though upheld in the Dail, was re-pudiated by the extreme wing of the Republicans and for most of 1922 there raged a civil war between the Free Staters and

* Now the 7th Earl of Longford.

the Republicans under de Valera. The Free Staters put down
the disorder and peace was restored. Ten years later the Free
State began its constitutional development into what has
become the Republic of today.

How the disorders consequent upon these events affected life
at Castle Townshend is revealed in a series of letters from
Edith to Ethel Smyth. At this time Edith's brother Cameron,
retired from the army, lived in Drishane with her. Her sister,
Hildegarde, married to Sir Egerton Coghill, lived in the Coghill family mansion, Glen Barrahane. Her brothers Boyle and
Aylmer were resident in England with their wives, though the
former planned to come over and live in Uncle Kendal's house,
The Point (or Cosheen). The younger brothers, Jack and Hugh,
were still serving in the army and navy. By a coincidence Hugh
was appointed to the command of the naval forces in Cork and
so was close to his ancestral ground. Castle Townshend was a
very isolated spot. Its connection by road to Skibbereen, five
miles away, was its only link with the outer world except by
sea. The County Cork in general had suffered badly in the
disorders. To be safe from murder, arson and robbery at the
hands of the ruffianly armed men who roamed about, the
residents had to keep on good terms with both sides, an
extremely delicate task, for if a resident, under threats, gave up
arms, horses, provisions and the like to one side, he was in
grave danger from the other. A small body of coastguards on
the shore of the haven below The Point afforded some protection. The police could not protect the public any longer.

In a letter to Ethel Smyth dated 16 February 1921 Edith
writes: 'Sinn Fein (i.e. the Republicans) make all communications between Skibbereen and the outer world very difficult.
All bridges round the town have been broken. We are cut off.
The post has just come out by a man on a bike who scrambled
over a gulf in the road.' Edith adds that she is working on her
new novel, *An Enthusiast*: 'I am copying, rewriting and
sweating blood, going to bed beaten but encouraged by Martin.'
She carries on as best she can, but Skibbereen, which is their

shopping centre, is so difficult to get to and its shops are so de-
pleted of goods, that supplies of food and household necessities
are hard to obtain. There are no authorities to whom it is safe to
complain. She has to be very careful what she says in her letters
and how she behaves in the state of anarchy which prevails.

In a letter of 23 February she declares that the Black and
Tans (the Crown forces) are worse than the Republicans. 'They
are as despicable as ever in most places. Here and there one
hears less shame-inspiring accounts of them.' In Ethel Smyth's
replies she is inclined to defend the Black and Tans; she cannot
believe that the forces of the Crown could be guilty of such
cruelties as are alleged.

Edith tries to work at her novel as if nothing was happening.
'I think there are some good bits. There *must* be because I know
Martin is working with me. But I don't know how many I
mayn't have foozled or stymied or bunkered (if you understand
these terms).' She liked to tease Ethel, who in fact was a confirmed golfer, though Edith never played the game.

On 9 March she recounts how a party of Republicans came to
the house and ordered Mike, the groom, to give them a horse.
Mike said: 'And why must I do that?' One of them gently
touched his breast pocket where his revolver was. They were
sorry, he said, and disliked having to do it, but were ordered
to bring back a horse. One of Edith's best mares was chosen,
worth with the saddle and bridle over £80, and taken away.
Edith notified the police and was told that the Black and Tans
would do nothing to help recover the animal, and that they
were powerless themselves. They warned her that a visit from
Black and Tans, on the plea of investigating the charge, would
be worse than the robbery.

A letter of 17 April contains some items to be noted. The
Republicans are said to be opening the mail and if they find
anything contrary to their side they sometimes burn the house
and shoot the writer. They had burnt down Derry, the house
mentioned where the parents of G.B.S.'s wife lived. But, Edith
goes on: 'We have been assured that we will be unmolested. I

was told that I was a nice lady always, with many allusions made to the hounds and the sport.' The country people enjoyed the West Carbery hunts. It was a big amusement in a dull place.

Edith tells Ethel Smyth that farm boys were press-ganged into joining the Republican bands. 'The wretched boys are dragged out by force and then captured and shot' by the Crown forces. The coastguards were a genuine protection. 'They can whistle a destroyer by wireless at any hour of the day or night.' The British destroyers, belonging to the Cork command, were prepared to take off resident gentry who lost their nerve. But Edith's nerve held. She was resolved not to be driven from Castle Townshend by ruffians of either side. 'The Crown outrages are appalling' she has in a following letter. And 'some people say the Republicans get £500 for killing a policeman.'

The situation looked so threatening to English eyes in June 1921 that Ethel Smyth urged Edith to leave Ireland. To this Edith replied that she must stay it out. 'Dearest, I can't come over,' she wrote. She could not desert her post at Drishane and those dependent on her there.

When the truce was signed at the beginning of July 1921 it was an immense relief. 'Martin has positively foretold peace,' she told Ethel. The truce was followed by negotiations in London between the Dail and the British cabinet, which dragged on for the rest of 1921.

Throughout these difficult months, made more trying by recurrent attacks of sciatica, Edith showed no trace of fear or despondency. Indeed, her spirits are so high that she inserts amusing anecdotes in her letters, like the following to Ethel on 9 August 1921. 'I heard a preposterous story the other day. A very nervous man went to the barbers to have his hair cut. A large bull terrier came and sat beside his chair and regarded him fixedly. The man got more and more nervous and at last asked the barber what the brute wanted. "Well, sir," said the barber, "Ye see it was that we had a little accident here yesterday—there was an ear got cut off—and may be it is he is waiting for another." '

In the same letter she states how her sympathies lie in the
Irish situation. She calls herself 'half rebel and a Miss-Facing-
both-ways'. Her heart is with the Irish but her tradition aligns
her with the establishment.

By August 1921 the negotiations in London between the
Irish delegation and the British cabinet had reached the point
where Dominion status was offered. The debate continued. She
knew, however, that Dominion status would not satisfy the
extreme Republicans. 'The widows of the war (i.e. the Anglo-
Irish fighting) who are called the Black Women, shriek out at
any hint of concession. One sees their point, poor creatures.
Why wouldn't they be bitter, their husbands whom they considered to be prisoners-of-war, hung like murderers. Whatever
their methods were, those men died for their country just like
any other patriots.' Such sentiments show a great advance on
Edith's former attitude to Home Rule. But she thought
Dominion status a good offer, which should be accepted. Peace
must be restored. Anarchy was ruining her and everyone else.
But her sense of humour was not damped; in this same letter
she repeats what she calls 'a highly improper story heard at the
church synod at Waterford' and related to her by a cousin. 'An
old woman said: "Oh the times is terrible altogether! What with
the Black & Tans one side o'ye and the soljers th'other, ye
cannot tell the minute ye'd not be pushed into Maternity".' In
spite of the truce, there was little change for the better in
County Cork.

As Edith's bank account was overdrawn, the farm not paying,
and a fair price for horses and cows unobtainable, she now
wondered whether money could be made from a play written
round the R.M. stories. Martin warmly encouraged the idea.
A young man called Maurice Hastings, an Oxford under-
graduate friend of her nephew, Nevil Coghill,, was staying at
Castle Townshend during the long vacation and was asked to
invent a plot. After getting his draft she 'called for the basin'
as it was so sickeningly bad. During this vacation Nevil had a
narrow escape. He and Hastings had gone to an agricultural

show and fête at Skibbereen. Suddenly they found themselves surrounded by a gang of excited ruffians who covered them with revolvers and ordered them to follow. They were hustled round a corner. It seemed that the gang intended to execute them as a reprisal for something or other. They were stood up against a wall and the gangsters were in the act of taking aim when a man rushed up shouting that they had got the wrong people. The fellows lowered their pistols. Nevill was given a chance to establish his identity and he and Hastings were released. It seems to have been a very close thing.

This same month of October 1921 saw the sudden death of Hildegarde's husband, Sir Egerton Coghill, the artist, who died while on a visit to England and was succeeded in the title and ownership of Glen Barrahane by his son, Paddy, the present baronet. Paddy, then twenty-five, was in Constantinople with the army. It was considered too risky for him to come home on account of the Republican habit of forcibly conscripting young men. Egerton was very popular with high and low in Castle Townshend because his manner was so natural. In her letter of 27 October Edith writes to Ethel Smyth: 'A man spoke to me of him yesterday and said how he loved him. I said, "Well, Jack, I know he was very fond of you too." "Ah, indeed, Miss, there was no love lost between us." That is really much the best sense in which to take the phrase.'

Three weeks later during a seance conversation with Martin, Edith received a message from Egerton asking her to get Hildegarde to communicate with him. 'Hildegarde doesn't feel able to try,' records Edith. 'It wrings my heart to see her so thin and colourless. But I hope that one day she will try and will succeed. It brings the peace past understanding.' Egerton was buried in Twickenham, but in 1923 his body was exhumed, brought over to Ireland and buried in St Barrahane's churchyard. Hildegarde, still grieving very bitterly, was unable to face a second burial service, a second interment, and stayed indoors. But Edith managed everything, the service, the music, the flowers, for she always could be depended on to rise to an

occasion. Paddy, who by now had got away from Constantinople, won his aunt's admiration by 'his care and devotion to
his mother which are quite delightful to see'.

On 6 December 1921, Griffith, the leader of the Irish delegation, together with his colleagues, Michael Collins and Robert
Barton, accepted, under threat of immediate war if they did not,
the offered Dominion status for Ireland and signed the treaty
under which the Free State came into existence. On Griffith
reporting to Dublin, de Valera speaking for the Republicans
immediately repudiated the treaty. But on 7 January 1922 the
Dail declared the treaty better than another war with England
and endorsed its signature. But de Valera was implacable. He
was determined on a full republic and carried with him the more
extreme members of the republican party. The result was a civil
war, Griffith and Collins leading one side and de Valera the
other. This turn of affairs infuriated Edith. She wrote to Ethel
Smyth on 23 December 1921: 'Everyone in the country is set
on the acceptance of the treaty. It was like that unspeakable
cad de Valera to look so noble a horse in the mouth and
pick holes in its teeth.' She was so angry that she threatened to
put a notice in *The Times*: 'E. Œ. S. has entered an idiot
asylum.'

At this moment of crisis, the idea of a play on an Irish R.M.
theme again occupied her mind, as a distraction. If youthful
Hastings had made a hash of the plot, there was always George
Bernard Shaw. She drew up a fresh plot, wrote the dialogue.
Charlotte Shaw, asked to find out whether G.B.S. would
read the play and advise, replied that he would. 'He is au
fond and behind the side he presents a very kind fellow.' The
correspondence between Shaw and Edith is amusing, but as he
finally said the play was no good, it is unnecessary to pursue
the matter. She sums it up in the sentence: 'He damns the
play utterly on all counts. He may be wrong but I fear he is
more likely to be right.' Martin however wrote: 'Don't give
in.'

But in fact it was no time for play writing. The civil war was upon them. What happened in the County Cork is vividly depicted in Edith's letters to Ethel Smyth.

The second half of 1922 was a most alarming period. Michael Collins, the commander of the Free State troops, was killed in action. Griffith died. Cosgrave took over. Robberies, burnings, murders were of daily occurrence. Cosgrave at first was unable to maintain law and order. A Free State supply ship in Cork harbour was seized by the republicans and its cargo of arms taken. In Drishane with Edith were Cameron, Hildegarde and Nevill. Edith writes: 'We are almost on the point of despair. Last night they broke into my sister's house, Glen Barrahane. Nothing was stolen. They were looking for arms. It is impossible to fortify such houses against raids. There is no authority to safeguard them.' If it wasn't for Martin's humour, it would be hard to keep up. In the seances she'd be her natural laughing self. On one occasion to tease Edith, Martin pretended she had met Tennyson, they had fallen in love, she called him Alf and sat on his knee. In recounting this to Ethel Smyth Edith remarked: 'It is so delightful to know that she can chaff and be as light hearted as ever.' The seances were always reassuring. Martin was felt to be watching over them. There was never a whisper of doom from the beyond.

Edith was made happier, too, by getting a pair of puppies. She became exceedingly fond of them, particularly of the one called Taspy, commemorated twenty-five years later in *Maria and Some Other Dogs*. But in spite of Martin and the pups she was not oblivious of the dangers that surrounded her. Any night ruffians might come hammering on the hall door. Many of her old friends, she says, had fled the country. She felt alone, but was sustained by her love for Ethel Smyth. 'It is more than I could ever have hoped for.' And she adds: 'The pups are really becoming saintly—and *very* clean!' And assures Ethel: 'Personally I would prefer to be shot rather than leave the house,' when a general massacre of Protestants was rumoured. 'The British navy at Queenstown is standing by to take them off.' Some of Edith's letters are in French to avoid the danger of

o   [209]

what she says being seen by the Republicans, who seize post offices and open letters. Ethel Smyth spoke French perfectly but Edith's French, she feels, is poor in comparison and she speaks of it as her 'dog French'. Hildegarde, who was also in correspondence with Ethel Smyth, does the same, but calls her French 'cur dog French'. 'Her cur dog lingo is magnificent,' says Edith. 'Her allusion to an overdraft at the bank is masterly —sur couronne d'air.'

A letter of 1 July 1922 contains some depressing facts but she laughs them off. 'We are all broke, Irish farmers and Irish writers alike.' There is no sale for anything. No one will buy horses. £4 for a good farmhorse, and the highest price for a hunter is £30. On top of this Edith cannot get any more from her publishers. 'I don't know how any English readers even looks at the word Irish without being sick.' However, all is not lost. The pups are improving. 'You will be glad to hear they are growing in grace and are almost impeccable in one important affair.'

At this date Skibbereen was occupied by Republican troops; the Free Staters were besieged in the police barracks. One of Hugh Somerville's destroyers lay off-shore near Skibbereen to put Cameron* on land. He was on his way home from England, and could not get through otherwise, as no trains were running. The Republicans thought the destroyer had come to reinforce the Free Staters, though the British navy was forbidden to interfere between the Irish parties. As a fight seemed imminent, the local inhabitants took fright. 'They fled with their children and their poor little household things, heaping mattresses on donkey carts and wheelbarrows, flying they knew not where,' wrote Edith. Such were the sufferings of the innocent rustic population during the civil war. As for herself, she has been lucky so far, she declares. Only four of her horses have been taken by the Republicans. Indeed, on the whole it looks more

* The Republicans had threatened to kill Cameron and he had been advised to leave Castle Townshend for a while. He was away in England and abroad for two months, and now, 6 July 1922, was returning.

hopeful. Cosgrave's main offensive against the Republicans has been launched and is succceeding. 'I remain as tranquil as I can.' The good news about the pups continues. 'They now ask to be put out.'

A week later, 13 August, Edith reports that the Republicans have been forced to evacuate the Skibbereen area and take to the mountains, as Free State troops have landed at many points along the coast. Before leaving they did as much damage as possible. 'Castle Townshend has escaped by dint of special help and effort from the Other Side. Martin says there has been an unwearied cordon of spiritual protection around us, 'provided by my father, Egerton, Uncle Kendal and many others. There is no other reason why we have escaped so easily. In comparison with other places, *nothing* has happened to us, although we have had some horrible people here. As the posts are so extremely bad and infrequent I think I will ask Martin if she can go to see you and tell me how you are.'

But though the Free State troops were able to take over a large part of the County Cork, they were not able to restore order at once. The Republicans made raids from the mountains. Houses continued to be burnt. Supplies were short. The roads were still unsafe. Martin's protection remained essential. As their guardian saint, it seemed right that a special altar should be raised to her in St Barrahane church. This Edith saw to; she made an altar from a sideboard belonging to Glen Barrahane House and put it in the church. How the rector regarded this worship of St Martin is nowhere mentioned.

But as we know Edith had a very practical side. 'We have been making history in West Cork and have not finished yet,' she tells Ethel Smyth in September 1922. 'Skibbereen is now held by the Free Staters. Cameron and I are doing all we can to help them and act as go-between with the destroyer captains.' The Republicans make sudden swoops down from the mountains. 'They bring off their ambush and then bolt back to the hills. So it is not safe for us here.' Drishane might be their next objective. However, a destroyer lies most nights in the haven, and a way of signalling to it in case of need has been arranged. But though the destroyer captains, under orders from brother Hugh, were ready to land a force and rescue them if necessary, their great reliance was on the ancestral ghosts.

Yet sometimes they received wonderful succour from a terrestrial quarter. The story of Father Lamb is here much to the point. During July 1922 a small raiding party of Republicans had entered Castle Townshend and occupied the coastguard station. Seven of them remained and the rest withdrew. On 30 July twelve more arrived by motor. Their orders were to demolish the pier and wharves, as Free State troops were rumoured to be about to land there. To effect the demolition the Republicans forced local labour to help, standing guard over them with loaded rifles. It was at this point that a Roman Catholic priest, Father Lamb, intervened. His exploit is given in a letter written next day by Edith to Hildegarde. 'A good deal of the end of the pier had been destroyed and was being thrown into the water when a boat was seen, coming at full speed. In it was the little R.C. curate, Father Lamb. As soon as he was within shouting distance he began to denounce the destroyers. Before the boat was alongside he leaped ashore, dashed up the slip and sprang like a wild cat at the throat of the biggest of the armed guards. Father Lamb is a little fellow, aged about thirty, in height at most 5 ft 5 in; he looks less than ten stone but he is tremendously wiry and athletic. The man he attacked went down like a ninepin. He was a big lubberly boy of nineteen, and while Father Lamb tore at his rifle to get it from him, he lay on the ground, feebly protesting "No Father! No Father!" One of the guards rushed to the Castle grounds to summon their leader, Jim Z, another rushed to the coastguard-station to bring up the rest of the gang. Father Lamb, transfigured by passion, with a dead white face and his very big light blue eyes blazing, ordered the pressed labourers to throw down their tools and go home at once. Then he caught the second in command, a burly young fellow, by the throat and dashed his head against the wall and, in the narrow lane leading to the

street, he met Jim Z, the big captain (a huge young man) and
his men, and stormed abuse and denunciation of the wickedness
they were committing. Meanwhile the wretched workers,
thankful for release, hurried away up the hill and gathered in
a knot outside a public house. It was at this point that I arrived
with Jem at the Two Trees.* A crowd of village people were
standing there and in highest excitement they told us that "the
priest had stopped the work and was below on the quay talking
to Jim Z". In about three or four minutes we heard rifle shots
from the coastguard station, and the sound of running feet,
and then we saw about a dozen Republicans coming racing
abreast along the Mall, one of them firing his rifle in the air
every few yards. When they got to the corner and saw the
group of workers they began to yell "Go back to your work".
The group fled down the hill again, the Republicans howling
after them, running as fast as they could. I saw a little sickly
boy of fifteen or sixteen (who had come to me to demand my
pony and trap the night before, and hadn't got it) racing and
howling with them. They had got about halfway down the hill
when I saw a little bareheaded black figure dash round the
corner by the schoolhouse and charge up the hill into the teeth
of the oncoming crowd. The fleeing workers checked their
flight, separating, and leaving the priest face to face with the
Republican pursuers. He charged on, shouting, and to our
incredulous amazement the twelve armed men turned as one,
and bolted back up the hill. They fled into the public house,
and the little priest bolted in after them like a terrier after
rabbits. (I have since heard that he rushed upstairs and caught
two of them in Mrs H's bedroom and there and then smashed
their rifles.) In what seemed less than a minute we saw him
burst out of the house with a rifle in his hand. Big Jim Z had
come up by this time. Father Lamb swung his fist round and
with a jump caught him heavily over the side of the head. Jim Z
made no return. Then the priest broke through the encircling

* The two trees in the middle of the main street of Castle Townshend, where it
joins the Mall.

people into the middle of the road. He tore the cartridges out
of the magazine of the rifle and then catching it by the barrel
he whirled it over his head and with a few furious blows he
smashed the stock and lock on the road and bent the barrels.
No one dared to go near him. This ended the fighting.' Looting
and arson continued in Castle Townshend until 300 Free
State troops landed on 8 August. They were, however, insufficient to drive out the Republicans who had considerable
forces in the neighbourhood. The British destroyer in the Haven
could not be asked for aid.

On 22 August Edith and Cameron went to Skibbereen on
hearing that Michael Collins, the commander-in-chief of the
Free State forces, had arrived there. They had an interview
with him and found him sympathetic, but he had no troops to
spare. Later that very day he was killed in an ambush. His
death set back the restoration of law and order in the County
Cork. The Republicans had it their own way again for a while.
Their bands continued to roam about pillaging and burning.
Castle Townshend, however, was not entirely defenceless. The
Free Staters who had landed, though too few to cope fully with
the situation, were able to prevent the complete destruction of
the place. Drishane, Glen Barrahane, and the other houses of
the gentry were not burnt down. Nevertheless Edith and the
rest had a frightening time as her letters to Ethel Smyth will
now disclose.

On 13 September Edith wrote to Ethel Smyth: 'Everything
is so troublesome, humiliating and dangerous.' She was tired of
it all and wished she were in England. Nevertheless she will
not abandon Drishane. She was alone there now with Cameron.
Hildegarde had gone over to stay in Dorsetshire with her
brother Admiral Boyle Somerville and his wife. Glen Barrahane
had nobody in it and had been raided several times. There was
nothing left there worth stealing but the raiders amused themselves by breaking up furniture. They also forced an entry into
Seafield, where the Chavasses were in residence, and took
saddles, bridles and bicycles. 'Martin told us,' wrote Edith,

'that the affair was a triumph for the Guardians.* I asked why and she said that "personal injuries had been intended" but that the Guardians had succeeded in changing the intention of the blackguards. . . . I forget if I told you that we had found at Glen Barrahane a bag full of bottles of wine ready to be taken away,† yet left on the floor of the dining room. The raiders had been frightened out of the house and forgot the loot in their panic. I asked Uncle Kendal, one of the Guardians, how he had done it, and he wrote *"Footsteps!"* The last time he wrote he said: "The scoundrels; I must say I longed for good old muscle and flesh for once in a way!" '

Edith remained immensely busy and undaunted, writing *Wheel-tracks*, family reminiscences like *Irish Memories*, and painting. 'These are the means by which I preserve my reason in this distracted country. It seems to get daily more hopeless. In County Cork all is chaos and our only safeguard is the destroyer which, thank heaven, remains in the harbour and can be summoned to our rescue if needed.'

Uncle Kendal was very active when it came to fighting. After his exploit of frightening raiders by ghostly footsteps we find him credited on 29 September 1922 with laying a trap for them, which failed owing to Cameron's negligence. 'We had a visit from raiders last night,' Edith tells Ethel Smyth. Several men battered at the drawing-room window about 11 p.m. and shouted they had come to search the house for arms. Cameron, who was woken by the noise, went downstairs, opened a shutter and told them there were no arms in the house. He heard a man say 'Fire a shot' but no shot was fired and they seemed to go away. He hastened upstairs to Edith's room and reported. It was decided to signal the destroyer, as it was hard to say what the raiders would do next. On its captain seeing a red light in Drishane, the agreed danger signal, he turned a searchlight on the house and 'we knew that our signal had

* The Guardians were the ghosts of deceased members of the Somerville and Coghill families, organized into a squad by Uncle Kendal.
† Sir Patrick Coghill writes: 'Alas! they got the wine later. When I got home the cellar was empty.'

been seen'. Meanwhile Edith tried to telephone the Chavasses at Seafield that raiders were about. No answer was received to the call. When the sailors arrived at Drishane they searched the stable yard and garden for trace of the raiders and found nothing. Edith then told Cameron to ask the lieutenant in charge to go to the Chavasses' house, in case the raiders had gone on there. Cameron, however, forgot to do this and the sailors returned direct to the destroyer. At that very moment Major and Mrs Chavasse 'were being held up by a man with a rifle. If only the sailors had gone straight there they would have bagged the lot'. As it was they took all Chavasse's clothes and his wife's jewellery. 'It is heartbreaking. My dear, how do you think I can leave here now? I couldn't desert Cameron. Even if there were no anxiety or danger it would be shabby to bolt.' The matter was reported to Martin and she wrote: 'Uncle Kendal has done nothing but rage over Cameron's stupidity in not sending the sailors to Seafield.' He had arranged to have the raiders trapped that way, he said, and they would have been if Cameron had not been so negligent.

'We are living hard and horribly here,' Edith writes on 11 October. Besides all the rest, Cameron had to be kept up to the mark. 'I have shifted my bed to a room opposite Cameron's, so as to wake him (he sleeps like a log) if I hear the thieves on the warpath.' Before this move, one night she had heard sounds below and 'crept up the passage in the dark, listened at Cameron's door. Silence.' She entered, called his name, but no answer; groped to the bed, found it empty, but warm. She thought they had got him and armed with a hunting crop started downstairs to rescue him. At this date she was sixty-four and very rheumatic, but brave as a lion. How many raiders there were, she had no idea, but she would face them with her hunting crop. The only dogs at the moment were the two pups, in her bedroom, fast asleep in their baskets, though some notion had penetrated their dreams for they made a bubbling sound as she left the room.

It turned out, however, there was no raid. Sailors had been

sent to see if all was well, and Cameron, on being woken by their knocking, went downstairs to speak to them.

Such alarms were of frequent occurrence. A week later a warning was received that a raid on Drishane to obtain warm clothes and blankets was imminent. Edith immediately took action. The destroyer captain was asked to send a lifeboat ashore and take off their stock of blankets. With the help of one of her servants she tied up six enormous bundles, got them on to the donkey cart and so down to the Haven and into the lifeboat. No raid occurred. 'We have got to stick it out,' she writes to Ethel. 'Dearest, I really am worrying along all right and am quite reasonably content. And the puppies are *quite good* now.' The last sentence in the letter is much in character—'There are some things too serious for anything but joking.'

One of her reasons for contentment was that she was coming round to the view that Cosgrave, who had succeeded Griffith as head of the Free State, could achieve a stable government and refurbish the administration. She had endured the Troubles in one of the most troubled counties of Ireland. She had experience of what it was like to live without the protection of the law, to listen for the knock on the hall door which might mean a bullet or a robbery without chance of redress. She couldn't help comparing herself with the Dublin literary set, who, living in perfect safety, laid down the law. 'There is too much written about Ireland as a nation by the Dublin literary set when anarchy is prevailing in the country places. I am feeling rather sick of their brag and bunkum.'

By 11 November 1922 her confidence in Cosgrave further increased. Hildegarde, who for several months had been staying in England with her brother Boyle, was encouraged to return to Drishane. The Free Staters were getting the upper hand at last, the civil war was perhaps nearly over.

Her hopes were justified by events. In December 1922 a *modus vivendi* was arranged between Free Staters and Republicans. There was to be no more official fighting, though at Castle Townshend the destroyer stayed, for brigand bands had yet to be rounded up. It was now possible to be openly on friendly terms with the destroyer crews. 'The officers play croquet at Drishane nearly every day.' One of the captains even bought two of her pictures for £30.

19

Attempt to materialize the spirit of Martin

On her return to Drishane Hildegarde was more inclined than
before to seek to communicate with Egerton through Jem.
Nevertheless, she remained reticent about it, and Edith asks
Ethel Smyth to keep off the subject when writing to her. 'I can
see what a wonderful help it has been to her and, Martin tells
me, what a joy to Egerton.' The memory of her own sorrow
breaks in. 'Seven years on 21 December since Martin went. She
won't let me talk of it to her now, but thinking is inescapable.
You will understand.' And a week later she writes: 'I suppose
there are plenty who would say I was either a fool or insane,
but I think you will understand that I am neither, even though
I tell you that Martin, Uncle Kendal, Egerton, all come and
talk to me and I to them, as if they had been here, as in fact they
said they were.' Yet the grief remains, as darting, as cruel as
ever. For seven long years she has not seen the darling of her
heart, only had letters, Oh to have a sight of her, even an
instant's sight! She would not be afraid of such an apparition.
To have a glimpse of her, to meet her eyes full of love, was it
too much to hope for? A few weeks back, when Dooley, the
last of the three much adored fox terriers was dying, Martin
seemed so close. 'I can't tell you, dearest Ethel, how it wrung
my heart to see that gentle little creature panting her life away
and looking to me for the help I couldn't give her. The only
comfort I had was that Martin was there, waiting for her, and

she wrote that as the little thing fell asleep (it was the gentlest thing, the heaving side gradually ceased to move—no more than that) she and Egerton were there and carried her away.' Martin so close, yet invisible. For seven years it had been like that.

The year 1922 passed away, a year so full of dangers and terror, sudden deaths, cruelties, violence of murder, shock of robbery, insult, disgust at nonsense shouted by demented men, lies, the denial of mercy. Such miseries could not be laughed off. Yet Edith had sought to ease them by laughter. And they had been eased by her absorption in a dream of the beyond, so real that it could hardly be told from reality, if indeed reality can ever be identified for certain.

All this had poured into Ethel Smyth's ears, Ethel who now wanted her old dead love, Henry Brewster, found and a message got from him by Martin. That was to come. The Government had recently conferred upon her the title of Dame. Edith would have liked the title of Dame. But she was not in the running for such public honours. In truth, she was too fantastic a creature, with her field of ghosts and the enlightenment she had gained by looking into the eyes of animals, to qualify. But Ethel was just right, with her society friends, at her concerts Royalty and Cabinet ministers, and elegant females and rich chaps.

In the course of 1923 Edith went over to London to consult her publishers and stay with Ethel Smyth. As before, she was asked out a lot and lunched with the Asquiths when she met Moseley and his wife. Her Irish friend, the Countess of Kenmare, gave a party for her, inviting such guests as Edmund Gosse, Eddy Marsh, Desmond McCarthy and Maurice Baring. Her publishers, Longmans, advanced her £400 for her new book of reminiscences, *Wheel-tracks*, of which *Time and Tide* bought the serial rights. She exhibited her pictures at Walkers in Bond Street and made a net profit of £230. Altogether it was a very pleasant change from being boxed up in Castle Townshend. But she was glad to get home in December 1923 to Cameron, Hildegarde and the dogs, and to her strange colloquies with the dead Martin.

On 20 January 1924, in the course of a seance conducted as usual, Martin wrote that one day she would try to become visible to them. It should be possible, she said, if conditions were favourable and she specified the required conditions. It was not, however, till 16 February that the Experiment, as Martin called it, could be begun, because Jem Barlow caught 'flu. On that day after tea Edith, Hildegarde with Jem Barlow took their seats in the library of Drishane. In an adjoining room Cameron was seated at the piano, playing softly a piece by Brahms. The rooms were in semi-darkness; no lamps had been lit. The three women sat very still for ten minutes. A chair had been placed, in which Martin would seat herself and where, it was hoped, she would become visible. These arrangements were in accordance with her instructions. The following description of what happened is taken from Edith's diary: 'Both Hildegarde and Jem were percipient, Hildegarde of a moving mistiness, Jem of the psychic waft. It seems to have been a good beginning.' In short, nothing happened. The form of Martin was not seen in the chair. But Edith was not disheartened. If she persevered, she would see that tender laughing face again. If the materialization sufficed, might she not touch her, even embrace her? Yet to embrace one from the dead, could that be?

The attempt was resumed the next evening. The diary has: 'At 6.30 we continued the experiment, Cameron playing for about half an hour. Hildegarde and Jem again percipient. I felt the waft, nothing more.' On 19 February a further attempt was made. Martin's chair seemed dimly lighted in part outline on this occasion. 'Hildegarde and Jem thought they saw a moving blur of whiteness (I not) coming from the chair towards us. We sat in total silence.' They tried again on 20 and 21 February. Martin did not appear, nor did she make any statement through automatic writing. It was impossible to say whether she was invisibly present as at the usual seances. Not a word was uttered, nothing was seen but a few spots of light.

Edith is not recorded to have sought again to see Martin, though she continued for another twenty years to communicate with her by automatic writing. There is nothing in the papers to show that Martin's failure to materialize was afterwards discussed with her. It must be supposed, however, that she was asked what had gone wrong. Were the conditions for a successful materialization not properly observed? Was it their fault or had she been unable to manage it for other reasons? If these questions were asked, they got no answers, or answers so vague as not to be worth recording.

20

Anecdotes

Edith had to keep up her writing because she couldn't afford not to; her royalties just about enabled her to balance her bank account. Since the death of Martin she had published *Irish Memories* (1917), devoted largely to memories of Martin; the novel *Mount Music* (1919); a collection of articles called *Strayaways* (1920), more than half of them written by Martin; the novel *An Enthusiast* (1921), about the closing days of the old order in Ireland. Now in 1923 she published *Wheel-tracks*, some twenty-six articles, some of which had already appeared in *Time and Tide*.

The book may be said to supplement *Irish Memories*. It is autobiographical, but does not cover recent times nor deal with the central event of Edith's life, her friendship with Martin and Martin's death. The Troubles are not mentioned, Ethel Smyth has no place. It describes early years in Drishane and has glimpses of the Ireland of pre-Free State days. 'Before the steam roller of Time obliterates all the old wheel-tracks I will try and retrace a few of them,' she writes.

The book is not comparable in quality or interest with *Irish Memories*, but it succeeds here and there in giving an authentic peep into nineteenth-century Cork. Take the following extract from the essay 'Chiefly concerning Beggars':

'An old man was one day announced as wishing to speak to me. I found him leaning on his stick (at the hall door), a

[223]

haggard gentle old fellow, with the tremor of palsy on him, clad in a long and ragged black coat. He curtseyed low to me. I asked him his history. Curtseying again, he replied, rolling each period with a skilled propriety: "I was a sexton in the town of Buttevant, my Lady of Honour! But I lost my hearing, Child, and the ladies of the place, Ladies of Honour, like yourself, my child, and Colonels' Ladies, they frowned upon me! . . . They frowned upon me, aweenoch, upon me that fretted them with my mistakes by reason of my infirmity, and I lost my situation in the Church o' Buttevant!" He paused and I uttered responsive and sympathetic sounds. "I'm going the roads ever since, my dear," he resumed; "If thrippence would take me to the Lord in Heaven, I couldn't give it!" I gave him a viaticum and he wished that God might have the Gate of Heaven open before me; which is as much as one can expect for a shilling.'

No need to believe his story, adds Edith, for mendacity and mendicity run close together, but she urges that for a being so old to be blown like a withered leaf along the rocky roads of the world was enough; 'beggars like the old sexton need have no propitiatory story to tell'.

As Edith penned this passage, so rich with feeling for the old Irish scene and so subtly worded, for the ancient beggarman does not speak the normal language of his class, but a stately diction invented by him for his act as a tragic personage, we seem to see the shade of Martin leaning over her and whispering the words in her ears, and do not find the visionary collaboration strange or unlikely, indeed find it certainly real, for the passage is pure Martin, the softly amused Martin, as in the passage where she described Paddy Griffy entering the hall of Ross and dancing with Mama, so that we are convinced that it was indeed whispered by her and thus become participants in the whole phantasmagoria.

In this book, *Wheel-tracks*, Edith looks aside from the Ireland of 1922 and finds reality in what she remembers of the deep countryside when she was young, perceptions not founded on history or legend, but which came to her direct. In the following passage she is not dishing up the fairies from the Gaelic but relating a childhood experience. 'The year that Cameron and I heard the fairy music was, I think, in the year *Alice in Wonderland* was published.' It was high summer as they read that book in a room at Drishane whose windows looked down towards the sea. 'Suddenly we heard from, as it seemed, the avenue a rushing outbreak of music richer and more delicious, as I remember it, than any music that I have heard before or since. It swept in through the windows in a wave of glory.' A German band had been on visit to the village and they ascribed the music to it and when it ceased rushed out to ask for more. 'But there was no band there and we two only had heard the music.' They learned later that on another occasion a gardener had heard it while working at the Chavasses' house. The music went down the hill past him to the wharf below Cosheen. The Fairy Queen was setting sail. It followed her down the Haven till she reached the outer sea.

Though ever mindful of 21 December 1915, the fatal day when Martin died, Edith decided in 1924 to give it special place by making the last week of December henceforth a Week of Remembrance. Martin's altar in St Barrahane's church was never without its flowers, but she multiplied them during the week dedicated to the sacred memory of her friend and prayed more fervently at the altar for an ever closer union with the celestial presence who encouraged and guided her in all matters of life. She also renewed Martin's cross in the churchyard. She was prompted in this not only by her love, but also because she felt in particular need of Martin's collaboration at the moment. She had started a novel, to be called *The Big House of Inver*, a book which owed its inception to a letter which Martin wrote to her on 18 March 1912 describing a visit she had just made to Tyrone House, one of the big houses which had gone to ruin. Quotations from this letter occur earlier in this book corresponding with the time when the visit was made. During the three and a half years between March 1912 and Martin's death in December 1915 the two women made no attempt to develop

P

the idea which had come to Martin at the sight of Tyrone
House. But twelve years had passed since then and now Edith
felt the moment had come to make the story the plot of a
novel. That Martin had wished to do this was a strong incentive.
If she still was of the same opinion, she would collaborate with
more enthusiasm than over a plot new to her. By the time of
the Remembrance Week in 1924 Edith had written a part of
the book. Access to Martin had been easier and her advice
clearer than was generally the case. *The Big House of Inver*
was published in 1925, a large edition of 10,000 copies, that
sold well and was praised by the critics. It stood for more
than the story of a particular family. Edith noted:* 'This is
the history of one of those minor dynasties that, in Ireland,
have risen, and ruled, and rioted, and have at last crashed in
ruins. They had their great days of peace and plenty, and
built fine houses that now stand empty. Their very names
are sunk in squalor, misspelt, mispronounced, surviving only
illegitimately.' They have their place in the history of the Irish
Landed Gentry, an exceptional part, for most of the gentry
survived, even through the terrible time of the great famine, a
financial calamity which greatly impoverished them. But they
became an anachronism. There was little place for them in the
political, economic and administrative structure of the new
Ireland. Yet they managed to retain their gentility. The
Somerville-Ross papers disclose in minute detail what they were
like, how proud they were of being Irish, how they loved
Ireland and how delightful and amusing they found the country
people. They no longer had any power, or at least no more
power than the landed gentry across the sea in England, but
they were still for the most part treated with the old respect,
so that it was possible for Martin to write how sad it was to see
the last of the St Georges in a donkey trap outside their once
palatial residence, looking like something between a lady and a
cook. The outward sign of the Irish gentry's survival was the
ancestral houses. As long as they could manage to keep them

* See *Hudson Bibliography*, p. 45.

up, some semblance locally of their old standing remained. The
Martins, as this narrative has revealed, could not keep up Ross
and are now scattered, the Coghills today no longer have Glen
Barrahane but the Somervilles are still at Drishane. That this
old house survived such difficult times was largely due to Edith's
extraordinary pertinacity. She toiled for over fifty years to keep
it going, she marshalled her family about her, and carried them
through. She stood head and shoulders above all the men, distinguished though some of them were, and above all the women.
She fought off time, she fought off death, till, aged ninety,
those twin destroyers bore her down. But her work was accomplished. The Somerville family still lived in its ancestral home
and, thanks to her genius, its name was more illustrious than
it had ever been. Such are the reflections that cross the mind
after reading *The Big House of Inver*, her last book of prime
importance.

At the date we have now reached, 1925, Edith was sixty-
seven. The 1924 Christmas had seen a great gathering of
brothers and cousins. Admiral Boyle Somerville, the brother
for whom she had the greatest respect, had retired from the
Navy and come to Castle Townshend with his wife. He made
The Point his residence, the Coghill house where Uncle Kendal
had lived till his death. Martin reported in a seance that Uncle
Kendal lost his temper, for he was just as touchy as ever, when
he heard that Boyle called the house The Point. His name for it
had been Cosheen, and he declared that it was an impertinence
on Boyle's part to change it. Edith's nephew, Paddy, was in
Baghdad but his brother Nevill was down from Oxford, where
he was soon to get a First in English Literature, followed by an
Exeter fellowship. The festive season passed off very well with
Edith seated at the head of the table. Only one contretemps is
recorded: 'Washed the dogs in icing sugar believing it to be
boracic powder.' But the outlook in the spring of 1925 was not
so comfortably amusing. The farm could not be made to pay. It
was £3,600 in debt to the bank, a frightening sum, far beyond
Edith's capacity to repay, when her personal account was also

overdrawn. The bank, however, was patient. She extended her dealing in horses from this date and eventually sold her hunters in America for sums far above the Irish market prices. The Cosgrave government of the Free State offered to make good the losses incurred by the public during the civil war. Edith claimed £165 for horses stolen by the Republicans, a moderate sum, but it helped. Royalties for old books also came in, but only £67. She was much cheered in a seance on 5 March 1925 by a jolly message from Uncle Kendal addressed to her, Jem Barlow and Hildegarde: 'Well, pretty ones, here's a kiss apiece for you.' She was also delighted by a letter from a friend Louise Keene, one of the Clare families, to say that when the country people heard that her uncle was selling the old family seat, 'they wrote threatening letters, in proof of their affection, saying he will get a bullet and they have pulled down his gates, all for love.' The Irish Landed Gentry had their fans. In September she went to stay with the Kenmares, leaving the dogs behind at Drishane. Hildegarde wrote that Taspy forgot herself and stole and ate the whole of her lunch.

By the end of 1925 it was reported that 8,000 copies of *The Big House of Inver* were sold and Edith was in funds again. In January 1926 she went over to London and stayed with Ethel Smyth's sister, a rich woman who moved in the best circles. We have one of Edith's typically caustic remarks: 'George Moore came to dinner. Don't like the drowsy old wasp, even though he said to me "What a pretty dress".' From London she took a trip to Spain, a visit she described long afterwards in her *Happy Days*. She was as usual disinclined to appreciate what was new to her. The splendid architecture of Burgos cathedral impressed her, but of a service that was going on inside she has: 'Sat in the cathedral and listened to the barbarous male bellowing, worthy only of Tibet, a sort of service for priests only.' This must have been the choir and priests singing an office. Cameron, left in charge of Drishane, reported 'Orphan dogs piano but good.' Back home in May they gave her 'a satiating welcome', knocking her down, tearing her stockings and licking her face. In entries thereafter the dogs figure prominently. Besides Taspy there seem to have been three others at this time, Cosy, Folly* and Kerry. On Martin's birthday, 11 June 1927, when the seance was going on, these three were shut out and became 'very noisy and interrupting'. Kerry was the naughtiest. One of the stablemen had called him 'a bloody old tramp of Hell'. The same month Taspy, who was the favourite, was allowed into the room when a seance was in progress and behaved in such a way that Edith concluded that Martin was visible to her. Martin, when questioned, confirmed that Taspy did see her. On her next visit to London (November 1927) Edith attended a mass meeting of spiritualists at the Albert Hall. There were eight thousand people in the audience. Conan Doyle was one of the speakers. 'Felt incessant cold wafts of air.' Her second exhibition at Walkers Gallery took place on this visit. But she only sold £100 worth. She was treated, however, as a visiting celebrity and the B.B.C. billed her as such in a broadcast. She lunched and dined out every day and immensely enjoyed herself. She was still on excellent terms with Ethel Smyth and, as has been said, was indebted to her, directly or indirectly, for many useful introductions. Ethel Smyth had also been a good influence in getting her to read more widely the best writing of the day. At this time, for instance, she read Feuchtwangler's *Jew Suss* and *The Ugly Duchess*, both of them books rather broad for her Victorian taste, but whose interest and quality she was now able to perceive. She seems, too, to have dipped into James Joyce's *Ulysses*. This work of genius was more than she could take, but it is noteworthy, as showing she was moving, though slowly, with the times, that when an edition of the book appeared in the U.S.A. with extensive cuts, she signed along with other writers a letter to the press disapproving of the mutilation. Ethel Smyth had now less cause to smile at her primness, and continued to inflict on her literary judgments in an aggravating manner, which, however, Edith took very well.

* An old pet dog that died of heart failure soon afterwards.

In March 1928, when back home, the death of her brother
Aylmer at the Red House, Castle Townshend, was a sudden
shock. His founding thirty-seven years back of the West Carbery Hunt had been a great boon. It provided her with material
for her books, as well as giving her enormous pleasure. It
created a bond between them, though she did not love him as she
did Cameron or admire him as she did Boyle. Her diary entry for
14 March 1928 is: 'Hildegarde and I covered a horseshoe with
violets for Aylmer. Went to the Red House. Mike (her groom)
and Desmond (Aylmer's son) arranged shifts of six bearers.
The funeral was at 3.30. We all went and I believe from the
other side they all came.' The belief that St Barrahane was
frequented by the ancestral spirits was a necessary corollary to
the ideology she had built up round the central figure of Martin.
She was now not only in communication with Martin, but
through her with the spirits of all members of the family
immediately after they died. Thus three days after Aylmer's
funeral she records in her diary that he sent messages via
Martin; and soon he and Egerton came regularly to write at
the nightly seances. It seemed to her that at all times she was
surrounded by presences. '8 April 1928. Jem stayed to dinner.
Played bridge. Taspy in my lap saw onlookers invisible to us,
though felt by Jem.' One of the bridge-four was the parson,
Canon Madden, whose bridge was so bad 'that it must have
amused the invisible ones'. There was nothing alarming about
the invisible ones in Edith's phantasmology. They were even
ready to laugh at an overbid or a revoke.

When her brother Boyle retired and took up his residence
at The Point, Edith found him an enthusiastic researcher into
the occult. He was the only brother with any literary talent and
was engaged on a biography of George Anson, the great
captain, who circumnavigated the world in 1740. This gave
him a special interest in old seafarers. In October 1928 Edith
records that with the help of Jem Barlow he raised the ghost of
a Spaniard who had been one of a Spanish force sent to invade
Ireland in Queen Elizabeth's time, and was buried in an old

deserted graveyard on the other side of Castle Haven. In a book dealing chiefly with the occult, called *Notions in Garrison* (1941) she devotes a long essay to this matter, called 'A Derelict's Story'. Jem and Boyle went several times to the old Spanish graveyard, a wild and deserted spot, above Atlantic cliffs, and called Galleon Point, as a tradition of a Spanish landing there in 1601 still lingered. There Jem sat on a rock in her mediumistic trance, ready to record in automatic writing whatever might be uttered by wandering spirits, if any were about. Boyle watched from a distance. Presently she found herself in touch with a Spaniard who had been killed during the Spanish raid and who told her its history. Boyle afterwards checked his statements with papers in the British Museum and found them to agree. He and Jem did not see the spectre but she heard him talking in Spanish, a language of which she was ignorant. Her automatic transcription of his words, however, was in English, as the meaning of what he said was subconsciously communicated to her. The derelict seadog was very miserable. For some mysterious reason he was tied to Galleon Point, though he longed to go home to Spain, whose bells he could hear. It is hinted that his office was to guard a buried treasure, as guardian ghosts in Asia, bound for ever by a magical formula, are reported to do. The seances continued off and on till 14 October 1929. It seems that the old spirit once materialized sufficiently for Jem to see that his appearance was wild, and his hair tangled and that he was wrapped in a large cloak. From her description Edith afterwards made a drawing of him, which she reproduced in *Notions in Garrison*. She herself did not attend the seances. But she was satisfied that Boyle and Jem had told her accurately what transpired. It was unthinkable to suppose otherwise. The account of the episode in *Notions in Garrison* is dramatically phrased and shows that she took it as a piece of serious psychical research. Boyle's notes she found 'cool and practical as became the official findings of a Senior Naval officer'. She reported the matter to Martin but it is not recorded that she asked her to help the derelict ghost to get home.

Anecdotes

Edith had made a habit for some years of recording in the space at the end of her diaries what amusing or striking stories she had heard during the year. As these have not been published and often are vintage Somerville, a few of them may be quoted here. They have to do in some cases with spiritualism, but treated with more humour than is usual with such a subject. Thus, a curate is quoted as saying that one day, returning to his rooms, he saw an old lady sitting in an armchair by the window. She gesticulated angrily at him and then melted away. He learned that a mad woman had lived and died in those rooms. On hearing that she was now acting in this angry way, friends of hers, believing her to be unhappy, asked him to pray for her. When he did so, she appeared again, and abused him in yet more trenchant terms before taking herself off. She was evidently not unhappy. It was just that she had taken a strong dislike to him.

Another ghost story came from Muriel Currey, Martin's niece. Two ladies of her acquaintance, she said, had rented a house for the summer on the Thames. From time to time they noticed a little old lady in a big black bonnet wandering in the garden and occasionally peeping into the house. It was some time before they realized she was a spirit. In the autumn they returned to London and at their own house proceeded to pay the taxi. The man said: 'That's not enough. There's the extra for the third person.' 'What third person?' 'The old lady in the black bonnet who has just got out and gone up the steps.' The point here is the reverse of the last. The ghost took such a fancy to the two ladies that she decided to change her address and haunt their London house.

Edith was such a humorist that she could make even ghost stories amusing.

As might be expected some of the anecdotes have to do with the Troubles. Thus, an old country woman is heard saying of the civil war: 'The Black and Tans are gone, and the soldiers are gone, and now the polis is going and the boys can fight in peace.' Another one is startling: 'A big Black and Tan with a

[232]

revolver in each hand went into a Cork tea-shop. He put his pistols on a table and called Maggie (a pretty gentle little girl) to bring him food. As she went for it, she was stopped by an I.R.A. man, who whispered to her to be quick, as the Black and Tan had to be shot by one o'clock and it was now half-past twelve. Maggie accordingly was as quick as she could and at one o'clock, as the Black and Tan left the shop, the back of his head was immediately blown away.'

Edith much relished stories about Catholic priests. Though a staunch Protestant she had nothing against them. We have seen how she admired Father Lamb. Here is a story to show how witty they could be. 'Fair Penitent (at confession) "I'm afraid, Father, my besetting sin is vanity." Father Healey: "Why do you think that, my child?" F.P. "Oh Father, when I get up in the morning and I look at meself in the glass, I think 'What a pretty girl you are'." Father H.: "Ah my child, that's not a sin. That's only a mistake." '

In another story the priest has been so bored by political clap-trap that even a murder fails to hold his attention. "A man shot a policeman and full of remorse went to confession.He made long and contrite explanations. At length the priest said: "Well, well, that'll do with politics now. Get on with your sins." '

Edith also relates what the famous Father Lamb said to Cameron about a certain Captain Boote of the Republican army. 'The I.R.A. pup (known as Captain Boote) was brought to him. "I hit him," said Father Lamb, "a smack on the puss and he burst out crying and gave me his revolver and said that was all he had. 'I don't believe you,' I said, 'I'll search you.' There wasn't a bit of him but he had dum-dum bullets, and split nosed and soft nosed bullets concealed on him. I beat him in earnest then, and I believe he's crying yet." '

Father Lamb was boasting a bit, but there is no doubt that the country ruffians were afraid to touch the priests.

On occasion Edith allows herself a joke at the expense of the Protestants. 'Sir Hugh Lane offered a very valuable old painting of the Virgin to an Ulster church. The vestry accepted it, but stipulated that a ring was to be painted on her third finger.'

That the next anecdote scene is also Ulster has perhaps some significance. 'A workman gives his seat to a lady who says: "I don't like to deprive you of it." The workman replies: "There's no depravity about it at all, Ma'am." '

Malapropisms of this sort always pleased Edith and she was also much taken with what the Countess of Kenmare told her one day. A very old countryman, met out in a bog, addressed her with the utmost respect, his hat in his hand: 'Are you Miss or Ma'am?' 'Ma'am,' said Lady Kenmare. The old fellow then remarked in a manner so simple and earnest as to be quite inoffensive: 'It is good, for I can be hoping that ye will attend to the increase of the population of the country.' Edith's contention was that no one but an ancient from the Kerry mountains would know how to address such a delicate admonition to a lady. The same affectionate regard prompted the following: 'In Dublin a bridegroom in dazzling white spats was accosted by an old woman, who whispered tactfully: "I beg your pardon, sir, but your dhrawers are coming down." '

Edith had a partiality for contretemps of the sort. The following was jotted down in 1928: 'Miss Hudson's* friend at a dinner party felt a bit of her underclothes drop as she was rising from the table. She kicked it clear and left with the rest, hoping for the best. She was followed by her hostess's dog, carrying her drawers in its mouth. She caught at one leg, the dog held on to the other.'

In spite of her primness Edith's love of humour sometimes led her to note down what was verging on the improper. Queen Mary, on her return from a visit to Queen Victoria's mausoleum chapel at Frogmore, where she was accompanied by Princess Beatrice and Princess Mary, then a child, went to call on Queen Alexandra, widow of Edward VII. The conversation, according to Charlotte Knollys, lady in waiting, was as follows: Queen Mary (shouting in Queen Alexandra's ear, because she was

* Edith's bibliographer, Elizabeth Hudson, an American.

deaf): 'There was a little bird flying about the chapel; we thought it was the spirit of Queen Victoria.'

Princess Mary (shouting): 'Yes, and it made a mess on Aunt Beatrice's hat.'

To which Queen Alexandra replied in grave rebuke: 'Queen Victoria would never have done that.'

It does not seem that this addendum to the legend of Queen Victoria has before seen the light.

Some may hold it absurd to term the above an impropriety, but will have to allow that Edith would not have recorded the following had not its humour absolved her:

'A man had a horse to sell for which he wanted £60. He took him to a fair and a buyer offered £50.

"I'll only take shixty."

"Will ye take fifty-five?"

"I'll take shixty."

"I'll give you sixty if ye'll take off ten per cent."

"I'll not take it."

He took his horse away and on the road home he stopped at a pub and had a drink. He was feeling unhappy about the deal and uncertain as to what he had refused. He told his story to the barmaid and said "Now, Mary, if I offered you shixty pound, what'd ye take off for ten per cent?"

Mary replied: "Every stitch!" '

It would be wrong to shut this private collection of anecdotes without citing one more—a dog story which, as far as I know, is not found among the innumerable dog stories included in her works. 'Dev Milburn, the great polo player, and his wife were lunching at a restaurant. A wild duck was brought to the table in a state of advanced decomposition. "Pity we haven't a dog here," said Mrs Milburn. "A dog wouldn't eat it!" said Milburn, "but he might roll in it." '

It is time to have done with these toys and turn again to the narrative of Edith's life. What did she do next? She went to America.

21

Edith in America

When in 1929 Edith was invited to go on a lecture tour of the States, she accepted with alacrity though she was seventy-one. She could not afford to refuse. By going she hoped to make enough money to pay her debts. It would be tiring, but she would enjoy it. Her books had a fair circulation in America. She had been assured of a good market for her paintings. Their exhibition in places like Washington and New York would give further publicity to her lecture tour. The bodies responsible for its organization would arrange for her to visit such states as South Carolina where her having been an Irish M.F.H. for many years would go down well in hunting circles. She persuaded Hildegarde to come with her. She adored her sister and her companionship would be a strength among strangers. Hildegarde, quiet, gentle and unassertive, had never minded taking second place. Indeed, any thought of rivalry with her brilliant sister had never entered her head. In point of fact she had an asset bound to be useful. To be Lady Coghill meant something in the United States, as it does everywhere else.

On 17 February 1929 they went on board the liner *Cedric* at Queenstown, County Cork. Martin, consulted about the trip, had given a favourable opinion, with the envoie: 'All your faithful band from over the Border want you to feel that they are ever present and powerful.' As Edith did not 'write with Martin', as the phrase went, during the tour, which lasted three months, this assurance of the presence of the invisible ones in America was not put to the test.

Edith had to leave her pet dogs behind and felt the separation as much as they did. Her drawing, used as the frontispiece of the travel book she wrote afterwards, *The States Through Irish Eyes*, shows her two little foxterriers, Taspy and Prinkie, on the steps of Drishane looking wistfully after the motor car carrying her away from them down the avenue. The family and staff held her U.S.A. tour to be a big occasion and as the *Cedric* on her way to New York passed within sight of Castle Haven, bonfires were lit on the headland visible to Edith through her binoculars, who also thought she could descry for an instant the dogs, like white spots.

In her luggage she had a curious article, which she was right in thinking was of the sort the Americans would be happy to learn Miss Somerville had with her. This was a fairy shoe. In the published account of her travels the shoe's provenance is set forth. It had been picked up a century earlier in a wild part of west Cork by a man of the hills who believed it to belong to a fairy. Not caring to keep so magical an object which might very well bring him bad luck he gave it to the local doctor, who passed it on to one of the Townshends, a first cousin of Edith's grandfather. In course of time it became Hildegarde's property. It was three inches long, made of leather as thin as silk. In America 'the Fairy Shoe had, everywhere, a reception which was at once enthusiastic and respectful. No one made the suggestion that it was a doll's shoe or a baby's.' The dons at Yale admitted they had never seen anything like it. There was nothing it could be, said Edith, except a fairy's shoe. Did not Conan Doyle believe in fairies? And A.E., too, once told her he had seen and painted them. His fairy paintings were much admired in Dublin at that time. Some members of the public believed that he had indeed seen the Little People, though others preferred to regard the pictures as symbolic only of the mystical beliefs which he had acquired from a study of Hindu metaphysics or, if at second hand, from Yeats's swami. One perceives, therefore, that there was respectable backing for the authenticity of Edith's shoe.

As the full details of her visit to the States are available in her own published text, no attempt will be made here to follow her in her travels. A few reflections, together with references to her diary for 1929, will suffice. After a short stay in New York to lecture and exhibit her pictures, she went to Aiken in South Carolina, where she and Hildegarde stayed with Mrs Thomas Hitchcock who had bought some of the Irish horses sent over from Drishane for sale in America. 'The Horse is the tutelary deity of Aiken,' Edith wrote. It was a great hunting and racing centre. As Mrs Hitchcock was an M.F.H. Edith felt much at home. The horses of the Aiken hunt, being thoroughbreds, were superior to those in the West Carbery, but Edith consoled herself with the thought that they would be quite unsuitable for the rough going in Cork.

Edith was carried away by American good spirits, their lavish hospitality, warmth of manner and the way they provided for her comfort. In comparison, Castle Townshend was a poor shabby place. Edith's clothes, too, seemed very cheap, her hats very wrong. The people at Aiken were too kind to tell them, but later in hotels they were stared at. They liked the Negro servants very much. Edith, who had an ear for Irish servants' amusing phrases, found the Negroes equally delightful and has preserved a 'coloured groom's delicate warning to a hard riding mistress offered during a check in a strenuous woodland hunt: "Mis' Mary, Mam, yo' done tore yore breeches clear tru' to de meat." '

Edith, indeed all the Somervilles, were passionately fond of music, and when she and Hildegarde heard for the first time Negro spirituals sung by the staff of a large southern mansion, they were enthralled. Edith was inspired by the memory to write one of her most heartfelt passages, so deeply felt as to contain not a bantering word, something very rare for her. 'That evening, after dinner, a dozen or so of the retainers, indoor women and fieldworkers and house-boys, all black as

night, led by the Chef, his white overalls and cap of office well
becoming his ebony complexion, assembled in the long shadowy
hall, and sang for us Spirituals, the real thing, loud, rough,
impassioned, infinitely more impressive, if not more beautiful,
than the sophisticated part-song that has been tamed to drawing-
room uses. The Chef would begin, setting the key and the tune,
and singing the first line in a strong baritone. A woman's
piercing voice would respond with a long wailing note, then,
gradually, like a storm rising, the rest would join, antiphonally,
one end of the line of singers answering the other, voice after
voice breaking in, haphazard, like gusts of wind, shouting the
theme, while the rest followed, with strange harmonies, and
windy crescendos and diminuendoes, and broken time, but with
unfailing rhythm.'

Edith had never heard anything 'as passionate, as utterly
inconceivable, had never had such an unforgettable experience'.
She had the heart of a true artist. She loved the Negroes after
hearing them sing. One should always keep in mind that for all
her foibles she was a great woman.

In another place she quotes the Irish saying: 'There are some
things too serious for joking, and one of them's potatoes.' And
adds 'And another of them is hounds.' Her only criticism of the
American way of life concerned hounds. Some of the packs she
saw were mangy and half starved, despite the affluence of the
hunt clubs. One may believe in fairies, but one boggles at that
assertion. I will not pursue the subject but go on to what she
says of Prohibition, which was in force at the time of her visit.
Some people told her that Prohibition had seriously interfered
with the liberty of the subject. Others assured her that 'every
citizen of the States went to bed drunk'. Her experience was
that 'few dinner parties failed of that trusty nourisher of conversation, champagne. Had I accepted all that was offered me,
I should soon have been eligible for deportation as an Un-
desirable Alien.' She admits, however, that at the first dinner
party she and Hildegarde felt 'cheated of a sensation that we did
not find ourselves rising from the table and leaving our fellow

guests under it'. Champagne did not always improve conversation. At a wedding party she got stuck between two men 'who were rather obviously Anti-Prohibitionists. Duller boon companions I have never met.' One would only discourse on crop prospects in the Middle West, the other on baseball. 'I would not borrow a shilling to get drunk with either of them.'

Coming from West Cork where motor cars were still a rarity, she was taken aback when, admiring the elegance of a car in the garage of a friend, she was told it belonged to the cook. 'I am sure,' she adds, 'that no self-respecting American ghost would now walk.' Had Martin's seances been in America she would have motored to them.

By April 1929 the sisters had moved up from the southern states to Boston. Edith's diary entries are of this sort: '29 April. Went early to Mrs Montgomery Sear's marvellous palace, the oldest and biggest and finest house in Boston.' On 1 May she is in Philadelphia and being fêted at the Cosmopolitan Club at a grand supper served by liveried negroes. Afterwards she read aloud one of the R.M. stories. 'All the hearers full of praise and worship.' At another rich house she was delighted when a woman, Nellie Donovan, who had been her parlourmaid thirty years before, introduced herself and inquired for 'Miss Hildegarde, Master Jack etc.'.

When she came to write *The States Through Irish Eyes* she found herself running short of material at this stage. Having handsomely declared the Americans to be most charming and hospitable people, whose parties, receptions and compliments had been so animating that days passed as in a dream, she saw little more to say about her tour. To give the book its proper length she was obliged to incorporate matters which, though amusing, had nothing to do with America. A complete chapter was given to a biography of her favourite dog, Taspy, a chapter which in 1949 she reprinted verbatim and without apology in her *Maria and Some Other Dogs*. It is immensely touching, and contains her belief that dogs, shorter lived than their owners, await them in Heaven, which is not Heaven till they turn up. She ended the travel book with a rich Irish anecdote which she pretends came into her mind because of the irritating habit American servants had of brushing away your bread at table before you had finished with it. The anecdote reveals her humorous self better than anything she ever wrote. It demands to be salvaged and can be included here as *The States Through Irish Eyes* is quite forgotten now and was never widely read. It is marvellously comic. What a treat it must have been to hear her recite it. Her whole personality will have played over her features. Those who saw her then will have been infatuated by the drollery of her expression and, no matter how well they knew her, will have felt they knew her better.

A Mr Mulrooney, a surveyor, tells the story: 'It was goin' on for one o'clock when I had me survey completed, and says I to meself, "I'll take me figures up to the Big House before I'll go home." What was in it when I gets there but his Lordship and her Ladyship, and they standing on the hall-door steps. "Come in, Mr Mulrooney," says they, friendly and agreeable, the way I ever knew them. "Come in and have a bit o' lunch," says they, "an' we'll see the map afterwards," says they.

'Well, for all I was in me dishabeel, and dirty old boots on me, I had a scruple to refuse them—(and begor' there wasn't bit nor sup went into me mouth since the dawning o' the day!)—So I thanks them, as in me manners bound, and we went inside to the parlour then and sot down to the table. I seen the big fella of a butler perceiving me boots, and a whipper-snapper of a snap-dragon of a tay-boy that was with him, in red plush breeches and white stockings, was making shnouts at them likewise. But little I regarded them. Well, I knew me manners, and I held me tongue, till his Lordship says to me "Mr Mulrooney," says he, "what'll ye ate?" "Mate, me lord," says I. (And God knows I was hungry!)

'Well, his Lordship cut off for me then two as nice slices of boiled beef as ever you seen, and a nice little bit o' fat attached, an' he gev it to the whipper-snapper of a snap-dragon of a fella in the plush throwshiers—breeches I should say—an' he puts it down before me. I had a nate forkful ready to put in me mouth when her Ladyship addressed a remark to me with regard of pigs. Now, swine is a subject I am familiar with, in an' out, from bonnives to bacon, and I puts down me fine forkful, as in me manners bound, to respond to her Ladyship. Well, I declare to ye, before you could say Shnipes, the Whipper-snapper of a snap-dragon of a fella in the plush throwshiers—breeches I mane—had the plate whipped away from me!

'I passed no remark. I held me tongue, as in me manners bound, and I was commencing to address a remark to her Lady-ship in regard of them fashionable poultry she had that time, when his Lordship sees me idle. "Mr Mulrooney," says he, "you're ateing nothing. What'll ye have?" says he. "Well, me Lord," says I, "I think I could do no better than have a couple o' slices of that elegant bit o' beef that's before your Lordship."

'With that his Lordship cuts me off two as nice slices as ever you seen, with a nice little bit o' fat attached. The owld butler fella puts it down before me, but before I had time to get to come at it, her ladyship addressed a remark to me in regard of fat cattle. Well, out of respect to her ladyship, and as in me manners bound, I puts down me knife an' me fork before I responds to her. But if I did, by the Gash o' War, if that Whipper-snapper of a snap-dragon of a fella in the plush throwsiers—breeches I should say—hadn't the plate whipped again from me! That now was the second time he done it, and says I to meself, "Wait awhile, me lad!" But I held me tongue.

'His Lordship then, that hadn't his own dinner hardly begun, and seeing me idle again this way, cuts off another couple of elegant slices for me, with a nice little bit o' fat attached, an' 'twas set down before me.

'When I reshumed me conversation with her Ladyship in regard of fat stock, I puts down me knife on the table beside me, but I retained me fork on me right hand, and when the Whipper-snapper of a snap-dragon of a fella in the plush throw—breeches, I mane, and may the divil sweep them!—

comes around the third time to grab me plate from me, I slews around in me chair and I says to him, "Move off with yourself!" says I, "ye whipper-snapper of a snap-dragon before I dam well sink this fork in your dirty fist!, says I. Well, with that her Ladyship got very red.'

On 4 May 1929 Edith embarked on the S.S. *Baltic* for home. She had made £1,500 from the sale of her pictures, which was very much more than she had ever made in London. What she got for the lectures is not on record. Her financial difficulties were at an end for the time being. Her diary for 11 May contains a very caustic account of her fellow passengers. Lately the centre of adulation she found herself suddenly among people who had never heard of her. It was natural she thought them all dreadful. 'Fellow passengers: Well-dressed and well-painted American ladies. Loud nasal talk about nothing. English parsons (2) all things to all men, even wearing lay tweed caps; one stoops to a grey sweater, but it is corrected by a gold cross and the ritual collar. Several depressed elderly couples. Dull bald men, grey twittering women. Hard to say which is most to be pitied (*both* I think). Table of bellowing youths, among whom one oldish man, who laughs deafeningly and talks incessantly, to prove he is younger than any of them. A scarlet-faced, stout young man, an embodiment of British heartiness. He tramps the deck from dawn onwards (after, no doubt, a cold bath) singing *Killarney* excessively out of tune. Three tall Irish priests, who have secret jests together, which they suppress with an effort when two spectacled Sisters of Mercy begin to walk the deck, importing to it the atmosphere of the convent garden. The usual undergrowth of fat-legged flappers, who squeal in companies, walking arm-in-arm. Occasionally harassed stewards, with thin intellectual faces, bring trays of tea to long silent row of mummies in chaises longues.'

On 12 May Edith landed at Queenstown where she was met by Cameron with Taspy in his arms. She had an ecstatic welcome.

Meanwhile a storm had blown up between Ethel Smyth and a

new friend of Edith's, a Mrs Anstey, whose pet name was Caz. She had met Mrs Anstey during one of her London visits and became very fond of her. Now in her diary she refers to the 'foaming letters' which were exchanged between Ethel Smyth and Mrs Anstey on the subject of the American tour. Mrs Anstey's letters are not preserved, but their tone and Ethel Smyth's state of mind in her letters, which are extant, can be gauged from the extracts which follow. It seems that Edith had written to Mrs Anstey letters in which she described the warmth of the American welcome in glowing terms. Mrs Anstey had then written to Ethel Smyth saying how distressed she was at the way Edith had lapped up American flattery. Ethel to Edith, 15 May 1929: 'I have defended you from what "distressed" her, and said that you were innocent and un-psychological and that that is really much nicer than sifting and rejecting, especially as you got over £1,000 from them. She now writes: "Her letters are instances of the curious twist of character you so ably define, but you see I love her so much and have so entirely concentrated on her interest," (ah! that hideous cloven hoof—fancy saying that, my God!) "that I am in the hollow of her hand, alas!" Oh, she really is a terror and I feel I shall never go near her again. One has to wipe off too much grease afterwards.'

Here is Ethel Smyth in a great rage. She often got into senseless rages. The underlying emotion in this case seems jealousy. She was not going to have her admired Edith criticized in a superior tone by a recently acquired friend.

Edith sent her a soothing reply, protesting that the Americans were really very nice. Ethel's rage against Mrs Anstey for intruding subsides and she assures Edith that the Americans always indulge in exaggerated praise, mistaking it for good manners. 'My dear, logic is not your strong suit, but I think you must see the difference between genuine admiration and gross flattery practised as a habit. According to you, everyone's first word was that your books were their bible. How disgusting!' Edith had written: 'It is delightful to be among people who are not ashamed to say what they feel,' a remark which Ethel considered very innocent.

In short, Ethel says much the same as what Mrs Anstey is abused for saying. One sees the point. It was permissible for her to lecture Edith, not for an upstart like Mrs Anstey. Aware that she is overdoing it, she rushes to flatter the Americans. 'I do believe in and admire their bottomless kindness.' But she turns again upon Mrs Anstey: 'I have heard poor Mrs A say and do things, even when you were there, which made me squirm.' By 20 May she had calmed down and wrote a letter which amounted to an apology, on which in Edith's handwriting are the words 'Amende honorable'.

This ridiculous episode—and Edith terms it so in her diary— is given because it throws further light on Edith's character. She was not temperamental. If her friends wrote insultingly, she passed it over. She continued to correspond with these two women till their deaths many years later. She showed no jealousy when in 1930 Ethel Smyth fell violently in love with Virginia Woolf. And on 28 June we find the entry that Mrs Anstey had arrived in Drishane for a stay of a month.

22

The calling up of Charles Bushe

As soon as Edith was back in Drishane she took up again her writing with Martin. In a seance dated 26 January 1930 Jem Barlow declared she could hear Martin pronouncing Edith's name. Edith tried all she could to hear the beloved voice but could hear nothing. The automatic script, however, showed that Martin was present.

Edith found writing the account of her American tour hard going as there was not much body in the subject, little real incident. She struggled on, however, taking regular counsel from Martin, though when the book came out in 1930 it carried Edith's name only on the title page, the sole departure from her usual practice. She has not stated her reason for omitting Martin's name, but several will occur to the reader.

The year 1930 began sadly, for her favourite dog, Taspy, died in March of distemper. She mentions that Martin, accompanied by Folly, an earlier pet, met Taspy's spirit. Then on 21 March, four days afterwards, she records of a seance: 'Very interesting but rather heart-breaking. The single hearted little dog came. Jem could feel her, but my earthly husk was too dense.'

Wanting a change of scene, Edith went over to Paris. To refresh her drawing she attended her old art school there and worked from the model. But the modern styles in painting which in her youth had been the exception were now the rule. She found herself quite out of sympathy with contemporary art. The Salon des Indépendants seemed to her full of absurdities.

In May she was back in London and went to stay with Ethel Smyth, who was now fully involved with Virginia Woolf. Edith did not seem to mind. She even read Virginia Woolf's *A Room of One's Own* and found it admirable. It would be wrong to assume any coolness between Edith and Ethel. An understanding existed between them solidly founded on twelve years' friendship and a vast correspondence. Edith could listen to 'Ethel's rhapsodies about Mrs Woolf' without irritation. Moreover she had her new friend, Mrs Anstey, 'dearest Caz', as she always called her in letters.

During the autumn of 1930, having finished the American book, she began to consider how she might write a biography of Charles Kendal Bushe (1767–1843) once Lord Chief Justice of Ireland, one of whose grand-daughters, Adelaide, was Edith's mother, and another, Anna Selina, always called Mama in this book, was Martin's mother. She admired him as a man because of his reputation for incorruptibility. That she and Martin shared him as great grandfather was a further attraction. Edith was not altogether fitted to write such a biography involving research into documents. Neither her knowledge of Irish history nor her experience was adequate. Though this is hard to believe, she set to work on manuscripts in the British Museum in November 1930, but found this sort of thing beyond her. The idea then occurred to her to call up the Lord Justice in a seance and get him to speak for himself. This way of getting round the labour of research is first mentioned in her diary on 5 December 1930. She was staying in London with Mrs Anstey at the time. They were both acquainted with a professional medium by the name of Geraldine Cummins, of Irish extraction, though resident in England. The diary has: 'The Chief Justice himself came and gave a long and very interesting account of himself.' The documentary source here is a notebook (No. 16), headed 'November 1930, Geraldine Cummins, C.K.B. messages'. As an example of its contents I cite as follows: 'Astor

said "there is a strong and forceful personality close to us".'
Astor was Geraldine Cummins's control. That he was the first
Viscount Astor, the millionaire, who died in 1919, is not alleged.
All professional mediums had controls, supernatural presences
who produced at the seances whatever spirit was desired. Astor
went on: 'He will have to be held back while this lady speaks.'
The lady was Martin, who after complimenting Astor on the
polite way he guarded the door, wrote to Edith 'My dear, I
have led the Chief to the circle. He is prepared to help; question
him.' The Lord Chief Justice Bushe then came through. 'I make
my bow to your generation,' he wrote in very strong large
characters, done very rapidly. He then hailed Edith as the most
intellectual of his descendants. She had made some study of his
life already but was short of material on certain subjects, among
others his first meeting with Nancy Crampton, his future wife.
A question on this point was put by Geraldine Cummins, the
medium: 'Can you speak of your youth and your meeting with
Nan?' Bushe's reply began with the words: 'Egad, it was a
brave time!' He then held forth at length about a ball in Merrion
Street, Dublin, where he was introduced to Nan, described
what she looked like, how she was dressed, how he was dressed,
how he proposed and eventually was accepted. These details and
a good deal more he poured out on 5 December 1930. Another
long seance was held on 22 September 1931 when he recalled
his speech in the Irish parliament on 15 January 1800 during
the important debate on union with the English parliament.

In Edith's diary of 2 February 1931 she wonders whether in
a scholarly biography founded on public and private records she
ought to use communications made by its subject through a
medium ninety years after his death. On reflection she felt
bound to do so. There could be no suspicion of fraud because
Martin herself had declared in the automatic writing that she
had found Bushe and brought him. Surely that guaranteed the
authenticity of Bushe's statements? How could she after fifteen
years' collaboration with the dead Martin doubt her in this
case? If she did, the whole fabric of her beliefs, built up since

the fatal December 1915, would be undermined. She must believe that Martin had brought the Chief Justice and advised he be questioned on matters where the documents were not full enough. Nevertheless she knew very well that testimony of the kind would not be generally acceptable. There seemed no alternative, however, and finally she decided to weave some of what Bushe said at the seances into the biography and leave the reader to assume that her source was his papers.

The book, called *An Incorruptible Irishman*, was published in May 1932. In chapter VIII are to be found the very words from the automatic script* where Bushe describes his first meeting with Nancy Crampton; and in chapter XXIV on the Union debate part of what the automatic script declared him to have said on that occasion, one of the most important in his life.

Nothing could reveal more clearly Edith's certainty that communication with the dead was possible and that their testimony was wholly reliable. But she did not face the corollary that all historians and biographers should, besides looking up the records, call up the principal personages for cross-examination. But, again, as Ethel Smyth points out, Edith's strong point was not logic.

* As preserved in Notebook No. 16.

23

D.Litt. Trinity College and Fellow, Academy of Letters

In February 1932, when the Bushe biography was finished but not yet published, Edith was offered by Trinity College, Dublin, the degree of Doctor of Letters. She accepted with great pleasure this recognition by Dublin of her labours as a writer. She was seventy-four years of age. Dublin was, of course, only following the opinion of the public in England and America. Indeed, it appears that Yale offered her an analogous degree, if she stayed on in the States until the date when honorary degrees were next bestowed, a condition it was impossible for her to accept.

The Dublin degree was conferred on 29 June 1932, a month after the publication of the book on Bushe. The Public Orator in his Latin oration* declared few women writers had ever reached her celebrity. When offered the degree, Edith had made it a condition of acceptance that Martin's name should be associated with hers. The Public Orator's reference to Martin was: 'I recall with veneration to your memory the cousin associated with her in so many works; whom living she loved more than the light of day, and whom, now that she is taken from her sight, she cherishes with no less love as though she were still present and helping.'

This delicate reference was as far as Trinity College, Dublin,

* The Latin text with its translation is in Elizabeth Hudson's *Bibliography*.

was prepared to go. Further cloaked as it was in the stately cadences of the Latin language, it was most unlikely to expose the University to ridicule. What was said satisfied the lady whom they desired to honour without admitting that her beliefs were in any way shared.

The biography of Bushe had a good press. Nobody detected that some of the statements attributed to him came from recent automatic writings. Edith had now two mediums, her friend Jem Barlow and Geraldine Cummins. The latter began making stays at Drishane and so was available more easily for seances. When writing with Bushe on one occasion, he declared to her that he had read his biography and was delighted with it. He was known during his lifetime to like punning jokes, and when he said 'Edith has grafted the Bushe on a good stock of laurel', the jocularity was held characteristic of his wit and his period. Jem Barlow, who added to her gifts as a medium the faculty to see ghosts, reported at this time to Edith how she saw one of the Coghill aunts, Aunt Florence, in St Barrahane church at Holy Communion one Sunday morning. The lady had died in 1883, fifty years back, and been buried beside the main door of the church. Edith's diary is the source for the following: 'Jem came to tea. She told me that at early service this morning she heard the rustling sound of a voluminous silk dress. Looking round she saw a tall lady walking up the aisle. She went into a pew behind Cameron. When they went to the rails (there were only seven) the lady knelt in the middle, between Jem and Cameron. Her dress was black silk with a purple pattern on it. She had a large black hat and no coat. When the Canon passed her, Jem realized she was a Visitor! After tea Jem and I wrote and the visitor was fetched by Martin and wrote "I am your Aunt Florence" and a few sentences more. She didn't like the window in the church and said briefly "Romish".' The window over the altar contained a representation of the Virgin. A short time afterwards Jem saw the ghost of Grandfather Somerville strolling in a top hat.*

* See his photograph with Edith as a young girl facing page 32.

Edith's interest in spiritualism had been growing steadily and was now at its height. She read all the books she could get hold of on the subject, attended spiritualist meetings when in London and discussed the subject with spiritualists in London society. Her closest friends, Ethel Smyth, Mrs Anstey and Lady Kenmare were all spiritualists. She had a battle in the pages of *Time and Tide* with Rose Macaulay, who had defined spiritualism as fraud and hysteria.

In the course of 1932 Yeats founded the Irish Academy of Letters and though hitherto he had paid Edith little attention he invited her to become a member of his Academy. When writing to her, however, he spelt her name wrong, which she thought characteristic of him.

In March 1933 she went to Dublin to attend a dinner given by the new Academy. It was her first introduction to the Dublin literary world. She found Yeats much more agreeable than she had supposed and describes him in her diary as 'very big, fine looking, with masses of wavy grey hair'. James Stephens she saw as 'tiny, hideous, like a sick monkey' but very entertaining. She met several people she liked at Walter Starkie's house, among others Sarah Purser, James McNeill and Lady Fingall. The Academy dinner was at Jammet's restaurant, the best in Dublin. She sat between Yeats and A.E. She was introduced to all the men, thirteen in number, among whom were Frank O'Connor and Joseph Hone. 'Lennox Robinson sent me a half bottle of champagne. We raised our glasses to each other. Then all stood up and drank my health and I stood up and did the same for them and all was peace and love.'

If there had ever been a coolness between Dublin and Castle Townshend that was the end of it. The fact had been that the Dublin intellectuals had underrated Edith Somerville. She had been written off as a follower of Lever who could do no more than dish up his stage Irishmen again. She was alleged to have repeated the stale old joke that all the Irish were figures of fun, to whom the government of their country could not possibly be handed over. But critical opinion had turned in her favour.

D.Litt. Trinity College and Fellow, Academy of Letters

She was now held to be a great Irish humorist in her own right. Her picture of the country Irish was taken direct from the model on his ground. She never used the machinery of the stage Irishman. In her works the Irish are not effigies performing set tricks and tumbles, but, far more amusing, real persons. Her sense of humour was very wide. She could laugh at anything, even if she thought it rather indelicate. Of what she called a 'nasty little nursery story' by Ethel Smythe, she quotes in her diary what an old country woman said of something of the same sort: 'I've thrown wather over cats for less than that'; and she laughed heartily when told that a notice, advertising a lecture on spiritualism to be given at Brighton by Geraldine Cummins, read: 'A lecture on the Road to Immorality with 25 years personal experience'. Her diary comment is: 'She had a crowded house.'

In 1941, nine years after the Irish Academy of Letters had made her a Fellow, it awarded her the Gregory Gold Medal, its highest award for literary excellence.

[253]

24

Edith fails as a playwright but succeeds as a horse dealer

In 1934 Edith increased the number of her seances and her reading of occult books. Automatic writing was not always the outcome. On 4 February 1934 she reports: 'Much violence, cold airs, table swinging and megaphone used as a weapon to express disapproval but nothing more definite.' She resented poaching on her preserves. 'Heard from Caz Anstey that she and Elizabeth Arbuthnot had "called" Martin to write with them. Wrote to both and said I was not pleased. Martin had responded, thinking it was my "call" and then did not like to refuse, but thought it was rather a liberty.'

Castle Townshend had always had its season every summer. The festivities in 1934 were more elaborate than usual because numerous American admirers and London journalists turned up. To amuse them a dog party was given. '14 dogs and 14 bones. I brought Cozy, Nancy and the puppies. All were good and enjoyed their bones.' In the evening there was a fancy dress dance for humans. Edith wore her doctor's robes. A cousin wore an old cloak belonging to Mrs Starkie and carried a live hen in a basket. A little cousin went as Gandhi leading a kid, while a smaller one danced a nautch.

But there was a depressing side. She could not make both ends meet. The two last books, the tour of the States and the

Bushe biography, sold very badly. The farm was monstrously
in debt again. But, 'like water in the desert', as she terms it, she
suddenly got a cheque for £497 10s. for the sale of horses in
America. Horse-coping had become her chief means of liveli-
hood. She also raised money by selling for £500 the MS. of
three of her books to Maggs of Conduit Street, W.1., who were
acting for the Comte de Suzannet. On leaving Maggs she was
in such high spirits that she treated herself to a taxi ride and
bought a wireless.

A fortnight later she went to a Menuhin concert at the Albert
Hall. Martin also heard the marvellous tone of the violin and
in a seance wrote: 'The boy is touched with heavenly fire.'
Ethel Smyth did not go, for she was now completely deaf, and
had exchanged musical for literary composition. 'She spoke in a
high raucous voice and trumpeted her woes.' They saw each
other when Edith was in London and corresponded at length
when apart. There are altogether 440 letters from Ethel Smyth
among Edith's papers.

Towards the end of 1934 Edith added two more mediums
to her occult entourage, Mrs de Crespigny and a Miss Lewis,
called the Flower Medium. In the diary is an account of how
Julian Huxley and his wife Juliette went to a private sitting with
these two mediums. Julian Huxley was so sceptical, says Edith,
that even when roses materialized he remained unconvinced.
After the seance he drove off in his open car with his wife. On
Hammersmith Broadway she called on him to stop. On the palm
of her hand a big bunch of violets had materialized. Julian
Huxley is reported to have been more impressed than he cared
to admit. 'If things were as they seemed to be, science would
have to reconsider' was his reported observation.

In her search for ready money Edith resurrected the old play,
which some years back George Bernard Shaw had criticized
so ferociously. Since then she had rewritten and offered it in
various directions but no one would put it on. Now in 1935 she
heard from Elizabeth Hudson, her American bibliographer, that
she was showing the play to various film people. But it was

no good; nobody would touch it. The typescript was put back in its drawer, where it remained till her death. The disappointment, however, was mitigated by the arrival of another cheque from America for horses sold, £315 10s. Suffering a good deal from her rheumatism, which had become chronic and which baths at Aix or elsewhere failed to alleviate, she had to lie up a good deal and, in an effort to become better acquainted with the English classics, on which she was very weak, she set to work on Jane Austen but thought all the men 'governesses in trousers and the girls impossible prigs'. She then tried Trollope's *Hunting Sketches*, but found them 'very dull and stodgy'.

On 3 December 1935, the twentieth anniversary of the day when she took Martin from Drishane to die in Glen Vera hospital, Cork, she communicated with the spirit of her beloved. Martin urged her to continue the automatic writing. For her, she said, the twenty years 'were like an evening past', but for Edith 'it is like ten years of years'.

An event, which was to be a profound shock, was close at hand, the murder of her brother, Admiral Boyle Somerville.

25

The Murder of Admiral Boyle Somerville

In March 1936 Edith was over in London staying with Caz
Anstey. Her brother Jack was also in London. On the 25th he
rang her up to say that he had just read in *The Times* that Boyle
had been murdered. The paper reported that the murder took
place the night before at The Point in Castle Townshend, where
Boyle and his wife Mab had resided since his retirement from
the Navy. They were in the dining room when at 9 p.m. a
knock at the hall door was heard. Boyle went into the hall and
opened the door. A man said: 'Are you Mr Somerville?' He
replied: 'I am Admiral Somerville.' Whereupon the man shot
him through the heart. Mab ran out of the dining room with a
lamp in her hand, which was extinguished by a gust of wind
from the open door. The man, and one or two others with him,
then bolted into the darkness. Boyle was stretched flat on the
hall floor, quite dead. The sound of a departing car was heard
at the avenue gate.

So much was in *The Times*. Edith and Jack left that night for
Castle Townshend, which they reached about 1 p.m. next day,
26 March. About forty hours had elapsed since the murder.
Rushing at once to The Point they found Boyle's body still
stretched on the floor of the hall, because the police, who had
been summoned from Skibbereen, would not allow it to be
moved till their investigations were complete, the necessary
photographs taken and a coffin delivered, which did not arrive

s

till later in the afternoon. The family had rallied round Mab. Hildegarde was there, and Hugh, the Vice-Admiral brother, and Paddy, Nevill and Ambrose, Boyle's nephews. Cameron was laid up in bed. The diary has: 'It was a heart-breaking home-coming, nothing but tears, incessant telegrams and letters. It had been a long agony for them all.' The funeral took place next day at 4 p.m. 'I spent the morning,' Edith continues, 'making a cross with white heather. Nevill and Ambrose got spring flowers from Glen Barrahane and made a cross themselves. Everyone in the country and Skibbereen and many from Cork came.' The Roman Catholic priest, Father Collins, who was devoted to Boyle, was 'near weeping with rage at the murder as well as with grief. A most comforting message from Martin was sent via Astor and Geraldine Cummins.'

The murder was evidently the work of gunmen of some irreconcilable group. But as the Troubles were over more than ten years before, how came it that Admiral Boyle, living in quiet retirement and much liked by high and low, was singled out? What had he done to rouse his murderers to so savage a reprisal? The murderers, it is said, left a note saying that he was killed because he had helped local youths to get into the British Navy by giving them certificates of good character. The plea that this action deserved death at a time when all major differences between England and Ireland had been settled was idiotic. De Valera, who had come to power in 1932 on the death of Cosgrave and was beginning to bring his Republic at last into existence by agreement, denounced the murder in the strongest terms, as did all groups. Not a voice was raised to declare Admiral Boyle had brought it on himself by acting against the interests of the Irish nation. But in any country, after a period of fighting and anarchy, a dissident remnant always remains, no matter how complete a settlement has been made. Admiral Boyle Somerville's murder was not the last outrage perpetrated by such relentless foes of England. The identity of Boyle's killers was never established. Despite the utmost efforts of the police no one was found guilty of the murder.

The Murder of Admiral Boyle Somerville

Edith lost no time in trying to get into touch with Boyle. On 5 April, ten days after the funeral, she records: 'After tea Jem, Hildegarde and I went to the studio and asked Martin if Boyle could write with us. Instantly he wrote "I am here myself".' A few sentences followed, fairly legibly written. He said he had one terrible moment of contact with evil when they looked at him out of the darkness, but afterwards was enfolded in an atmosphere of love when he was met by familiar faces. Other short seances followed but not till 5 June did he describe his murder. He professed to knowing the name and appearance of the man who had fired the shot that killed him. 'He raised the hand and a blinding flash came from that hand. I felt no pain, but had the sensation of sinking into a deep well of night.' His next feeling was one of sudden release. He found himself soaring and presently was aware that his mother, Uncle Kendal and his brother Aylmer were gathered round him. The seances were continued for some days, but nothing more definite was revealed.*

At the time of his death Boyle had nearly finished a book on Will Mariner, a contemporary of Captain Cook, who was for some years a prisoner in Tonga, the Pacific group of islands. Edith revised his MS. which was published later by Fabers.

A much more curious collaboration with him was shortly to take place. During his lifetime he and she had planned to write a history of the Somerville family. Boyle, as has been mentioned, became interested in spiritualism after his retirement from the Navy. The line he specialized in was what he termed psycho-metry. In this form of communication with the dead, the medium is put in touch with some object or place once closely associated with a deceased person. When Jem Barlow, accompanied by Boyle, sought information from the ghost of the Spaniard, one of the soldiers stationed at an encampment in Castlehaven at the time of Queen Elizabeth, it was the ruins of the old Spanish encampment which enabled them to summon him. Such was the

* In the Notebook numbered 43 is preserved a quantity of automatic writing from Boyle covering several years. It has little interest.

psychometric belief. Inasmuch as Boyle had been a practising spiritualist of this kind, Edith now proposed to ask him to help her to write the family history by getting in touch with the ancestors. The matter was put to him at one of the seances. He professed every willingness to help. During the researches into the family which he had made while alive he had come upon a letter written by William Somerville, the first of the family to come to Ireland. (The Somervilles had fled from Scotland in 1690 to avoid religious persecution.). His son, Thomas, became in the thirties of the eighteenth century rector of Castlehaven. On 22 September 1938 Boyle wrote in a seance: 'I would like you to give Geraldine Cummins that old letter of William Somerville's to hold. It will draw William or his son Thomas from the distant place where they now reside.' In the family history subsequently written, Edith described what happened. 'I compiled a list of questions and extracting William Somerville's letter from the old portfolio I laid it on the table in my studio in front of Geraldine Cummins. On this occasion we had not long to wait. Astor announced: "Here comes your brother in company with a black-coated gentleman who wears a white tie".' The automatic writing then gave the name—Thomas Somerville, William's son. Some biographical information then came through from him in the automatic script. When the power began to fail, he promised to return later.

At a seance two days afterwards, he was again reported present. On this occasion he gave a detailed account of the family's escape across the strait from Scotland in a small boat, the weather stormy, he violently seasick. There followed some details of how he grew up in Ireland and became in due course rector of the parish of Castlehaven.

Edith, though aware that the authenticity of these statements was debatable, decided to accept them, where they did not clash with the known facts, and included them in her account of the Somervilles, which was printed by a Cork firm of publishers in 1940 under the title of *Records of the Somerville Family of Castlehaven and Drishane from 1174 to 1940*. She joined her name as author with Boyle's, the title page reading: 'Compiled by Edith Œnone Somerville and Boyle Townshend Somerville.' This is the only case where the name of a collaborator other than Martin appears in her works.

During the period between the appearance of *An Incorruptible Irishman* (1932) and *Records of the Somerville Family* (1940) Edith, who was eighty-two years of age at the latter date, managed to get out three more books, *The Smile and the Tear* (1933), *The Sweet Cry of Hounds* (1936) and *Sarah's Youth* (1938), a wonderful feat for a woman who was not only very old but much enfeebled by chronic sciatica and other forms of rheumatism. The two first-mentioned books were collections of essays, of the character of Irish reminiscences, easy to read, humorous and amounting to a small addition to her existing œuvre, into which they neatly fit. *Sarah's Youth*, however, was a full-length novel, a more exhausting undertaking than the two volumes of essays, some of which had already appeared in periodicals. In its review in *Punch* the book is called a happy revival of the Somerville and Martin Ross style of fiction, its characters 'all worthy to be hung on the line in the portrait-gallery of Irish types given us in earlier years by the authors of the R.M.'. It is the mixture as before, but quite pleasantly stirred.

These books sold moderately well, but of course Drishane could not be maintained on royalties. It was Cameron's pension which kept the place going. The farm, planned as a steady source of revenue, had become a liability. Edith could not bear the idea of disposing of it and discharging her employees, several of them faithful old servants. The only substantial source of revenue was the sale of horses in America, carried on in partnership with her friend, Sylvia Warren of River Bend, Dover, Massachusetts, who in July 1936 was staying at Drishane, helping Edith to buy likely horses in County Cork. '1 August. I've been motoring all over the country with Sylvia Warren hunting for horses,' sound weight-carrying animals of the cob type. When bought they were smartened up by her groom, Mike

Hurley, for whom she felt the closest affection she had ever felt for any man outside her own family, and shipped to America in his charge, where Sylvia Warren took delivery and sold them at a good profit.

Six months after Boyle's death Edith went to Massachusetts to stay with Sylvia Warren, accompanied by her niece, Katharine Coghill, sister of Paddy and Nevill. This American visit was a business one, not the tour of a literary celebrity. She sought to acquaint herself on the spot with the American horse market, prices, types of horses required, etc., and went about the country regardless of her age and disabilities. She overdid it for a woman of seventy-eight. In October, twelve days after her arrival, a small varicose vein in her left leg suddenly became tender and swollen. A doctor pronounced it phlebitis, a dangerous clot in the vein which might lead to a thrombosis, and ordered her to lie up. She remained in bed till 22 November, when she was well enough to start for home.

26

The death of Cameron

Edith had thirteen more years of life, for she did not die till she was ninety-one. As was inevitable, since no mortal can keep age at bay, she became more and more feeble, though her mind remained clear. Her last lap was made harder still by coinciding with the second World War. There was more to eat in Ireland than in England, but supplies of such necessities as coal and oil were more limited. Her sources of income dried up. The severest blow of all was the death in 1942 of her brother Cameron, owner of Drishane. He was nearly eighty-two, she was eighty-four. Her diary entry for the event read: '30 January 1942. C. left us at 10 mins. to 6 a.m. in sleep, quite peacefully, without awaking. Martin, writing at night, said he was still asleep and that they thought it too long till they could tell him where he was, with his poor body restored to health and youth. He was my earliest friend and his love has never failed me for all but 82 years.'

The diary contains other touching details. Cameron had had a long and painful illness. 'Grief is almost forgotten in the thankfulness that he has no more to suffer and has escaped.' One of the telegrams of condolence read: 'May his gentle soul have eternal rest.' He *was* a gentle soul. All these years he had lived quietly at Drishane with Edith and Hildegarde, in perfect amity and self effacement under Edith's firm and loving rule. Now his body lay among flowers, with a small Union Jack spread by it on which his M.V.O. cross was placed. On

2 February, the day of the funeral, Mike Hurley, the groom, now general factotum, head retainer and manager of the household under Edith, collected twenty men. 'At 3 o'clock they carried the coffin to the church. Hildegarde and I had driven there.' They stayed in the Baptistery during the service. They were worn out with grief and weeping, these two ancient ladies.

A financial crisis followed. Cameron's pension died with him. As he had no children, he left Drishane to his nephew Desmond, Aylmer's son, who was in the Army and now failed to get leave. It was one of the worst moments of the war; Singapore had fallen, the Japanese had entered Burma, the American fleet had been sunk at Pearl Harbour; France was occupied by the Germans, England only just holding on. The Somerville brothers, Jack and Hugh, elderly retired officers, were present in Castle Townshend, the former over from London where he lived, the latter resident in the village at a house called Malmaison. What was to be done? How maintain Drishane? The Coghill ancestral seat, Glen Barrahane, an even larger mansion than Drishane, had to be kept up by its owner, Paddy, become Sir Patrick Coghill, the head of his family. Edith Somerville had no money except what she could make by books and horses, both hazardous enterprises, which the war had largely ruined. A bomb had hit Longmans and destroyed their stock of her books, which they refused to reprint on the plea that paper for reprints was unobtainable. Export of horses across the U-boat infested Atlantic was, of course, impossible. How was she to live, how was Hildegarde, Lady Coghill, to live? Edith's rule as mistress of Drishane, under the benign eye of her brother, Cameron, was at an end. Her nephew Desmond, the new owner, would no doubt give her shelter. But as he was married, it would not be the same as in bachelor Cameron's time. Moreover, he could not leave the Army and settle in Drishane till the war was over. And who could foretell when that would be? In her desperation Edith wrote off to Hermon Ould, the P.E.N. Club's secretary, to inquire what prospect she had of getting a pension from some literary benevolent society or the Civil List.

The death of Cameron

In the course of February 1942 it occurred to her that perhaps her most sensible course would be to abandon Drishane and move into a nearby cottage called Furzy Mill. But this drastic plan was not followed up. On 24 February Desmond Somerville arrived on leave from the Army. She notes: 'Hildegarde, Desmond and I discussed financial and domestic points.' When would Desmond be free to take up residence in Drishane; was he agreeable to allow Edith and Hildegarde to remain there till he did so; could he afford to pay towards its upkeep what Cameron had paid? There was no provision in Cameron's will giving Edith the right to remain there during her lifetime. But now, she says, her brother Jack 'with unexampled generosity' came to her financial rescue, providing enough money to tide her over the crisis and make it unnecessary to press her application for a benevolent grant. Desmond had to return to his command on 2 March, leaving Edith and Hildegarde in possession of Drishane for the time being, secured by Jack's grant of money.

At this period Edith's rheumatic disorders increased. On top of that she contracted shingles, but somehow managed to administer the affairs of the farm from her bed, giving instructions to the faithful Mike Hurley. A nurse visited her daily. Through all this she kept her diary, methodically cataloguing her symptoms and the nerve pain she suffered from the shingles, but without weakness or lamentation. Very slowly she got over the shingles, for not until 31 March was she able to go downstairs. Even by then she was far from well. Throughout this evil time she maintained her nightly communication with Martin, for she could now manage alone the automatic writing well enough for short messages.

To this period belong a few extant letters of hers written to Maurice Baring, the celebrated man of letters, for whom, since they first met at Elizabeth Kenmare's in 1919, she had a liking which grew warmer with time. On 13 April 1942 she wrote informing him of Cameron's death: 'I have been rather ill ever since and could hardly write any letters. He was the best and most devoted brother in the world.' (Her extant letters to him number 363.) 'This has been a dark year for us.' Her nephew, Philip Somerville, Hugh's son, commanding a destroyer, had lately been killed in action. Elizabeth Kenmare's husband, Lord Kenmare, had just died. 'I only wish that her and your religion would allow you the unspeakable consolation of an occasional message from those who have gone over. I have known it now for five and twenty years when an unexpected, volunteered word from my cousin Martin Ross came and saved me.' The letter contains the sentence: 'I have taken to reading, quite a new amusement for me, who had read nothing but newspapers since the war began.' One of the books she read was Enid Starkie's autobiographical *A Lady's Child*. In another letter she cites the hardships of having only candles*—sometimes only one candle—to read by at night. And she does not hide the drying up of her literary income. 'I shall have died in the workhouse long before Longmans reprint.' This was before Jack came to her assistance. She signs herself 'yours affectionately'. Maurice Baring died during 1945.

At the end of the 1942 diary Edith transcribed a message from Martin, dated 10 November. 'In 1943, when the war starts to lift, you must press Longmans to reprint those of our books not in stock. Suggest a complete or collected edition. Meanwhile we must work at short pieces. I want to have a book ready.'

A year after the publication (for private circulation) of *The Records of the Somerville Family* in 1940, Edith had got Methuen to publish a book of her essays called *Notions in Garrison*, notions, as she writes in a foreword, 'that are as ready to laugh at misfortunes as to lament over them, and are ready to accept Marvels with an open mind'. The essays, phrased autobiographically, included one on poltergeists, another entitled 'Some Ghost Stories', two giving a full account of Boyle's colloquy in the old Spanish graveyard in Castlehaven with the derelict

---

* There was no oil for lamps. Electric light was not installed in the village of Castle Townshend till 1945.

spectre, and six others on miscellaneous marvels. The book is forgotten now, but it should not be, for it is true Somerville vintage, humorous, touching, fanciful, smiling, poetical and very Irish. Well, Martin is represented as commanding her to buckle to and get ready yet another book. She was eighty-four, but had still two books of essays in her, *Happy Days* (1946) and *Maria and Some Other Dogs* (1949) the year of her death.

27

Last Days

From 1942 to the end of the war Edith and Hildegarde hung on at Drishane, trying to make the best of a hard time like everyone else. In the month of May 1944 Edith lost two of her best friends, for whom she wrote two notable valedictions. Ethel Smyth died on the 9th. 'She was 86, born on April 23, 1858, ten days before me. She was a splendid creature and I am thankful to have known and loved her and to have been loved by her.' On 24 May Elizabeth Kenmare died. 'I shall never know another creature as perfect in all ways as she. It is a poor thing to outlive one's best friends.'

As soon as the war was over, Desmond Somerville and his wife Moira (*née* Roche) took up their residence in Drishane. Hildegarde withdrew to her son, Paddy's, house, Glen Barrahane, but Edith stayed on. She had been *de facto* mistress of Drishane since her mother died in 1895, half a century ago. It was not an easy situation. She had to abdicate or leave.

An early intimation of what was afoot is to be found in a letter dated 11 November 1946 written to Martin's nephew, Richard Martin, who lived in London. 'Paddy Coghill has let his house, Glen Barrahane, and is providing another home in Castle Townshend for his mother Hildegarde. I am therefore leaving Drishane in order to live with her.' The other house was Tally Ho, the property of Paddy's brother, Ambrose, which had become vacant. It was situated in the main street of the village. In another letter two months later to the same person, she wrote from Tally Ho: 'For various good reasons Hildegarde and I had to uproot ourselves and set up on our own here.'

Edith's letters to her brother Jack (who like Richard Martin lived in London) and the entries in her diary bring us closer to this drama of a very old and famous woman having to leave at eighty-eight the house where she had presided for half a century. In a letter of 24 September 1946 she mentions to Jack that Tally Ho will be vacant in November. 'It has two good bathrooms and when (or if) I go there, there will be three as I shall bring my own bath with me.' On 7 October she wrote to him: 'The Transit of the two Venuses to Tally Ho has been indefinitely postponed.' (The house required redecoration and repair.) 'I got down there after tea and surveyed the rooms I am to have. I cannot say that they compare well with my beloved old rooms here (Drishane) but they have at least the merit of no stairs and I'm now so awfully lame that this is really a boon.'

The removal was fixed for 11 November 1946. On 28 October Edith told Jack: 'Hildegarde and I feel that we have no abiding city here. No one but myself knows how I detest turning out of my studio and my bedroom. I most fervently wish I had been left to die at Drishane in spite of the stairs.' But perhaps she will feel better 'when this damnable move is accomplished. It's the anticipation that keeps me awake at night.' And on 1 November: 'I am now, in view of this dread move to Tally Ho, beginning to sort books and letters.' There were the accumulations of nearly ninety years. 'Tidied and collected and classified rubbish in the studio, so soon to be forsaken, and felt perfectly wretched, head giddy and legs tottering.' For 10 November her diary has: 'Began the great effort of preparing for what may be called the Hegira or Flight of E.Œ.S.' On 11 November Hildegarde moved ahead into Tally Ho. 'Awful work of demolition and depredation and transportation. Destruction of masses of treasured rubbish, disturbing most ancient beds of cats. Under everything there was something.' On 12 November Edith moved: 'The tumbril arrived at 9 a.m.

and fell upon the studio and had gutted it by lunch. I, a useless incapable cripple, was carted to Malmaison,' Hugh's house, where with Hildegarde she waited till all their effects had arrived at Tally Ho.

The first thing they got on entering Tally Ho was a telegram from Jack to cheer them up. He knew how they felt. The transfer of these two old ladies, miserable and protesting, was, indeed, a pitiable event. Edith was exhausted by having had to sort the vast accumulation of treasured letters, papers, little personal possessions, drawings, periodicals, a thousand things she had to say goodbye to for ever. She left all her paintings, except those in her studio, hanging on the walls of Drishane, where they still hang. It was like an enactment of her death while still alive, and was infinitely depressing. But there was no help for it. Not that its inevitability was any solace at the cruel moment of farewell.

Nevertheless, Tally Ho was a good house. On the right of the photograph here reproduced is the wing chosen for Edith, as it was one storey. She could be wheeled into the garden comfortably in her bath chair. In Drishane her apartments were upstairs. To the left are Hildegarde's quarters, and in the centre a dining room and drawing room with spare bedrooms upstairs. The windows commanded a more open view of the sea than at Drishane. It was less damp than the other house. All these advantages, however, did not serve to abate Edith's disenchantment at her departure, compared by her to Mahomet's flight from Mecca to Medina, and to the horrid transit of an aristocrat in a tumbril to the guillotine. She did not accept as inevitable what had befallen. Surely she could have been left, she exclaims, to die quietly in a house which though not her own legally was hers by every reason of the heart. That Edith held these views at the time was human and natural. The day after the move, as she looked at her belongings jumbled in her new quarters, she was appalled by the reflection that she would never be able to locate 'where any single necessity belonging to me is'. A week later she wrote to Jack: 'I am very far from being settled in and down and having any of my property under control. You would not believe without seeing the chaos in this big room.' She feels that she needs Jack's comfort, that only he can comfort her and she asks him and his wife to come over from London and spend Christmas at Tally Ho. It goes against the grain to have to couple her invitations with the request that they pay 30s. each for board a week, but so poor has she become that she has to ask for the money. 'I must bore you with my difficulties, but please consider them as strictly private. I am too old to have been transplanted. It makes me mad I am useless and a cumberer of the earth.'

But she was never a person to give way for long to lamentations. As always, she soon saw there was another side to the matter. By 20 December, a month and a bit after the move, one finds her telling Jack: 'As a matter of fact my departure has been a blessing.' And another month on, as noted, she told Richard Martin how there were various good reasons for having to uproot herself. Nevertheless, her last diary entry for the year 1946 was a cry of despair: 'Superfluous lags the Veteran on the stage in vain defiance of relentless age', a cry however not against the move but pitiless death which had already 'slammed life's door'. She was in her eighty-ninth year and an incurable invalid. Her last words for 1946 were from Landor:

'I warmed both hands before the fire of life.
It sinks and I am ready to depart.'

Early in 1947 she suffered another shock. Jem Barlow, her friend, the clairvoyant and medium, who for so long had helped her to communicate with Martin, died. But she had Geraldine Cummins, a more professional and experienced medium, who had by this time become a close friend.

Very appropriately she had published just now a volume of essays called *Happy Days*, wherein she called to mind happinesses of the past. The title page, as before, bears the two names, though one notices that now Edith adds 'Hon. Litt.D.' to hers. She was proud of the Trinity College, Dublin, degree, so proud that she does not see how it serves on a title page to distinguish her from Martin, the very last thing she wanted. All these essays had appeared at one time or another in such journals as *Time and Tide*, *Blackwood's*, *Country Life* and *The Field*. The subject of one of them is the happy time at Étaples, painting, with Martin as her companion. In another she describes the tour of Sicily during the first months of her infatuation with Ethel Smyth. Happy too were the days when hunting with her own pack and the smart hunts she had with the Quorn in England. The best essay is that in which she asks whether horses are more delectable than dogs. One sees her trying to take the horses' side, pointing to their nobility of character, willing service to the needs of man, obedience and readiness to sacrifice even their lives, as in battle or steeplechasing. Quoting Landor, she alters his line: 'Nature I loved and, next to Nature, Art' to 'Horses I loved, and, next to Horses, Art.' Yet it is clearly a losing fight for the horse. She loved dogs more. When you died you found your dogs waiting to welcome you on the other side. In the seances her pet foxterriers, though invisible, were often reported present. The medium saw them, even felt them. But of all the horses she rode not a sign, not even of the lovely Bridget, one time her favourite mare. There were no horses in heaven. Martin, once an intrepid horsewoman, never came mounted. Astor, Geraldine Cummins's haughty control, was always afoot. And this, though horses, she contends, were endowed with as acute a supernormal consciousness as dogs. And she recalled how a tired old cart-horse, lumbering back from a fair in the dark, madly bolted when an abominable female spectre popped out of a bush and caught hold of the cart at the back.

By 1947 Edith was half in and half out of this world. Gone though were her father and mother, Uncle Kendal, her brothers Cameron, Boyle and Aylmer, and most of her closest friends, she was still in communication with them through Martin, who received them lovingly when they died, gathered them about her, summoned them when required, for she was a

goddess in that realm, ever at hand to encourage, to prophesy
and, above all, to collaborate. Edith felt she would soon be
reunited to her. It was towards that rapturous meeting that she
strained her old eyes.

Despite these anticipations of death, she kept up her diary
on everyday events. In 1947 she had reached her seventy-fifth
volume. Her daily entries throughout averaged about a hundred
words. That gives a total of some two and three-quarter million
words, which exceeds the number in all her published books
combined. No other woman has ever left such a mass of detailed
information about her daily life. She completed the volume for
1947 and, with some gaps, the volume for 1948, in the May of
which year she entered her ninety-first year. She did not keep
a diary for 1949, the year she died, because she became too
blind to see what she was writing. Her vast correspondence
also ceased in 1948. But she managed the extraordinary feat of
putting together another book of essays, the *Maria and Some
Other Dogs*, published in 1949, where are collected from her
books and articles the most amusing, most touching and most
intuitive anecdotes and observations on the life and death of
the many dogs she had adored.

The diary of 1947, though written under great physical
disabilities, is not without its amusing touches. She was born a
humorist and she died a humorist. For instance on 9 August 1947
she records how a friend came to see her and told her how on
her way to Cork her car was punctured. Having no spanner to
change the wheel, she waited for a car to pass. At last she saw
one, a hearse with a coffin inside. The driver stopped and
volunteered to do the job, saying pleasantly: 'The gentleman
I have inside here won't be in a hurry.'

On 19 January 1948 she recorded her wishes in the matter of
bequests. 'I wish while I still retain my senses to make a few
notes. I believe I have about £700 in the bank together with
£300 in securities.' She was not certain the figures were
correct but hoped they were. 'Legacies could be given with my
love to the following dear friends (leaving their bestowal to the

discretion of my beloved and faithful sister Hildegarde, helped in this troublesome job by my dear godson, Paddy). As far as possible, £50 each, to Mike, Nurse O'Riordan (for long her nurse), Geraldine Cummins, Muriel Currey' (Martin's niece). Two old servants are also named. 'I had hoped to leave Mike considerably more, but unless *Maria and Some Other Dogs* turns up trumps, I shall not be able to do so.'*

For the year 1948 Edith's letters to her brother Jack, now a retired Colonel of over seventy living in London, are a good authority and will be dipped into here. The handwriting of the letters becomes increasingly unsteady. On 19 April, a fortnight before her 90th birthday, she wrote: 'You see how vilely I write but my mind is quite clear.' Her heart had begun to give trouble and she had had a damaging fall in May 1947. On her 90th birthday her doctor declared her to be quite well. There was nothing wrong with her except that she was dying of old age, whose disabilities of blindness and rheumatic joints and muscles prevented her from doing anything. She was well enough, however, to be wheeled out of the house to her pony trap and taken a drive by Mike Hurley. She got forty telegrams on her birthday, she told Jack, and her nephew, Nevill, broadcast a talk about her on the B.B.C. 'I could have wished he said more of Martin but I suppose a live dog is always more effective than a dead lion.'

In June 1948 she wrote: 'I am certainly improving but I can't walk two steps. My writing is nearly out of control.' Some days the letters to Jack are almost illegible, on others the writing is clear but wobbly. On 20 July she wrote him a pitiable letter, the writing hardly decipherable. 'I'm sorry I can't see what I'm doing. If I sent you and Mildred twenty pounds would you come here to us for a week. I can get out of bed and drive in Desmond's car, but alas! I can't see. Think it over. I should love to see you and I have more money than I spend. Do believe that I'm not crazy but only that I can't see. *Do come.*'

---

* On Edith's death the family pensioned Mike Hurley.

Last Days

In November she was still struggling to write to Jack: 'I'm good for nothing, so you must just accept this scrawl with all my love and assurances of my deep and faithful love to you both.'

She felt helpless, lonely and entirely immobilized. To write, she had, she says, 'to grope along somehow'. She refused to dictate and declined Geraldine Cummins's offer to write her letters for her. In a last letter, before Christmas 1948, she says: 'I don't think I can live much longer, but I will struggle on if you and Mildred will come over. It would be an enormous pleasure and my only hope of seeing you before I die. Darling Mildred and Jack, don't refuse this last request.'

Her diary of 1948 supplements these letters. On 1 January she listed the people in Tally Ho. Paddy and Nevill were there over Christmas. The permanent residents were Hildegarde, her nurse, four servants, a gardener, the faithful groom Mike Hurley, now an odd job man, as there was only one pony. The dogs were reduced to one, Porgy the 2nd. Geraldine Cummins often came to stay. When not there, she wrote regularly, as did Jack, their letters 'being a wonderful help and pleasure'. Visitors from the other gentry houses were frequent. On 10 January there was even a sherry party at Tally Ho, a large gathering of 'about 30 people crushed into a solid mass, yelling to each other at the full power of their lungs'. Ancient invalid though she was, Edith found the occasion enlivening. But sometimes she fell into a stupor for days. Emerging from this state, she would read letters, look at new books which people sent her, enter up her diary and get Mike Hurley to take her for a drive. The news on 7 February that the Oxford University Press was including *The Real Charlotte* in its series, The World's Classics, greatly pleased her, though when the book came, the blurb annoyed her, as her heroine, Francie Fitzpatrick, was compared to Thackeray's Becky Sharp. She had spirit enough left to write to the publishers that: 'Anything more idiotic can hardly be imagined.'

Nevill's broadcast on her 90th birthday, 2 May 1948, came

in for very special praise in the diary: 'He read it most beautifully and it couldn't have been more gracefully written or in
better or more well-bred taste.'

Next day she notes: 'Tired after the excitements of yesterday
and did not get up till after lunch. I have now become very
blind. I can still read good print, but with difficulty'. The broadcast was followed by a flood of letters from strangers who had
heard it. 'It has brought strange creepy creatures out of their
dens to glare through the darkness at me.'

From this on Edith's handwriting deteriorates very much.
Her fall the previous year, when she tripped over Porgy, had
gravely damaged her hearing, her sight and her power of
movement. Her entry for 27 July was just the two words
'Eheu fugaces', the opening of Horace's Ode 14, Book II. That
Edith was acquainted with this great classic ode must have
been due to her friend, Maurice Baring, having sent her his
anthology of choice pieces from the Latin, Greek, Italian,
French and English, called *Have You Anything to Declare* (published in 1936). He drew special attention to this ode, of which
he gave various translations in the hope of achieving one that
truly mirrored the original, a hopeless task as he well knew.
'Alas! how glide away the flying years, my Postumus. Piety
cannot delay wrinkles nor the advance of old age and uncon-
querable death.' The words exactly fitted her case.

There are extant two or three letters written this same
July 1948 to Elizabeth Hudson, the American friend who compiled her Bibliography, and whose pet name was Huz or Huzzie.
Here quoted are some phrases from them: 'Dearest, I don't
think I have much more to stand in this world. I shall be much
nearer you when I get over the Border. I don't want to stay
here. This may be my last letter to you (22 July 1948). I feel
very weak and incapable today. My head is clear enough but
my hand won't respond. I was most grateful to you for the two
bottles of whiskey, a great help. We are too poor to live anywhere.'

On 13 September is the last entry in the 1948 diary, the final

volume of this huge work: 'Continued as before unchanged since
May 1947 when Porgy tripped me up. I have not done a day's
work since; and never thought I would have to end a good active
hardworking life dying like a worn out old horse in a corner of
a field.'

Edith lived for another year and twenty-five days. As her
diary and letters stop one must look elsewhere for information.
Some is provided by Geraldine Cummins in her biography
Dr. E. Œ. Somerville, published in 1952. She had no access to
the Coghill papers on which the present book is founded, but
she got to know Edith very well, stayed often at Drishane and
Tally Ho, and preserved the letters they exchanged. She was
on a visit to Tally Ho in August 1949. Edith, though somewhat
weaker than in the previous September, was still mentally all
right. She could sit in her wheel chair and even take short drives.
She suffered little pain now from the sciatica. Before the end of
August, however, she had a heart attack one night. During
September she seemed better and on 3 October went for a
drive in her trap with the nurse and Mike Hurley. This was too
much for her. That night a slight congestion of the lungs was
diagnosed. Geraldine Cummins, who had returned to her own
house near Cork, but was keeping in touch, heard in a letter
received on 8 October a reassuring report. But Edith's heart
failed that very afternoon and at 3.15 p.m. she passed away.

Her funeral was on 11 October. On the coffin were placed her
doctor's hood, her hunting crop and horn, and her palette and
brushes. It was carried by men of the place from Tally Ho to
the church. The grave was next to Martin's. She had expressed
the wish to have as headstone an uncarved boulder like a
menhir from the neighbouring hills. Desmond Somerville saw
to this and it stands today as he placed it. A very short and
simple inscription was cut under the boulder on a piece of
limestone. Inside the church is a long memorial inscription
placed there by her American friends and admirers.

This is the end of the story. Edith's biography does not continue, as in Martin's case, in the form of automatic scripts.

There was no practical need, of course, for such messages since the collaboration was at an end. Curiosity might have tempted the family; if so they resolved not to yield to it. Distaste and doubt may have had a part in this decision. It was a sobering reflection that in all the long years Edith had never succeeded in materializing Martin, never saw Martin's ghost, never heard her voice, the sound of her step, the rustle of her dress. She longed for such a confirmation of the automatic writings. She was not afraid, though an apparition can be very frightening. But she failed and had to be content with the written messages. These, in fact, sufficed to console her and gave her heart to continue her writing. Her surviving close relatives decided to leave it at that, a very sound decision.

Note on manuscript sources

Diaries

Edith Somerville 1873–1948 (1876 missing)—75 volumes (2¾ million words).

Violet Martin (Martin Ross) 1875–1915 (1876, 1877, 1881 missing)—38 volumes (2¼ million words)

Letters

from Edith Somerville:

to her sister Lady Coghill (1883–1949)	368 letters,	1,793 pp	
to her brother Cameron (1879–1941)	363	,,	4,359 ,,
to her brother Jack (1905–1948)	911	,,	3,413 ,,
to Violet Martin	97	,,	376 ,,
to Ethel Smyth (1921–1930)	276	,,	1,193 ,,
to Mrs Anstey (1930–1938)	97	,,	335 ,,
from Violet Martin to Edith Somerville	172	,,	745 ,,
from Ethel Smyth to Edith Somerville (1919–1930)	438	,,	2,043 ,,

In addition to these major sources there are several hundred miscellaneous letters and a great quantity of note-books, which contain accounts of the farm, etc., correspondence with publishers, Hunt accounts; records of the seances held, some amusing stories and sayings of the local people, etc., recorded as they were heard. There are also many papers of smaller interest, not tabulated here. Sir Patrick Coghill himself possesses the complete list of all the items in the MSS.

No bibliography beyond the MS sources is appended, as this book is founded almost entirely on the manuscripts. Where any other source is drawn upon, a footnote is appended.

The holders of the copyright have not given anyone but myself access to any of the above-mentioned papers.

Index

AE (George Russell), 187
Altar to Martin, 225
America, E. Somerville's trips to, 236 seq. and 262
Annagh, Wood of, 54
Anstey, Mrs (Coz), 244, 257
Astor, a spectre, 248–9; 260

Balfour, Arthur, 85, 95
Baring, Maurice, 188, 265, 276
Barlow, Jem, 164, 177, 230, 271
Barrahane, seat of Coghill family at Castle Townshend. Also name of the church there, 28
Barret, Nurse, 52, 53, 69, 78, 80, 83
Barton, Robert, 208
Black and Tans, 202, 204, 206, 232–3
Brady, 56
Bridget (maid), 117
Brontë, Duke of, 193, 194
Buckley, Jack, 109, 110
Bushe, Charles Kendal, Chief Justice, 19, 28, 247–8
Butt, Clara, 198

Coghill, Ambrose, 268

Coghill, Egerton (husband of Edith's sister Hildegarde), 30, 84, 90, 96, 97, 102, 108–9, 207, 211
Coghill, Ethel (sister of Egerton). Marries Jim Penrose, 32; 173
Coghill, Hildegarde (Edith's sister), 34, 66, 81, 84, 90, 96, 110, 114, 147, 207, 210
Coghill, Sir Joscelyn, 30, 90, 102, 138
Coghill, Kendal (Uncle Kendal), 22, 28, 102, 161, 185, 215, 227
Coghill, Nevill, 14, 124, 206, 207, 227, 275, 276
Coghill, Patrick, 14, 112, 113, 124, 138, 227, 275
Collins, Michael, 208, 209, 214
Collis, Louise, 15
Connor, Thady, 57, 105
Cosgrave, 209, 217
Crespigny, Mrs (medium), 187, 255
Cummins, Geraldine (medium), 247–8, 251, 253, 272, 276, 277
Currey, Muriel, 14, 275

Dail, 201, 202, 205, 208

Index

Darley, Bishop of Cavan, 20
Davin (nurse), 100
Davy, Ann (maid), 77, 79
Dawson, Edith (sister of Martin), 48, 136, 148
Drishane (Somerville's house), 30, 120-1
Dogs, 39, 42, 62, 70, 96, 115, 116, 117, 119, 143-4, 147, 161, 180, 187, 205, 209, 211, 219, 227-9, 234-5, 237, 240, 246, 254
Doyle, Conan, 229

Evans, Mrs (cook), 114

Fairy shoe, 237; fairy music, 225
Fay (of Abbey Theatre), 130
Firr, Tom, 99
Florence, Aunt, her ghost, 251
French, Percy, 133, 142

Garston, Miss, 198
Gonne, Maud, 130, 133
Gorham, Dr, 101
Gormanston, Lord, and spectral foxes, 147
Gregory, Lady Augusta (*née* Persse), 22, 128, 130, 162
Griffy, Paddy, 53
Guardian spirits, 215

Hodgson, family of at Currare-vagh, 56, 58
Holloran, Shanneen, 100
Hone, Joseph, 252
Hudson, Elizabeth, 276
Hunting, 94, 99, 124; in R.M. stories, 126; 133, 135, 156, 160
Hurley, Mike, 204, 262, 264, 274, 277

Huxley, Julian and Juliette, 255

Kenealy (retainer), 150
Kenmare, Lady, 188, 267, 268
Kineary, Anne, 105
Kipling, Rudyard, 166

Lamb, Father, 212, 233
Lane, Sir Hugh, 162, 166, 233
Lang, Andrew, 104
Leary (a maid), 96
Lodge, Oliver, 182
Lusitania, 166

Martin, Anna Selina (called Mama), 19, 20, 23, 49, 50, 51, 53, 56, 60, 74, 101, 117, 138, 139
Martin, Archer, 61
Martin, Connie, 23, 74, 76, 138, 140
Martin, James (father of Violet Martin), 18, 54
Martin, Oliver, (founder of the family), 17
Martin, Richard, 15, 268
Martin, Robert (brother of Violet Martin), 18, 19, 23, 50, 74, 76 seq, 136-7
Martin, Selina (sister of Violet Martin), 36
Martin, Stella, 14, 100
Martin, Violet (the Martin and the Martin Ross of the text). Birth, 17; leaves Ross for Dublin (1873), 19; visit to Bishop of Cavan, 20-2; visits London (1882), 23-4; meets Edith Somerville 24, 28, 36, 38; friendship for Edith Somerville grows, 38 seq; first collaboration with her (in 1886),

Index

Martin, Violet—*cont.*
38; with Robert Martin in London, 39; visits Edith in Paris (1887,) 43; in London, 43; first book with Edith, 45; returns to Ross, 49, 51 seq; 54, 55; her night drive to a dance at Currarevagh house, 58; first novel with Edith accepted, 63; Connemara tour (1890), 75; Richard Martin and Connie come to stay at Ross, 77 seq; *The Real Charlotte*, 84; 98, 103, 104; bad fall hunting, 124; publication of vol. 1. of R.M. stories, 126; and Yeats, 129, 130; refuses to join Abbey Theatre group, 131; leaves Ross after death of Mama, 139; her will, 146; illness and death of 168 seq; 187, 209, 211
Mary the Monkey (maid), 114, 144
Moore, George, 159, 228
Mulloy, Mary, 80, 81

Norris, Mrs (a retainer), 113

O'fflaherties, the, 78
O'Grady, Standish, 142–3
Ould, Herman, 264

Packenham, Frank (now Lord Longford), 202
Parker, Lady and rats, 147, 148
Penrose, Jim, husband of Ethel Coghill, 31
Pete-een, (fiddler), 144
Pinker, J. B., 123, 124, 146, 148, 160

Rickeen (retainer), 143

Ross, description of house and demesne, 54

Shaw, George Bernard, 127, 146, 208, 255
Sinnett, 165, 166
Smyth, Ethel, 229, 244–5; death of, 268; 272
Somerville, Adelaide (Edith's mother), 28, 29, 33, 34, 91, 92, 93; death of, 106
Somerville, Aylmer (Edith's brother), 29, 40, 90, 94, 108, 110, 114, 116
Somerville, Boyle (Edith's brother), 29, 34, 90, 133, 227; murder of, 257; 259, 260, 266
Somerville, Cameron (Edith's brother), 28, 33, 89, 92, 109, 117, 120, 160, 166; letters to, 172 seq; 203, 210, 216, 221; death of, 263, 265
Somerville, Desmond (Edith's nephew), 264, 265, 268, 277
Somerville, Edith, 13, 14; meets Violet Martin, 28; youth in Drishane house, 29; goes to London, 29; the affair of Ethel Coghill, 29, 32; paints Martin's portrait, 35; goes to Paris, 36; hunting, 39; method of collaboration with Martin, 45 seq; meeting with Oscar Wilde, 48, 49; first novel accepted (in 1888), 63; letter on death of dog, 66; Connemara tour (1890), 75; begins work on *The Real Charlotte*, 84; death of mother (1895), 106 seq; goes to Aix for cure, 123; horse dealing, 133; becomes M.F.H. (1903), 175; attempt

Somerville, Edith—*cont.*
    to communicate with spirit of
    Martin, 177; meets AE, 187;
    meets Ethel Smyth, 188; ex-
    hibits her paintings in London,
    190; Sicilian tour with Ethel
    Smyth, 193 seq; and the
    Troubles, 203 seq; her play,
    208; visits America 236; and
    Bushe, 246 seq; and D.Litt,.
    T,C,D, and Fellowship of Irish
    Academy of Letters, 250; her
    play, 256; again in America
    262; leaves Drishane, 270;
    death of, 277
Somerville, Hildegarde (Edith's
    sister), *see* Coghill
Somerville, Hugh (Edith's
    brother), 29, 30, 90, 203, 212
Somerville, Jack (Edith's brother),
    90, 161, 266, 270, 275, 276
Somerville, Thomas (Edith's
    father), 28, 34, 91, 92, 107,
    110n, 117, 118, 119, 120
Spiritualism, 95, 102, 121, 122,
    133, 164

Starkie, Enid, 266
Stephens, James, 252

Tally Ho, house, 268, 269, 270
Townshend, Castle, 23, 25; plan
    and aerial view of, 26, 27, 28
Troubles and unrest, 33, 84, 85,
    201 seq; 267
Two Trees, 213

Victoria, Queen, 133

Warren, Sylvia, 261, 262
Waterford, Lady, 43
Welsh Tour, 60
Wilde, Oscar, 48
Wills, Willie, 24, 42, 94
Woolf, Virginia, 247
Woolley (maid), 98

Yeats, W.B., 128 seq; 163, 252

Zetland, Lady, visit of to Ross,
    84 seq
Z, Jim, 212, 213